BET YOU DIDN'T KNOW

BET YOU DIDN'T KNOW
Hundreds of Intriguing Facts about Living in the USA

CHERYL RUSSELL

 Prometheus Books

59 John Glenn Drive
Amherst, New York 14228–2119

Published 2008 by Prometheus Books

Inquiries should be addressed to
Prometheus Books
59 John Glenn Drive
Amherst, New York 14228–2119
VOICE: 716–691–0133, ext. 210
FAX: 716–691–0137
WWW.PROMETHEUSBOOKS.COM

12 11 10 09 08   5 4 3 2 1

Library of Congress Cataloging-in-Publication Data

Russell, Cheryl, 1953–
    Bet you didn't know : hundreds of intriguing facts about living in the USA / by Cheryl Russell.
        p. cm.
    Includes bibliographical references and index.
    ISBN 978–1–59102–635–8 (pbk. : alk. paper)
    1. United States—Social life and customs—1971—Miscellanea. 2. United States—Social conditions—1980—Miscellanea. 3. United States—Economic conditions—2001—Miscellanea. 4. Social surveys—United States. I. Title.

E169.Z83R87 2008
973.923—dc22

2008026157

Printed in the United States of America on acid-free paper

For Sky, Julie, Jimmy, Charlotte, and Colleen

CONTENTS

INTRODUCTION

Why should you read this book?

Here's why: by opening these pages, you have shown yourself to be someone who wants to know how the world works. This book tells you how hundreds of things work—not things like computers or microwaves, but marriages and money. *Bet You Didn't Know* explains the how and why of life in the United States. Each page of this book is another page in the story of your life.

How come I know so much about you? Because I am a demographer and demographers are trained to stick their nose into other people's business. Demography is all about sex and babies, marriage and divorce, moving in and moving out, how long you will live, and how well you will live. This books answers the kinds of questions you probably ask yourself every day: Why do so many unmarried women have babies? Are children worth the trouble? Do we own more dogs than cats? Why do we need so much self-storage space? How often do people feel like they're going crazy? Why is it so hard to make ends meet? Are immigrants willing to learn English? What do blacks really think about whites? How happy are other people's marriages? Is anyone a virgin on their wedding day? Is a college education still worth the cost? Why have we gained so much weight?

If you are a curious person—and if you've read this far, I would say you qualify—you have enough questions to keep the Google search engine busy for a lifetime. But you don't have to bother searching for the answers because you now hold them in your hand. As the former editor of *American Demographics* magazine and once dubbed the "Trend Cop," I have made a career out of tracking the facts and spotting the trends. Long embedded in the frontline of American life, I am trained to separate the real stories from the distractions. Think of *Bet You Didn't Know* as the social science equivalent of "two-minute mysteries." On each page I tackle another of life's vexing questions and untangle the answers. I may not always solve the mystery, but in a few paragraphs I might have you thinking differently about the answer.

LOOK OVER HERE!

Let's talk about distractions. Thanks to the demands of the twenty-four-hour news cycle, there are lots of them. Both television and newspapers face the daunting task of producing fresh headlines 24/7 just to keep you coming back to their advertisers. That's the media's bottom line. To improve the bottom line, reporters are always on the hunt for stories that will keep you coming back for more. What you too often get from the frantic hunt for headlines are glib reports meant to entertain rather than enlighten.

Bet You Didn't Know entertains *and* enlightens. It will not waste your time by restating the obvious, as so many headlines already do ("Population is Growing!" "Some Richer than Others!" "Women Earn Less than Men!"). Rather than recite old news, *Bet You Didn't Know* brings you the breaking news. Prepare for some "ah ha" moments.

Bet You Didn't Know is intended to be a fun read, but it is also a challenge to our deeply imbedded and often wildly wacky beliefs about love, marriage, children, jobs, and money. These are tales from the trenches as we try to hold on to the ground gained by our parents and grandparents. That acreage is being eroded by technological change, denial, and a deeply powerful and primitive embrace of belief over evidence, faith over facts, and judgment over action. *Bet You Didn't Know* connects the dots, revealing the good, the bad, and the ugly about life in the United States today.

YOUR CHEAT SHEET

Bet You Didn't Know examines hundreds of issues—201 to be exact, with one issue per page. Each page highlights a demographic fact, telling the story behind it, revealing the trends driving it, and arriving at an often-surprising conclusion. All this is accomplished in a few paragraphs of about three hundred words. It is not easy to explore topics as big as out-of-wedlock births, our obsession with race, the impact of immigration, or the decline of the middle class in three hundred words. These topics have filled entire books. But by boiling down the issues to their essence, my hope is that more will read to the end—the bottom line—and discover the depth beneath the many stories too often trivialized by the media. The generalizations, finger pointing, and sloganeering that pass for news are intended to do little more than fill time and space, yet they too often keep us from the work we need to do—preparing for a future that will be very different from our past.

Bet You Didn't Know is filled with issues dear to my heart. I have been talking about them for a long time to anyone who will listen—friends, family, colleagues, readers of my *American Consumers* newsletter and *Demo Memo* blog. As you thumb through *Bet You Didn't Know* you will notice several themes emerging—not all of them happy, but none that can be ignored. The Internet has ended the centuries-old isolation of the United States from the rest of the world. This isolation long protected us from a variety of global pressures and allowed us to attain a far higher standard of living than anyone else. Now the protection is gone. Many of the stories on the following pages describe the consequences.

MANY THANKS

I would like to thank my longtime editor Linda Regan, who kept bugging me to write another book. You win. Thanks also to my wonderful family, a willing audience whenever I climb on the soapbox—an all-too-frequent occurrence. You were warned this project would keep me busy, and it did. Now that my yips have been captured on paper, you probably think I will shut up for a while. Sorry, no such luck. Also, thanks to my many colleagues throughout the years—from *American Demographics* to *The Boomer Report*, *Money* magazine, and New Strategist Publications—you made this a very fun ride. Someone once said demography was dull. It isn't anymore.

PART I

YOUR RELATIONSHIPS

Chapter 1
FAMILY

PERCENTAGE OF HOUSEHOLDS
WITH DOGS OR CATS: 56

Pets. This is where it begins. Any serious scrutiny of family life must start by acknowledging the importance of pets. American households, in fact, are now more likely to include a dog or a cat than a child. But are we substituting pets for children? The answer appears to be yes.

The average person spends only about half of his or her adult life raising children. This is a new turn of events for *Homo sapiens*, few of whom survived into old age until recently. Over the past couple of centuries, two trends have converged: family size fell and adult life expectancy rose, leaving humans facing decades of life without something cute and cuddly to care for. The average number of children per family plummeted from more than five in 1850 to just two children today. At the same time, life expectancy at age 20 climbed from about 40 years to almost 60 years.[1] How to fill the time? We got pets.

Specifically, we got dogs and cats. A Gallup survey finds that more than half of us own a dog or cat.[2] According to the American Veterinary Medical Association, 36 percent of households own a dog and 32 percent own a cat.[3] Households with dogs have an average of 1.6 dogs. Cat owners are more indulgent, with an average of 2.1 cats.

As the nest empties, we devote more of our time and money to our pets. Beginning in the 45-to-54 age group, people are more likely to care for pets than for children on a given day, according to the American Time Use Survey.[4] The biggest spenders on pets are householders aged 45 to 64—most of them empty-nesters. Spending trends confirm the nation's growing focus on pets. The average household spent $316 on pets in 2006, a substantial 29 percent more than in 2000 after adjusting for inflation.[5] During those years, spending on children's toys fell 39 percent.

Factoid source: Frank Newport et al., "Americans and Their Pets," The Gallup Poll, December 21, 2006, http://www.gallup.com/poll/25969/Americans-Their-Pets.aspx (accessed November 25, 2007).

PERCENTAGE OF HOUSEHOLDS
WITH CHILDREN: 35

The typical American household does not hear the pitter patter of little feet. It does not need to bother with bedtimes, curfews, or allowances. The average American household is a child-free zone. With barely one-third of households today containing children under age 18, some say the needs of children have fallen by the wayside as adult lifestyles increasingly dominate the nation's priorities.

How times have changed. In 1950, nearly half of households were home to children under age 18. It was the *Father Knows Best* era when women stayed home, men went to work, and children were (supposedly) seen but not heard. Some refer to the family of the 1950s as "traditional," but it was anything but. The idealized nuclear family of the 1950s was a temporary phenomenon growing out of the booming postwar economy. "At the end of the 1940s, all the trends characterizing the rest of the twentieth century suddenly reversed themselves," explains Stephanie Coontz, professor of history and family studies at Evergreen State College in Olympia, Washington, in her groundbreaking work *The Way We Never Were*.[6] Women's median age at first marriage fell to 20 in the 1950s—meaning half of women married in their teens. Family size grew from 2.3 children in 1940 to a peak of 3.8 children in the late 1950s as the baby-boom generation was born.[7]

Today, the average woman marrying for the first time is nearly 26 years old. She will have only two children in her lifetime, and she will live most of her life child free. The nuclear family of the 1950s was nothing more than a waypoint between the extended family of the past and the individualism of today. In a few years, the most common household type in the United States will be people living alone.

Factoid source: Bureau of the Census, 2007 Current Population Survey Annual Social and Economic Supplement, http://pubdb3.census.gov/macro/032007/hhinc/ toc.htm (accessed September 16, 2007).

PERCENTAGE OF CHILDREN
LIVING WITH BOTH PARENTS: 67

A strange thing happened to the nuclear family over the past few decades. It began to disappear. As a percentage of the nation's households, nuclear families (meaning mom, dad, and one or more kids) fell from 44 to just 23 percent.[8] That is what you might call a downfall. In 1960, nuclear families were the most common household type. Today they rank third in the household line-up behind married couples without children at home (most of them older, empty-nesters) and people living alone (many of them elderly widows).

Divorce and out-of-wedlock births have turned nuclear families into single parents. Since 1960, the percentage of children living with both parents has plummeted from 88 to just 67 percent. At the same time, the percentage of children living only with their mother has nearly tripled, rising from 8 to 23 percent. Few children (just 5 percent) live only with their father. What about all those grandparents who are shouldering the burden of raising their children's children? This is one of those stories that begins as filler on a slow news day and then takes on a life of its own. In fact, only 5 percent of children live in the home of a grandparent—a figure that has barely changed over the decades. And for the 60 percent majority of those children, one or both of their parents also lives in the home.

How far we have come from the extended-family living arrangements of our agricultural past. According to the 2000 census, the 55 percent majority of American households include only one generation. Another 41 percent are home to two generations, and just 4 percent include three or more.[9] A handful of long-lived families need a traffic cop to manage the bathroom. The census counted 269 households with five generations under one roof.

Factoid source: Bureau of the Census, Families and Living Arrangements, Historical Time Series—Families, http://www.census.gov/population/www/socdemo/ hh-fam.html (accessed September 16, 2007).

PERCENTAGE OF PARENTS WHO BELIEVE CHILDREN ARE WORTH THE TROUBLE: 97

So you think having kids is the holy grail of happiness? You are not alone. When Americans are asked whether watching children grow up is life's greatest joy, fully 86 percent say yes, according to the General Social Survey.[10]

The overwhelming consensus on the joys of children explains why most women under the age of 45 have already had children (58 percent), expect to have them (33 percent), or cannot have them (3 percent), leaving only 6 percent who do not want children.[11] With all this enthusiasm for children, you might think most men and women would be devastated if they could not have kids. Yet only 42 percent of childless women and 30 percent of childless men say it would bother them a great deal if they ended up childless.[12] Maybe they are familiar with the social science research. Studies show childless adults to be just as happy, if not happier, than people with children—and without all the work.

Parents will argue, of course, that the rewards of children outweigh the work. When parents under age 45 are asked whether being a parent is worth it, a nearly universal 97 percent say yes.[13] But according to psychologists, we are just kidding ourselves. When people think about having children, they expect to feel happy and rewarded, says Harvard psychologist Daniel Gilbert in his book *Stumbling on Happiness*.[14] Similarly, when parents look back on parenthood, they remember it as happy and rewarding. But, says Gilbert, "Careful studies of how women feel as they go about their daily activities show that they are less happy when taking care of their children than when eating, exercising, shopping, napping, or watching television."[15] The happiness that mothers experience while looking after children, says Gilbert, ranks only slightly above the happiness they feel while doing housework.

Factoid source: National Center for Health Statistics, *Fertility, Contraception, and Fatherhood: Data on Men and Women from Cycle 6 of the 2002 National Survey of Family Growth,* Vital and Health Statistics, Series 23, No. 26, 2006, pp. 110–11.

PERCENTAGE OF CHILDREN WITH A WORKING FATHER AND A STAY-AT-HOME MOTHER: 22

The working mother: perhaps no figure has been more controversial over the years than this often-unwelcome messenger of modernity. It has been decades since most housewives untied the apron strings and joined the commute to work. Yet, there are preachers and pundits who still wait for mom to surrender her car keys and return to the kitchen. These sentinels are a testament to the powerful nostalgia for the exuberant postwar era of the GI bill, affordable housing, cheap mortgages, and the rising wages of a booming manufacturing sector.

Times have changed. We can no more return to those heady days than we can relive our senior year in high school—not that most of us would want to. The fact is, during the past half century, the cost of the American Dream has grown much faster than men's incomes. Consequently, most husbands no longer earn enough to support the middle-class lifestyle of homeownership, health insurance, college for the kids, and a secure retirement. Since 1980, housing prices alone have nearly doubled relative to the median earnings of a man with a full-time job, according to Census Bureau statistics.[16] As rising costs threatened the nation's middle class, mothers answered the call.

Working mothers once faced a hostile public. In 1977, most Americans believed a working mother could not establish as warm and secure a relationship with her children as a mother who did not work, according to the General Social Survey.[17] Two out of three Americans believed preschoolers suffered if their mother worked. A few still feel that way today and wait for mom's return. The rest are looking for daycare.

Factoid source: Bureau of the Census, America's Families and Living Arrangements: 2006, Detailed Tables, http://www.census.gov/population/www/socdemo/hh-fam/cps2006.html (accessed November 25, 2007).

PERCENTAGE OF PRESCHOOLERS
IN DAYCARE: 60

Most children have working mothers. Most are also in daycare. During a typical week, 60 percent of the nation's preschoolers are cared for by people other than their parents, according to the National Center for Education Statistics.[18] The experience of daycare differentiates the young from the old. When asked whether their mother ever worked for pay for as long as a year during their childhood, fully 84 percent of 18- to 24-year-olds say yes, according to the General Social Survey.[19] Among people aged 65 or older, only 45 percent had a mother who worked.

Although some believe daycare harms children, most of today's parents would disagree. Daycare has become a plus rather than a minus in the lives of children. For some parents, it is even a status symbol like a luxury car or a designer purse. The children most likely to be in daycare are not the disadvantaged. Rather, they are the children of the nation's elite. Just over half of children from the lowest income families (with an annual income of $25,000 or less) are in daycare during an average week compared with a much larger 79 percent of children from families with incomes above $100,000.[20] Similarly, only 35 percent of the children whose parents dropped out of high school are in daycare compared with 66 percent of those whose parents are college graduates.

When parents are asked to list the most important qualities of a daycare arrangement, the largest share (89 percent) cite the reliability of the daycare provider. No surprise there. But next on the list are the positive experiences daycare offers—learning activities (cited by 75 percent) and time with other children (65 percent). The average child in daycare spends 29 hours a week in nonparental care. Today's parents regard that as time well spent.

Factoid source: National Center for Education Statistics, National Household Education Survey, Initial Results from the 2005 NHES Early Childhood Program Participation Survey, http://nces.ed.gov/pubs2006/earlychild/tables.asp (accessed February 18, 2007).

PERCENTAGE OF MIDDLE-SCHOOL STUDENTS IN POVERTY WHO TAKE PART IN AFTER-SCHOOL ACTIVITIES: 30

When children apply to college, it is not hard to guess which ones will have the most impressive resumes. Families with money literally buy their children's way onto the nation's college campuses—not by funding a new building, but by giving their children the experiences that colleges increasingly demand from applicants.

Families with money can provide their children with a variety of experiences beyond the reach of the poor. The differences are stark by middle school, where participation in after-school activities among poor children (30 percent) is less than half the rate among children from high-income families (66 percent).[21] The gap persists in high school, where teenagers from low-income families are less likely than those from high-income families to participate in extracurricular sports (22 versus 59 percent), clubs (20 versus 52), or lessons (16 versus 46 percent), according to the Census Bureau's Survey of Income and Program Participation.[22]

What accounts for these differences? The Centers for Disease Control and Prevention has been trying to find out. In one study, it asked parents why their children did not participate in after-school physical activities. The number-one problem was cost, mentioned by nearly half the parents.[23] Transportation was the second biggest problem, and a lack of time was third. Many low-income families are headed by single parents with full-time jobs. They do not have time to shuttle their children from one activity to another. Many do not even own a car.

Unfortunately, income does not differentiate the hopes and dreams of parents. More than 85 percent of parents, regardless of income, want their children to graduate from college.[24] But reality does separate the rich from the poor: Among young adults from high-income families, 63 percent attend college. Among young adults from low-income families, the figure is just 24 percent.[25]

Factoid source: National Center for Education Statistics, National Household Education Survey, Initial Results from the 2005 NHES Early Childhood Program Participation Survey, http://nces.ed.gov/pubs2006/earlychild/tables.asp (accessed February 18, 2007).

PERCENTAGE OF PARENTS WHO SAY THEY NEVER FEEL ANGRY WITH THEIR CHILDREN: 49

Someone is in serious denial. What kind of parent "never" feels angry with her children? The question, "I feel angry with my child. How often do you feel this way," is one of many included in the Census Bureau's Survey of Income and Program Participation (SIPP). It is meant to probe the quality of the parent-child relationship, but the large percentage of parents who deny feeling angry says more about people's relationship with the government than with their kids.

Anger is just one of the emotions that parents are quick to deny. Fatigue and frustration are two others. More than half of parents (51 percent) say their child "never" takes up more time than they expected.[26] Forty-six percent of parents report, with a straight face, that their child never does things that bother them a lot. Even the parents of teenagers are loath to admit tearing their hair out occasionally. Conversely, when the survey asks whether they praise their child regularly, parents cannot gush enough. Among the parents of teens, a substantial 40 percent report praising their child not just once but at least three times a day. Even Ozzie and Harriet were not that good.

Parents may equivocate when probed about feeling angry with their children, but the public at large is not shy about letting parents vent their anger. When asked whether they agree or disagree with the statement, "Sometimes it is necessary to discipline a child with a good, hard spanking," a 72 percent majority of the public agrees, according to the General Social Survey.[27] The fact that this ferocity largely disappears when the government asks parents about their angry feelings suggests that survey respondents are fearful of the government's purpose in asking the question. If they admit to feeling angry, could Child Welfare Services be far behind?

Factoid source: Bureau of the Census, A Child's Day: 2004 (Selected Indicators of Child Well-Being), Survey Income and Program Participation, Detailed Tables, http://www.census.gov/population/www/socdemo/2004 _detailedtables.html (accessed October 31, 2007).

PERCENTAGE OF PEOPLE WHO THINK OBEDIENCE IS THE MOST IMPORTANT QUALITY TO INSTILL IN A CHILD: 18

"Because I said so," is not as popular a comeback among parents as it once was. That's because parents themselves don't buy it. Few parents today want to raise a child for whom obedience is rule number one. They want more from their children than obedience: they want them to think for themselves.

It wasn't always this way. In our agricultural past, obedience was one of the most important qualities parents wanted to instill in their children. In a survey taken more than a century ago in 1890, 64 percent of mothers cited "strict obedience" as one of the three most important characteristics that needed to be emphasized in childrearing, behind only "loyalty to church." Just 16 percent of the mothers cited independence as one of the top three characteristics, according to an analysis of historical data by Duane F. Alwin, director of the Center on Population Health and Aging at Penn State.[28]

Parents are in the business of raising successful offspring. As the United States evolved from an agricultural to an industrial and now an information-driven society, independence became increasingly important to getting ahead. Consequently, parents changed their priorities. The percentage of the public citing obedience as one of the most important traits to instill in children plummeted from the 64 percent of 1890 to just 18 percent in 2006, according to the General Social Survey. To most of the public, teaching children to be obedient is about as significant as teaching them to help others (considered most important by 16 percent) or to work hard (19 percent).[29] The number one trait, cited as most important by the 46 percent plurality of the public today, is teaching children to think for themselves.

Factoid source: Survey Documentation and Analysis, Computer-assisted Survey Methods Program, University of California, Berkeley, General Social Surveys, 1972–2006 Cumulative Data Files, GSS Variable OBEY, http://sda .berkeley.edu/cgi-bin32/hsda?harcsda+gss06 (accessed September 16, 2007).

PERCENTAGE OF CHILDREN
WALKING OR BICYCLING TO SCHOOL: 16

Being a kid is a lot easier than it used to be. Take the walk to school, for example. Most kids don't have to do it anymore. In 1969, a substantial 42 percent of school children walked or biked to school. Today, only 16 percent of children get to school on their own, according to travel studies by the federal government.

Are kids lazy or spoiled? Neither, it turns out. Children no longer walk to school because, for most, school is too far away. In the past thirty years, the number of school children has expanded by 2 million, but the number of schools has fallen by more than 1,000.[30] School consolidation means fewer children attend a neighborhood school. Here are the numbers: Among children aged 5 to 18, the percentage living within one mile of their school fell from 34 to 21 percent between 1969 and 2001. The percentage living three or more miles from their school climbed from 33 to 50 percent. According to researchers at the Centers for Disease Control and Prevention, 62 percent of parents with children aged 5 to 18 say distance is the greatest barrier that prevents their children from walking to school.[31]

Even for students living within a mile of school, fewer are walking or biking to class. Over the past three decades, the number fell from 87 to 63 percent. Again, laziness is not a factor. Instead, a lack of sidewalks and traffic congestion make walking not only dangerous, but exceedingly unpleasant. In the CDC study, parents cite traffic danger as the second biggest factor preventing their children from walking to school. But parents may be trapped in a catch-22 situation. By driving their kids to school, parents themselves are causing much of the traffic congestion. According to the CDC study, the percentage of children getting to and from school by car climbed from 16 to 46 percent over the past three decades.

Factoid source: Centers for Disease Control and Prevention, "KidsWalk: Then and Now—Barriers and Solutions," http://www.cdc.gov/nccdphp/dnpa/kidswalk/then_and_now.htm (accessed August 13, 2007).

PERCENTAGE OF ADULTS WHO LIVE WITHIN A ONE-HOUR DRIVE FROM THEIR PARENTS: 85

Remember the bumper stickers proclaiming, "I'm spending my children's inheritance," or the stories about middle-aged adults shipping their elderly parents off to nursing homes? Don't believe them. For most Americans, the parent-child relationship is one of the strongest and most enduring bonds, and it does not disappear just because the kids have grown up.

Here is the evidence: most adults do not live far from home, and they are in frequent contact with their parents. Apparently, our chaotic, overly scheduled, high-tech lifestyle has strengthened rather than weakened the parent-child connection. Eighty-seven percent of adults describe their relationship with their mother as close. Seventy-four percent feel that way about dad.[32]

Many adults feel close to their parents because they still need them, maybe more than ever. Burdened with college loans, a mortgage, daycare expenses, and health insurance costs, young and middle-aged adults are having a hard time making ends meet. Parents are coming to the rescue. According to researchers at the University of Michigan, parents provide their adult children with substantial material support. The numbers are not trivial. The researchers estimate that parents give their children $38,000 in material support from ages 18 through 34, on average, with the amount ranging from more than $3,000 a year for those at the younger end to about $1,500 a year for those in their early thirties.[33] Parents also spend an average of 367 hours a year helping their grown children with babysitting and household chores— the equivalent of nine weeks of full-time work. Far from spoiling them, today's parents are trying to secure for their children the same middle-class lifestyle they enjoyed while growing up.

The payoff is closer family ties. Forty-two percent of adult children see or telephone a parent at least once a day, up from the 32 percent who did so in 1989.[34]

Factoid source: Pew Research Center, *Families Drawn Together by Communications Revolution*, February 21, 2006, p. 8.

PERCENTAGE OF ADULTS
WITH A BROTHER OR SISTER: 90

Pop quiz: which living relative are people most likely to have? Give yourself an A if you said a brother or sister. Nine out of ten people aged 18 or older have a sibling, according to a survey by the Pew Research Center. That beats the percentage of adults with children (73 percent) and the percentage with living parents (68 percent).[35]

Most of us have fond memories of sharing a bathroom with a big brother or little sister. Well, the memories may not be so fond, but most of us have them. Even today, with family size greatly reduced from what it used to be, 79 percent of the nation's children are sharing a home (and usually a bathroom) with at least one sibling.[36] The sibling rivalry of childhood has a way of turning into one of the closest family relationships, second only to the bond between parents and children. Seventy-eight percent of adults with siblings say they are very close to at least one brother or sister, reports the Pew survey. Most see a brother or sister at least once a month and are in contact with a sibling at least once a week, according to the General Social Survey.[37] Only 6 percent of adults with siblings say they have no contact with their brothers or sisters.

When we need help, our brothers and sisters are there for us. Siblings rank third as the people to whom we are most likely to turn for advice when we have a serious personal problem—following friends and mom, and even ahead of dad.[38] Eleven percent of adults say they would be most likely to turn to a brother or sister for advice if necessary. This equals the proportion saying they would be most likely to turn to God—but maybe that's because our siblings convinced us they were God.

Factoid source: Pew Research Center, *Families Drawn Together by Communications Revolution*, February 21, 2006, p. 13.

NUMBER OF PEOPLE IN WHOM
THE AVERAGE AMERICAN CONFIDES: 2.08

Social scientists are worried about you. They think you do not have enough friends. They have even gone so far as to count your friends, coming to the depressing conclusion that the circle is small—and shrinking.

Why should anyone investigate your social life? This is why: in every society, the strength of social networks is critical to well-being. According to some—but not all—these networks are eroding in the United States. One intriguing study published in *American Sociological Review* examined responses to a General Social Survey question asked in 1985 and repeated in 2004: "Who are the people with whom you discussed matters important to you?"[39] The researchers counted the number of people mentioned, finding the median falling significantly over the decades, from 2.94 to 2.08. Alarmed, they searched for what might explain the decline. One of the most likely suspects is technology, the researchers suggest. The Internet and cell phones allow more contact across the miles, but could reduce face-to-face contact and shrink our circle of confidants.

Not everyone agrees, however. Parents with texting teenagers in their home are probably scratching their heads at the notion that the Internet and cell phones have reduced friendships. A survey by Pew Research Center also challenges the notion that our circle of friends is shrinking. Pew investigated the matter by broadening the social network question to capture evolving forms of communication. It asked respondents how many people they discussed important matters with, *or* were in frequent contact with, *or* from whom they seek help.[40] After widening the net in this way, they discovered that the average American has a median of 15 friends—much greater than the number reported by the General Social Survey. Pew does not think the Internet is making people antisocial. "To the contrary," concludes Pew, "the Internet is enabling people to maintain existing ties, often to strengthen them, and at times to forge new ties."[41]

Factoid source: Miller McPherson, Lynn Smith-Lovin, and Matthew E. Brashears, "Social Isolation in America: Changes in Core Discussion Networks over Two Decades," *American Sociological Review* 71 (June 2006): pp. 353–75.

Chapter 2
MEN AND WOMEN

THE MEN MOST LIKELY TO BE
VERY HAPPILY MARRIED: COLLEGE GRADUATES

The Dating Game explains a lot about family life in the United States. If you want to understand out-of-wedlock childbearing, divorce, and absentee fatherhood, then take a turn playing the game. Two bachelors are in the competition today, each aged 25 to 34 and trying to get ahead in our increasingly competitive economy. Which bachelor will appeal to the nation's women? Let's meet them and see.

Bachelor Number One is a high school graduate and represents 32 percent of men aged 25 to 34. He works in construction and has no retirement or health insurance benefits. This year, if he's lucky, he might earn as much as $29,000 (the median earnings of men aged 25 to 34 with a high school diploma).[1] Because of the slowdown in the housing market, he could lose his job.

Bachelor Number Two is a college graduate, representing 28 percent of men aged 25 to 34. He recently earned his degree in civil engineering. He landed a job with an engineering firm at a starting salary of $46,000 (the median earnings of men aged 25 to 34 with a bachelor's degree), plus retirement and health insurance benefits.

Which one will women choose? Not Bachelor Number One. The less educated the man, the less success he has in the marriage market. Few women will commit themselves for long to a man with poor job prospects. Women's reluctance to stay married to men at the bottom of the food chain explains why, among men under age 45, those with no more than a high school diploma are more likely than college graduates to have a child out-of-wedlock (31 versus 6 percent), live apart from their children (29 versus 14 percent), and divorce (40 versus 17 percent).[2] Given the choice, women will take Bachelor Number Two. In the marriage market the bottom line is not love, but money.

Factoid source: Survey Documentation and Analysis, Computer-assisted Survey Methods Program, University of California, Berkeley, General Social Surveys, 1972–2006 Cumulative Data Files, GSS Variable HAPMAR, http://sda .berkeley.edu/cgi-bin32/hsda?harcsda+gss06 (accessed September 26, 2007).

CHANGE IN REAL MEDIAN EARNINGS OF MEN WHO WORK FULL-TIME, 1980 TO 2006: DOWN 2 PERCENT

Men are in trouble. They no longer make enough money to support a middle-class lifestyle. The cost of the American Dream is greater than ever, and men's earnings have not kept pace. The $42,261 median earnings of men who worked full-time in 2006 were 2 percent less than a generation ago in 1980, after adjusting for inflation. Meanwhile, the price of admission to the middle class has soared. Here's how men have fallen behind.

Homeownership. Men are having a harder time buying a home. In 1980, the median sales price of a new home ($64,600) was 3.5 times the median earnings of men working full-time.[3] Today, the median price ($246,500) is six times men's earnings. Translation: The cost of homeownership relative to men's earnings has nearly doubled since 1980.

Health insurance. Out-of-pocket health insurance costs for the average household climbed from $718 in 1984 (the earliest year available) to $1,465 in 2006, after adjusting for inflation. Like the cost of homeownership, the cost of health insurance relative to men's earnings has doubled over the past few decades.[4]

College education. In 1980–81, one year of college (including tuition, fees, room, and board) at a four-year public university cost $2,550, according to the National Center for Education Statistics.[5] At the time, the figure was only 14 percent of the median earnings of men working full-time. By 2005–06, the annual expense for attending a public university had grown to $12,108—or 29 percent of men's median earnings. The cost of college relative to men's earnings has also doubled over the years.

What kept American families afloat over the past few decades? The answer is the working woman. Between 1980 and 2006, the median earnings of the average woman with a full-time job climbed 25 percent, after adjusting for inflation.

Factoid source: Bureau of the Census, Current Population Survey, Historical Income Tables—People, http://www.census.gov/hhes/www/income/histinc/incpertoc.html (accessed September 25, 2007).

CHANGE IN REAL MEDIAN EARNINGS OF WOMEN WHO WORK FULL-TIME, 1980 TO 2006: UP 25 PERCENT

How convenient. Just when men's earnings were falling, women's earnings were rising, saving the middle class in the nick of time. But did women play the role of Mighty Mouse or The Joker in this saga? Let's ask the question more scientifically: Did women go to work because their husbands incomes were falling, or did men's incomes fall because women were taking their jobs? Whose fault is it, anyway?

Let's examine the Mighty Mouse theory first, which suggests women were forced to go to work because their husbands could not earn a decent living. Not true, according to long-term studies of married couples by analysts at the National Bureau of Economic Research.[6] The wives of low-earning men, whose incomes have plummeted over the decades, have experienced the smallest increase in labor force participation. The wives of middle- and high-earning men have boosted their labor force participation the most. Conclusion: women were not out to save the day, just responding to opportunity.

Now let's examine The Joker theory, in which women are stealing jobs from men and driving down their wages. Interestingly, as women's earnings have grown relative to men's, men's earnings have diverged, becoming much more unequal. The two trends have occurred in lockstep, according to economist Finis Welch writing in *American Economic Review*, which suggests it is no coincidence.[7] His analysis of the phenomenon shows that men's incomes have fallen because men with below-average incomes have lost ground. But men with high incomes are still making gains. In other words, in a marketplace demanding brains over brawn, the brawny men have been pushed down the wage scale while the brainy men have been pushed up, according to Welch. With more brains than brawn, women have filled in the gaps (although, on average, they still make less than men). It turns out women are neither heroes nor villains, but—like men—innocent bystanders to sweeping economic change.

Factoid source: Bureau of the Census, Current Population Survey, Historical Income Tables—People, http://www.census.gov/hhes/www/income/histinc/incpertoc.html (accessed September 25, 2007).

PERCENTAGE WHO FAVOR
TRADITIONAL SEX ROLES: 36

Nothing is more egalitarian than time. Each of us gets 24 hours a day, 168 hours a week. How we spend that time is our own business—and everyone else's apparently. Just ask a working woman.

It wasn't easy for women to go to work, and finding a job was not their biggest problem. The biggest obstacle was the hostile public. In 1950, just 34 percent of women aged 16 or older were in the workforce. It took a generation before working women became the norm, reaching 50 percent in 1978.[8] The cluck-clucking and tut-tutting were deafening. At that time, traditional sex roles—where men went to work and women stayed home—were favored by 66 percent of the public, according to the General Social Survey. Two out of three Americans believed preschoolers suffered if their mother worked.[9] Young women could not afford to listen. The economy was shifting under their feet, requiring two earners rather than one to achieve the same middle-class lifestyle enjoyed by their parents. Women's labor force participation stands at 59 percent today. Among mothers, an even larger 71 percent have jobs.

After decades of nail biting, finger pointing, and hand wringing about working mothers, there is good news to report: the kids are all right. In fact, they are better than ever. A definitive study of time use by sociologists at the University of Maryland shows that today's parents spend more time with their children than their counterparts did forty years ago—despite the increase in the hours women spend on the job. Married mothers devote 12.9 hours a week to their children as a primary activity today, up from 10.6 hours in 1965.[10] How do they do it? By ending their romance with Mr. Clean, freeing up more time for the kids. Married mothers cut the time they spend doing housework almost in half, from 34.5 to just 19.4 hours a week.[11] When you visit, don't mention the dust bunnies.

Factoid source: Survey Documentation and Analysis, Computer-assisted Survey Methods Program, University of California, Berkeley, General Social Surveys, 1972–2006 Cumulative Data Files, GSS Variable FEFAM, http://sda .berkeley.edu/cgi-bin32/hsda?harcsda+gss06 (accessed September 25, 2007).

PERCENTAGE OF NEW FATHERS WHO CARRY PICTURES OF THEIR CHILD WITH THEM WHEREVER THEY GO: 66

Men are reveling in fatherhood. This is the conclusion that must be drawn from surveys of men's attitudes toward their children and studies of how much time they spend with them. With both parents working in most of today's families, men and women have readjusted many of their priorities. But for both mothers and fathers, children remain at the top of the priority list.

The federal government actually keeps tabs on these things, using surveys to probe the quality of family life. One survey, sponsored by the National Center for Education Statistics, is following a group of infants born in 2001.[12] When the children were 9 months old, the government interviewed their biological fathers, if they were living with the child, to find out how they felt about fatherhood. Bursting with pride doesn't begin to describe it. Obsessive is more like it. Two out of three fathers said they talk about their child all the time. Three out of four said they are always thinking about their child, and 66 percent said it was more fun to buy something for the kid than to get something for themselves. Most strongly agreed that they should be as heavily involved as the mother in childcare. And they appeared to be doing their part. Compared to fathers forty years ago, today's dads spend twice as much time taking care of the kids, according to time use research. In 1965, fathers spent 2.6 hours a week caring for children as a primary activity (about one-fourth the amount of time spent by mothers). Today, the figure has more than doubled, rising to 6.5 hours a week (about half the time spent by mothers).[13]

Men's newfound enthusiasm for family life is showing up in other areas as well. With women reducing the hours they spend doing housework, men have picked up some of the slack. Married fathers now devote 9.7 hours a week to housework, up from the 4.4 hours done by their counterparts in 1965.[14]

Factoid source: Frank Avenilla, Emily Rosenthal, and Pete Tice, "Fathers of U.S. Children Born in 2001: Findings from the Early Childhood Longitudinal Study, July 2006," http://nces.ed.gov/pubsearch/pubsinfo.asp?pubid=2006002 (accessed August 23, 2007).

PERCENTAGE OF WOMEN DOING LAUNDRY ON AN AVERAGE DAY: 27

Maybe it is the satisfaction of winning the war against dirt. Or the warm feeling that comes from folding clean clothes. Whatever the reason, American women practically insist on doing the laundry. On an average day, women are four times more likely than men to be in the laundry room—27 percent of women and just 6 percent of men, according to the American Time Use Survey.

Laundry is not the only chore dominated by women, however. Despite the fact that most women now work, they continue to shoulder the bulk of stereotypically female tasks. On an average day, 61 percent of women but only 34 percent of men prepare meals.[15] Thirty-three percent of women but only 10 percent of men clean up the kitchen. Thirty-seven percent of women, but only 12 percent of men clean the house.

It is not as bad as you think. Men are not idling on the couch while the wife vacuums under their feet. (Well, maybe they are. On an average day, men spend more time than women watching TV.) Husbands have their jobs around the house, too. Men are more likely than women to mow the lawn, repair leaky faucets, and change the oil in the SUV. Those tasks don't seem to cut it with their wives, however. When married couples are asked about the division of chores, 59 percent of wives say they do *more* than their fair share, according to the General Social Survey.[16] Yet an even larger 67 percent of husbands say they do a fair share. Who is right? It all depends on how you define "fair." Time use research shows husbands and wives with children working an almost identical number of hours per week. Considering both paid and unpaid work, wives work 65 hours a week and husbands 64 hours.[17] The average husband spends less time doing housework, but more time on the job.

Factoid source: Author's calculations based on Bureau of Labor Statistics, unpublished data from the 2005 American Time Use Survey.

PERCENTAGE OF MEN LIVING APART FROM THEIR CHILDREN WHO THINK THEY ARE DOING A 'VERY GOOD' JOB AS A FATHER: 27

A man's home is his castle. But divorce and child custody battles have banished many men from their kingdom. In parenting, men are the underdogs. When they marry and have children, they risk being torn from those they love the most—their children. More than 40 percent of marriages today are destined to end in divorce, and when they do, mom usually gets the kids. Women account for 83 percent of custodial parents, according to the Census Bureau, a figure that has not changed in the past decade.[18]

This is reality for men today: twenty-seven percent of fathers do not live with one or more of their children.[19] Ironically, men have become much more involved in parenting just when the outcome—a closer relationship with their children—is becoming more doubtful. Perhaps this is why fathers harbor grave doubts about their parenting skills, especially those living apart from their children. When asked how good a job they are doing as a parent, only 46 percent of men living with at least some of their children say "very good." Among men living apart from their children, the figure is an even lower 27 percent.[20]

It's not like they aren't trying. Three out of four men with children living elsewhere are in contact with their kids.[21] But on a scale of 1 (very dissatisfying) to 10 (very satisfying), they rate the satisfaction they get from visits with their children a lowly 4.6. The joys of being a part-time parent are piddling indeed.

Perhaps this is why only 74 percent of adult children describe their relationship with their father as "close," less than the 87 percent who say they are close to their mother, according to a Pew Research Center survey.[22] But fathers are making some emotional inroads. The percentage of adults who feel close to their father has climbed 5 percentage points since 1989.

Factoid source: National Center for Health Statistics, *Fertility, Contraception, and Fatherhood: Data on Men and Women from Cycle 6 of the 2002 National Survey of Family Growth*, Vital and Health Statistics, Series 23, No. 26, 2006, p. 106.

PERCENTAGE OF WOMEN WHO THINK
THEIR MOTHER DID AN EXCELLENT JOB
OF RAISING THEM: 69

Thanks, Mom. You did a great job of raising such a wonderful person: me. Most women are enthusiastic about the job their mother did raising them, according to a Fox News poll. How nice, but a wee bit self-serving—especially considering the fact that most women are not as generous when asked to rate the job today's mothers are doing with the current crop of youngsters. The 54 percent majority of women say today's mothers of young children are doing a worse job than mothers did several decades ago, according to a Pew Research Center survey.[23] If true, the future looks bleak.

In fact, the Pew survey shows that each succeeding generation of women thinks that mothers in the past did a better job of raising children than today's mothers are doing with their youngsters. If this were actually true, then by now women would have had to abandon parenting altogether, and social services would have been called in to rescue the kids. Apparently, it is human nature to judge others more harshly than one judges oneself—especially with advancing age. Those most likely to think today's mothers aren't up to snuff are older women—those past childrearing themselves but watching in alarm as their daughters and granddaughters make a mess of it. Among women aged 50 to 64, the percentage who think today's mothers are doing a worse job than mothers twenty or thirty years ago rises as high as 66 percent, according to Pew.

Mothers are not the only ones getting blamed for falling down on the job. The feeling that things are getting worse is a common theme in public opinion—and probably always has been. Even Socrates is supposed to have complained about the younger generation: "The children now love luxury; they have bad manners, contempt for authority; they show disrespect for elders. . . ." Yada, yada, yada, it was all downhill from there.

Factoid source: Fox News/Opinion Dynamics Poll, May 5, 2005, http://www.foxnews.com/story/0,2933,155635,00 .html (accessed August 26, 2007).

Chapter 3
SEX

AVERAGE AGE AT
FIRST SEXUAL INTERCOURSE: 17.3

Those who urge young adults to wait until marriage before having sex have not looked at a calendar lately. This is not the 1950s, when half of women married in their teens. The median age at first marriage in 1950 was just 20 (meaning half married for the first time before age 20 and half after).[1] Back then, it might have made sense to wait. But with the median age at first marriage now 25.5 for women and 27.5 for men, asking young adults to wait until marriage is like asking a popsicle not to melt in the sun.

This is not rocket science; it is biology. By the time they turn 18, most young adults have had sex—54 percent of men and an even larger 58 percent of women, according to the National Survey of Family Growth.[2] By the time they reach age 25, more than 90 percent of single men and women have had sex. The timing of the "first time" differs by a matter of months, not years, regardless of whether a teen is male or female, black or white, fundamentalist or atheist.

Casual sex it is not—at least in most cases. More than two out of three women say their first sexual partner was a steady boyfriend.[3] Far from regretting their loss of virginity, most young women who had sex before age 20 wanted it to happen. Thirty-four percent say they really wanted to have sex, and another 53 percent partly wanted it to happen. Only 13 percent say they did not want to have sex the first time around.[4]

Is sex education in the public schools to blame for all this teenage sexual activity? Hardly. In sex education classes—which most high school students have endured by tenth grade—teens are more likely to have been taught how to say no (85 percent) than how to use birth control (66 percent).[5] At least they paid attention to some of the lectures: three out of four teenagers used birth control the first time they had sex.[6]

Factoid source: National Center for Health Statistics, *Fertility, Family Planning, and Reproductive Health of U.S. Women: Data from the 2002 National Survey of Family Growth,* Vital and Health Statistics, Series 23, No. 25, 2005, p. 73.

PERCENTAGE OF AMERICANS WHO SEE NOTHING WRONG WITH PREMARITAL SEX: 46

"Free love" was one of the rallying cries of the 1960s counterculture. Older Americans were shocked when they discovered that their children were having sex before marriage. The difference in attitudes toward sexual behavior was one of the defining characteristics of the generation gap emerging at the time. Does the gap still exist today, or did it disappear as those freewheeling young adults grew up? Let's find out.

The American public once strongly disapproved of premarital sex. In 1972, only 27 percent of people aged 18 or older agreed that sex before marriage was "not wrong at all," according to the General Social Survey. By 2006, the figure had grown to 46 percent. Generational replacement explains the change. The prim and proper adults of the past have been replaced by more open-minded younger generations.

Look at the size of the generation gap in the early 1970s: at the time, 47 percent of people aged 18 to 29 saw nothing wrong with premarital sex compared with 16 percent of their middle-aged parents—a yawning gap of 31 percentage points.[7] How wide is the generation gap today? The attitudes of 18- to 29-year-olds have barely changed, with 51 percent of today's young adults seeing nothing wrong with premarital sex. The attitudes of middle-aged people (the parents of today's young adults) have been transformed, however. Now, a much larger 43 percent of that age group thinks premarital sex is "not wrong at all." The generation gap has shrunk to a crack of just 8 percentage points.

Of course, today's middle-aged were the young adults of the early 1970s. Few changed their minds about premarital sex as they matured. Instead, they changed our society—and they are still at it. Only 29 percent of people aged 65 or older approve of premarital sex—a figure that will soon change.

Factoid source: Survey Documentation and Analysis, Computer-assisted Survey Methods Program, University of California, Berkeley, General Social Surveys, 1972–2006 Cumulative Data Files, GSS Variable PREMARSX, http://sda .berkeley.edu/cgi-bin32/hsda?harcsda+gss06 (accessed October 4, 2007).

PERCENTAGE OF CATHOLIC WOMEN
WHO USE BIRTH CONTROL: 60

It may be hard to believe, but birth control was once as controversial an issue as abortion is today. Not until 1965 did the Supreme Court strike down the last of the state laws prohibiting the use of birth control. In *Griswold v. Connecticut*, the court ruled unconstitutional the law prohibiting Connecticut residents—married or single—from using any drug or instrument for the purpose of preventing conception. Most of Connecticut was ignoring the law anyway, just as most American Catholics ignore their church's ban against the use of "artificial" birth control.

The use of birth control may yet be controversial in the Vatican, but it is a done deal in the United States. Among American women of childbearing age, the 62 percent majority currently uses birth control—just slightly above the 60 percent figure for Catholics.[8] Among birth control users, Catholic women are as likely as the average woman to be on the pill (32 percent), use condoms (18 percent), or be sterilized (25 percent).

To understand just how universal birth control use is today, take a look at why 38 percent of women of childbearing age do not use contraception. Are they religious fanatics who refuse to interfere with God's will? Are they irresponsible numskulls risking an accident? Did they mean to take the pill but were so busy they forgot? Almost none of the above. Nearly half of them are not using birth control because they are not sexually active.[9] Others are already pregnant, trying to become pregnant, or unable to have children. Only 7 percent of women of childbearing age are numskulls—defined as sexually active, not wanting to become pregnant, and keeping their fingers crossed as their method of birth control.

Factoid source: National Center for Health Statistics, *Fertility, Family Planning, and Reproductive Health of U.S. Women: Data from the 2002 National Survey of Family Growth,* Vital and Health Statistics, Series 23, No. 25, 2005, p. 99.

PERCENTAGE OF AMERICANS AGED 15 TO 44 WHO HAVE EVER USED A CONDOM: 90

The back seat of the car is not what it used to be. Once a place of unbridled passion, it is now where teenagers dispense birth control with all the seriousness of a family planning clinic. The percentage of men and women who used a condom the first time they had sex climbed from just 22 percent in the years prior to 1980 all the way up to 70 percent today, according to the federal government's National Survey of Family Growth.[10] Condoms are the birth control method of choice for those in the process of losing their virginity.

The popularity of condoms soared after AIDS emerged in the early 1980s, adding urgency to their use. In 1982, only 52 percent of sexually active 15- to 44-year-olds had ever used a condom. The 90 percent figure of today is the type of behavior change that occurs in social science statistics only when the survival instinct comes into play. Condoms have become as common as credit cards in the American wallet. Still, those most likely to have unrolled a condom recently are singles rather than married couples. Only 27 percent of married men used a condom in the past year compared with 67 percent of their unmarried, sexually active counterparts.[11] Many married couples depend on the pill and, with increasing age, sterilization.

Condom use is so widespread that the embarrassment factor has greatly diminished—at least in the bedroom. The 55 percent majority of young men aged 15 to 24 say there is "no chance" they would be embarrassed to talk about using a condom with a new sexual partner.[12] Store clerks are another matter. "Furtive," is how *Drug Store News* describes the way consumers feel when they buy condoms. According to the trade publication, condoms today remain in the "brown bag category."[13]

Factoid source: National Center for Health Statistics, *Use of Contraception and Use of Family Planning Services in the United States: 1982–2002,* Advance Data, No. 350, 2004, p. 15.

PERCENTAGE OF PREGNANCIES
ENDING IN ABORTION: 24

When South Dakota passed a law early in 2006 banning most abortions, many thought it might be the challenge that would finally overturn *Roe v. Wade*. But it never got that far. Opponents of that law—which outlawed abortion even in cases of rape or incest—soon gathered enough signatures to put it to a vote. In November 2006, the state's voters overwhelmingly rejected the ban by 56 to 44 percent. The vote wasn't even close because most Americans support the right to an abortion—at least in some circumstances. According to the General Social Survey, 40 percent of the public supports abortion for any reason.[14] A larger 78 percent support abortion in cases of rape or incest, and fully 88 percent support a woman's right to an abortion if her health is seriously endangered.

Over the years, abortion foes have succeeded in restricting access to abortion in many states. The number of abortions (about 1.2 million a year) and the abortion rate have been falling—but not just because abortion providers have been driven out of town. Something else is at work. Emergency contraception, or the "morning-after pill," is eliminating the need for abortion, reducing the number of abortions by 51,000 in 2000 alone according to a study by the Guttmacher Institute.[15] And that was before the FDA approved the sale of emergency contraception (or Plan B) from pharmacies without a prescription. With Plan B now available, abortions are likely to become less common and the issue may recede in importance.

Or will it? The battle may be shifting from the abortion clinic to the pharmacy counter, where antiabortion forces are urging pharmacists to refuse to dispense the contraceptive. But they are fighting a losing battle with the American public. According to a Pew survey, when asked whether pharmacists should be able to refuse to sell birth control (a category that includes the morning-after pill), 80 percent of the public says no.[16]

Factoid source: Guttmacher Institute, "Estimates of U.S. Abortion Incidence, 2001–2003, August 2006," http://www .guttmacher.org/sections/index.php?page=stats (accessed June 20, 2007).

PERCENTAGE OF MEN WHO IDENTIFY THEMSELVES AS HETEROSEXUAL: 90

The government does ask and it does tell. According to the National Survey of Family Growth, nine out of ten adults under age 45 (the survey is limited to the under 45 age group) say they are heterosexual. The percentages are almost identical for men and women.

Does this mean 10 percent of Americans are gay or lesbian? Maybe. When answering the survey, respondents could identify themselves as "heterosexual," "homosexual," "bisexual," or "something else." Among men, 2 percent identify themselves as homosexual, 2 percent as bisexual, 2 percent refuse to answer, and 4 percent say they are something else. Among women the proportions are pretty much the same. According to government analysts, those who say they are something else may not understand the terminology.

The survey probes sexual orientation from a different angle as well. It asks respondents whether they are attracted to people of the same or the opposite sex. On the attraction question, 92 percent of men say they are attracted only to females.[17] Among women, 86 percent say they are attracted only to males. The government digs even deeper, asking about sexual experiences. The answers: Six percent of men have had oral or anal sex with another man. Eleven percent of women have had a sexual experience with another woman.[18] (The survey asks men and women different questions, making it difficult to compare results by gender.)

No doubt, many would never tell the government about their sex life, although the researchers conducted the interviews in a way to minimize this hesitancy. Respondents wore headphones and entered their responses directly into a computer, preventing the interviewer from knowing their answers. Nevertheless, homosexuality is certain to be underreported, making the 10 percent figure as good a guess as any.

Factoid source: National Center for Health Statistics, *Sexual Behavior and Selected Health Measures: Men and Women 15–44 Years of Age, United States, 2002,* Advance Data, Vital and Health Statistics, No. 362, September 15, 2005, p. 30.

PERCENTAGE OF AMERICANS WHO THINK HOMOSEXUALITY SHOULD BE ACCEPTED BY SOCIETY: 49

On the issue of homosexuality, Americans stand shoulder to shoulder with the citizens of the less-developed countries of the world. Just 49 percent of the public thinks our society should accept homosexuality. Some may take heart in the fact that at least the number willing to accept homosexuality is larger than the number rejecting it (41 percent), but the figure is far below the acceptance level in Canada, Germany, France, Great Britain, and Italy. Our attitudes are similar to those of Bolivia and Bulgaria.

How come the most affluent and educated citizens of the world share the attitudes of the poorer and less-educated populations of less-developed countries? Why is our thinking so different from our socioeconomic equals? Here is the reason: Among the developed countries of the world, the United States stands alone in its enthusiastic embrace of religion. More often than not, religious teaching equates homosexuality with immorality, which shapes the attitudes of millions of Americans.

Nothing separates the men from the boys more than religiosity. Regular churchgoers are most likely to see homosexuality as a moral failing. In contrast, those who rarely attend church are most likely to see homosexuality as something people are born with and cannot change. When asked whether homosexuality is an acceptable lifestyle, the 64 percent majority of people who attend church at least weekly say it is not acceptable, according to a Gallup poll.[19] Seventy-five percent of regular churchgoers are against gay marriage, 60 percent oppose civil unions, and 54 percent believe gays and lesbians can change, according to a Pew survey.[20]

Statistics like these make you wonder what brand of morality is being taught in Sunday school. One thing is certain, churchgoers do not have to worry about bumping into gays and lesbians at the coffee hour—or so they think. When asked whether they are in or out of the closet with friends, family, coworkers, their boss, or at church, the largest share of gays and lesbians—72 percent—say they hide their orientation at church.[21]

Factoid source: Pew Global Attitudes Project, *World Publics Welcome Global Trade—But Not Immigration*, October 4, 2007, p. 35.

Chapter 4
MARRIAGE AND DIVORCE

COUPLES LIVING TOGETHER OUTSIDE OF MARRIAGE AS A PERCENTAGE OF TOTAL COUPLES: 8

The United States is all about big numbers. Geographically, we are the third largest country in the world. Demographically, we are the third most populous country. The nation's 116 million households include 59 million married couples and 5 million couples who live together outside of marriage.

Hold on—just 5 million cohabiting couples? In this great country of ours, a minuscule 8 percent of couples live together without being married? The number hardly deserves all the attention it receives, being no more than a footnote in the Census Bureau's vast spreadsheets of detail about who lives with whom.

In the United States, cohabitation, once seen as a threat to marriage, is almost always a transitory state en route to wedded bliss or heartbreak. Although half of women under age 45 have lived with someone outside of marriage, most do not remain in legal limbo. Fifty-two percent of cohabiting women eventually marry their partner, 35 percent break up with their partner, and only 13 percent continue to live with their partner without marrying, according to the National Survey of Family Growth.[1]

Clearly, few Americans are willing to make cohabitation a permanent lifestyle. Compare the US experience with Sweden, where cohabitation is much more permanent. A substantial 28 percent of Swedish couples live together outside of marriage. What explains our lack of enthusiasm for life outside the legal bonds of matrimony? Call it "matrimoney" and the reasons will become clear. In the United States, our financial status depends on our marital status, explains David Popenoe, codirector of the National Marriage Project at Rutgers University, with benefits such as health insurance and lower tax rates accruing to married couples.[2] It is not that way in Sweden, where government benefits (including health insurance) and taxes are determined by individual factors rather than marital status. For Americans, it literally pays to marry, which is why most of us are eager to get to the altar.

Factoid source: Bureau of the Census, 2007 Current Population Survey, http://pubdb3.census.gov/macro/ 032007/hhinc/toc.htm (accessed September 24, 2007).

PERCENTAGE OF BRIDES WHO ARE VIRGINS: 15

The average woman walking down the aisle has never been older. The median age of first-time brides is 25.5, according to the Census Bureau—an all-time high. Women are marrying more than five years later than their counterparts in the 1950s, when half of first-time brides were teenagers.[3] Back then, couples did not wait until marriage before having sex, they married to have sex.

The top priority for today's young women is college rather than marriage. Most women graduating from high school enroll in college a few months later. Given these priorities, it is no surprise that the percentage of women in their early twenties who have not yet married has surged along with college enrollments. Among women aged 20 to 24 today, 75 percent are single, up from only 32 percent in 1950.[4]

Going to college does not make women less likely to marry. It just changes the wedding date. Women with a college degree are less likely to marry young. Only 38 percent of women with a bachelor's degree are married by age 25 compared with a much larger 59 percent of women who went no further than high school.[5] Ultimately, however, the college-educated are just as likely to marry as those with less education. By age 35, more than 80 percent of both groups have said "I do."

Staying married is a bigger problem than getting married for most women today. The rise in divorce over the past half century means fewer couples are celebrating marriage milestones. Among women marrying for the first time in the late 1950s, 67 percent eventually celebrated their 25th wedding anniversary. Among those marrying for the first time in the late 1970s, the figure was a much smaller 46 percent.[6]

Factoid source: National Center for Health Statistics, *Fertility, Family Planning, and Reproductive Health of U.S. Women: Data from the 2002 National Survey of Family Growth,* Vital and Health Statistics, Series 23, No. 25, 2005, p. 81.

PERCENTAGE DESCRIBING THEIR MARRIAGE AS VERY HAPPY: 61

Marital bliss is harder to come by these days. The proportion of married men and women who describe their marriage as very happy fell from 68 to 61 percent between 1973 and 2006, according to the General Social Survey. The proportion describing their marriage as only "pretty" happy—basically, a shrug of the shoulders—grew from 30 to 36 percent.

These changes are not monumental, but they may be important. Many Americans are worried about the decline in marital happiness and the institution of marriage itself—enough, in fact, to form special interest groups. These groups survey the public, issue reports, and lobby Congress. The National Marriage Project at Rutgers University and the National Fatherhood Initiative based in Gaithersburg, Maryland, are two of the organizations promoting marriage and stable family relationships.

How strange to promote something most of us already want—a happy marriage. But wanting a happy marriage is not the same as having one. In fact, those who believe most heartily in marriage are the ones having the greatest difficulty keeping their marriages together. The least educated women—high school dropouts—are the ones most likely to think it is better to marry than to go through life being single, according to the National Survey of Family Growth.[7] Yet this group is most likely to divorce. College graduates, in contrast, are less likely to think marriage is better than single life. Yet once married, they are least likely to divorce.

According to sociologist Norval D. Glenn of the University of Texas–Austin, the erosion in marital happiness is due to the decline of what he calls the "ideal of marital permanence."[8] With divorce commonplace, today's husbands and wives are always in the market for a better marriage partner. In the new marriage market, where sales are never final, the all-too-familiar spouse can look a bit shopworn.

Factoid source: Survey Documentation and Analysis, Computer-assisted Survey Methods Program, University of California, Berkeley, General Social Surveys, 1972–2006 Cumulative Data Files, GSS Variable HAPMAR, http://sda .berkeley.edu/D3/GSS06/Docyr/gs06.htm (accessed September 24, 2007).

PERCENTAGE OF WIVES WITH
A BETTER-EDUCATED HUSBAND: 23

Even in a supposedly upwardly mobile society such as ours, Cinderella stories are rare. Most husbands and wives are from the same socioeconomic
class. The 55 percent majority of couples share the same level of education.
Few women (or men) marry "up." These trends appear to be solidifying as
education becomes increasingly important to getting ahead.

In the marriage sweepstakes, the winners keep on winning thanks to the
college sorting process where men and women destined to become the
nation's elite meet and marry. Together, these powerhouses form dual-
income couples whose median household income is often in excess of
$100,000 a year. Many of these couples can afford to send their children to
private school, summer camps, and enrichment programs, boosting their academic performance and putting the shine on college essays. Once in college,
the cycle starts all over again. Socioeconomic status is the most significant
factor in determining whether a child is in a gifted program, takes AP or
honors courses in high school, or enrolls in college.

If Cinderella stories are uncommon, Anna Nicole Smith stories are even
harder to find. The age difference between 26-year-old bride Anna Nicole
Smith and 89-year-old groom J. Howard Marshall was a jaw-dropping sixty-
three years. Most couples are much closer in age. In fact, 60 percent of husbands and wives were born within two or three years of one another.[9] A
twenty-year age gap is rare. Only 524,000 husbands are twenty or more
years older than their wives—which amounts to less than 1 percent of all
married couples. Among wives, just 183,000 are twenty or more years older
than their husbands.

Factoid source: Bureau of the Census, Families and
Living Arrangements, http://www.census.gov/population/
www/socdemo/hh-fam.html (accessed September 24,
2007).

PERCENTAGE OF WOMEN
WHO HAVE EVER DIVORCED: 23

You have heard it before: Half of all marriages end in divorce. Although this figure is widely quoted and believed, reality is more complex. The notion originated from a statistical fluke. Back when the federal government collected detailed data on marriage and divorce (it has not done so since 1996), there were about half as many divorces as marriages in a given year. Leaping to conclusions, more than a few reporters interpreted the figures to mean that half of all marriages would end in divorce.

In fact, estimating the fraction of marriages that will end in divorce is no easy task. The probability of divorce is not the same for everyone. For reasons not well understood, the year you were born—your birth cohort—influences your probability of divorce. Everyone knows younger generations are more likely than older generations to divorce, but this may be less well known: people born between 1945 and 1954 have a higher probability of divorce than anyone else.

In a study of marriage and divorce patterns, the Census Bureau finds women born between 1945 and 1954 most likely to have ended a marriage, with 41 percent experiencing a divorce.[10] Even so, a larger 44 percent of women in the age group have been married only once and are still married. Among men, divorce also peaks for those born between 1945 and 1954, with 38 percent having experienced a marital breakup. But a larger 50 percent of men in the age group have been married only once and are still married.

Divorce has not yet reached the 50 percent probability level, although the 1945-to-1954 birth cohort is pushing it. Why are these men and women most likely to divorce? No one really knows, but one theory is that the changing roles of women in the 1960s and 1970s caught them off guard, creating marital strife and leading to higher levels of divorce.

Factoid source: Bureau of the Census, Number, Timing, and Duration of Marriages and Divorces: 2004, Detailed Tables, http://www.census.gov/population/www/socdemo/marr-div/2004detailed_tables.html (accessed September 24, 2007).

PERCENTAGE WHO BELIEVE DIVORCE IS THE BEST SOLUTION FOR COUPLES WITH MARRIAGE PROBLEMS: 43

Divorce has become commonplace, and most Americans are not happy about it. Fewer than half the public thinks divorce is the best solution for couples with marital problems, according to the General Social Survey. The 46 percent plurality of the public wants to make it more difficult for couples to divorce.[11]

A nearly universal 94 percent of Americans regard divorce as a serious national problem, reports the National Fatherhood Initiative.[12] Eighty-eight percent agree or strongly agree with the statement "couples who marry should make a lifelong commitment to one another, to be broken only under extreme circumstances." These strong feelings against divorce would warm the heart of the pope, but are they genuine?

Maybe for those who are not yet divorced. Men and women who have been through a divorce feel differently. Apparently, divorce is a serious national problem until you need one. Most of the divorced think divorce *is* the best solution when couples can't work out their marriage problems, according to the National Survey of Family Growth.[13] And when the divorced are asked whether it should have been more difficult for them to get a divorce, the resounding 80 percent say no.[14] As is true with abortion and many other national issues, divorce is disapproved in general but tolerated in the specific. When questions about divorce are more narrowly focused, smaller percentages of the public disapprove. Only 43 percent think unhappy couples should stay together until their children are grown, for example.[15]

Do the divorced have any regrets? You decide: When asked whether they wish they had worked harder to save their marriage, fully 74 percent of the divorced say no.[16] But when asked whether they wish their spouse had worked harder to save the marriage, the 62 percent majority says yes—proof, perhaps, that the marriage could not be saved.

Factoid source: Survey Documentation and Analysis, Computer-assisted Survey Methods Program, University of California, Berkeley, General Social Surveys, 1972–2006 Cumulative Data Files, GSS Variable, DIVBEST, http://sda .berkeley.edu/D3/GSS06/Docyr/gs06.htm (accessed September 24, 2007).

PERCENTAGE OF EVER-MARRIED ADULTS
WHO HAVE CHEATED ON A SPOUSE: 20

It is a testament to the monogamous nature of human sexual relationships that only 20 percent of ever-married adults have had an extramarital affair. Of course this figure is an underestimate of the incidence of cheating, since it is a volunteered response to a question on the General Social Survey. Even after adjusting for discretion, however, it is safe to say that most spouses are faithful to one another.

But that doesn't change the fact that happily ever after is an ending found mainly in fairy tales. Fewer than half the nation's adults have married only once and are still married.[17] Among men, the figure is 44 percent. Among women an even smaller 41 percent still live with Prince Charming—the man with whom they first walked down the aisle. "Life is what happens to you while you're busy making other plans," John Lennon once said, and many of the divorced would agree. When asked why their first marriage failed, the 55 percent majority of the divorced say infidelity was a major reason, according to a survey by the National Fatherhood Initiative.[18] But they cite other reasons as even more important for the breakup, including a lack of commitment (73 percent) and too much arguing (56 percent).

Our increasingly complex relationships have changed the course of adult life. In 1960, men and women could expect to spend 62 percent of their lives with a spouse and children.[19] Today, we spend less than half our life in a nuclear family, thanks to the postponement of marriage, smaller families, and the greater likelihood of divorce. And divorce is not the only D-word bringing an end to marriage. Death also intervenes. Among women aged 70 or older, only 29 percent are still married and living with the man they first married because most have been widowed.[20]

Factoid source: Survey Documentation and Analysis, Computer-assisted Survey Methods Program, University of California, Berkeley, General Social Surveys, 1972–2006 Cumulative Data Files, GSS Variable EVSTRAY, http://sda .berkeley.edu/D3/GSS06/Docyr/gs06.htm (accessed September 24, 2007).

PERCENTAGE OF WOMEN AGED 85 OR OLDER WHO LIVE ALONE: 58

At one time, it was unusual—perhaps even suspect—for people to live by themselves. In 1950, only 5 million Americans lived alone, just 3 percent of the population. Today, more than 30 million people live by themselves.[21] Single-person households account for more than one-fourth of the nation's total households, and lone living is poised to become the most common living arrangement in the United States.

Why has living alone gone from odd to ordinary? Three trends have conspired to make lone living one of the most popular lifestyles. One, the postponement of marriage boosted the number of young adults who live alone. Two, divorce added the middle-aged to the mix. Three, and most important, the aging of the population resulted in many more older women living by themselves.

Sad, but true: wives are far more likely than husbands to be widowed. Not only are women less likely to die than men at every age, but most women marry men who are slightly older—increasing the odds that they will outlive their spouse. Among the nearly 1 million Americans who lose their spouse each year, more than 70 percent are women.[22]

In our agricultural past, most elderly widows lived with their grown children—not because they moved in with the kids, but because the kids never moved out. On the family farm, children grew up and took over the chores. Mom remained at home until she died. Most of today's older Americans want the same thing—to stay at home, even if it means living alone. When asked in an AARP survey whether they agree with the statement, "What I'd really like to do is stay in my current residence for as long as possible," a nearly universal 95 percent of people aged 75 or older want to stay where they are. Eventually, this will mean living alone.[23]

Factoid Source: Bureau of the Census, Families and Living Arrangements: 2006, http://www.census.gov/population/www/socdemo/hh-fam.html (accessed September 24, 2007).

Chapter 5
BABIES

PERCENTAGE OF BIRTHS
TO UNMARRIED WOMEN: 38

Out of control. That's how some might describe the trend in out-of-wedlock births. Of the 4 million children born in the United States each year, more than one in three are born out of wedlock, according to the National Center for Health Statistics. In 1950, the figure was just 4 percent.[1] Once upon a time, single women who found themselves in a family way were thrown out of school, shipped to homes for unwed mothers, and had their babies farmed out for adoption. Today, public schools provide daycare centers, friends host baby showers, and the proud parent sends out birth announcements. Out-of-wedlock childbearing has become socially acceptable, if not yet the norm.

But it is the norm for some. Among blacks, for example, seven out of ten births are to single mothers. It wasn't always this way. Single mothers did not account for the majority of black births until the mid-1970s.[2] Black women are not alone in choosing, increasingly, to have children outside of marriage. Other women are following in their footsteps, with a doubling in the proportion of babies born out of wedlock among non-Hispanic whites and Hispanics over the past few decades. Today, nearly half of babies born to Hispanics are out of wedlock, as are one in four babies born to non-Hispanic whites.[3]

What sparked this profound change—some would call it disintegration—in the family? The demographics tell the story. The most disadvantaged segments of the population are the ones with the highest rates of out-of-wedlock childbearing—the poor, the uneducated, and the young. Some argue that moral standards have declined. That's the easy answer. The pattern of single parenthood shows the reasons to be more complex—and more troubling—than any moral failings among today's young women.

To unravel this mystery, follow the money.

Factoid source: National Center for Health Statistics, *Births: Preliminary Data for 2006,* National Vital Statistics Report, Vol. 56, No. 7, December 25, 2007, p. 6.

PERCENTAGE OF MOTHERS UNDER AGE 45 WHO HAVE BORNE A CHILD OUT OF WEDLOCK: 42

Having a child out of wedlock is not just for "bad girls" anymore. With more than 40 percent of mothers aged 15 to 44 reporting an out-of-wedlock birth, single parenthood is close to becoming the norm. In fact, it is the norm for mothers under age 30, high school dropouts, and women raised by a single parent.[4]

What do these women have in common? It's what they don't have in common that matters more—and what they don't have is a lot of money. Neither do the fathers of their children. To understand out-of-wedlock childbearing, look no further than Economics 101 and the daily struggle to maximize the "utility function." That's an economist's way of saying that each of us—rich and poor alike—is looking for the best deal whether we are in the market for a mate or a melon.

Many disadvantaged women avoid marriage because it makes no sense to commit themselves to a man with little earning power. Marriage is an economic partnership, and no woman—rich or poor—finds it advantageous to marry a man with little economic potential. Rather than limiting themselves to one impoverished provider, poor women build networks of fathers and families to help them raise their children. In the classic ethnographic study of the urban poor, *All Our Kin*, anthropologist Carol B. Stack shows how these relationships stabilize the volatile economy of poverty—an economy characterized by minimum-wage jobs, unemployment, illness, vehicle breakdowns, evictions, and ever-changing living arrangements. "As long as the father acknowledges his parental entitlement, his relatives, especially his mother and sisters, consider themselves kin to the child and therefore responsible for him," observes Stack.[5]

Having a child out of wedlock is not a moral choice, but an economic strategy. The fact that out-of-wedlock childbearing is growing speaks volumes not about morals, but about the increasingly dire prospects for millions of American men.

Factoid source: National Center for Health Statistics, *Fertility, Family Planning, and Reproductive Health of U.S. Women: Data from the 2002 National Survey of Family Growth,* Vital and Health Statistics, Series 23, No. 25, 2005, p. 52.

PERCENTAGE OF WOMEN UNDER AGE 45 WHO THINK IT IS OK FOR AN UNMARRIED WOMAN TO HAVE A CHILD: 70

Which comes first, the chicken or the egg? Does the growing percentage of women having children out of wedlock change attitudes toward single parenthood—the "Everybody's doing it so it must be OK" defense? Or does a change in attitude encourage more women to have children outside of marriage—the "You did it, so why not me" defense?

Whichever way it works—and it probably works both ways—attitudes have reversed course from the days when pregnant single women were spirited away to homes for unwed mothers. Among Americans of all ages, the 54 percent majority now says it is morally acceptable to have a child out-of-wedlock, according to a Gallup poll.[6] Not surprisingly, young adults (many of them single parents) find out-of-wedlock childbearing more acceptable than their parents or grandparents, according to Gallup, which could guarantee its continued rise toward the norm.[7]

Regardless of their demographic characteristics, the majority of women under age 45 say it is OK to have a child out of wedlock, with one exception: Women who describe themselves as fundamentalist Protestants are more likely to disapprove than to approve of out-of-wedlock childbearing.[8] Even among the fundamentalists, however, the 49 percent who say single parenthood is OK outnumber the 45 percent who object.

Some of the women most approving of single parenthood are those who have had a child out of wedlock themselves (77 percent). Why is this not surprising? Here is something more unexpected: Even among women who have not had a child out of wedlock, the 67 percent majority thinks single parenthood is OK. The pope can't even rally Catholics to rail against the growing trend. Among Catholic women under age 45, the 72 percent majority says out-of-wedlock childbearing is OK.

Interestingly, men are more likely than women to disapprove of out-of-wedlock childbearing. Even so, the 59 percent majority of men under age 45 think it is OK for a single woman to have a baby.

Factoid source: National Center for Health Statistics, *Fertility, Contraception, and Fatherhood: Data on Men and Women from Cycle 6 of the 2002 National Survey of Family Growth,* Vital and Health Statistics, Series 23, No. 26, 2006, p. 123.

MINORITY BIRTHS AS A PERCENTAGE OF TOTAL BIRTHS: 46

Diversity. It may be the most overused word of the twenty-first century, evoking among some a clench-teethed tolerance of differences in skin color, religion, and lifestyle. Diversity's breeding ground, literally, is the nation's hospitals, where 46 percent of newborns are Hispanic, black, Asian, or American Indian—approaching half of births.

Like a slow-motion tidal wave, diversity is flowing from the maternity wards into the elementary schools, where 42 percent of the nation's public school students are Asian, black, or Hispanic.[9] Diversity is surging up the age structure and transforming the entry-level workforce. Hispanics, blacks, and Asians account for 38 percent of food service workers, 50 percent of janitors, and 55 percent of laborers at construction sites.[10]

At the other end of the pay and power scale, however, diversity is little more than a discussion point. Take the S & P 1,500 companies, for example. Blacks, Hispanics, and Asians account for only 10 percent of those sitting on their boards of directors, according to Institutional Shareholder Services.[11] In the US House of Representatives, only 17 percent of lawmakers are black, Hispanic, Asian, or American Indian. In the Senate, the figure is just 6 percent, according to the Congressional Research Service.[12]

In fact, business leaders and politicians will be the last to diversify. Their older age, for one, insulates them from the mix. The average senator today is 60 years old, an age group overwhelmingly dominated by non-Hispanic whites. The Senate is monochromatic for another reason, too. The US Constitution guarantees each state two senators, regardless of the size of the state's population. Consequently, the nation's smallest and least diverse states are vastly overrepresented in our nation's most important legislative body, observes University of Texas law professor Sanford Levinson.[13] This is why so many politicians can ignore the wants and needs of minorities. Blacks, Hispanics, and Asians are not their constituents.

Factoid source: National Center for Health Statistics, *Births: Preliminary Data for 2006*, National Vital Statistics Report, Vol. 56, No. 7, December 5, 2007, p. 6.

ON A SCALE OF ONE TO TEN, HOW HAPPY WOMEN ARE TO BE PREGNANT: 7.9

"You're pregnant." Are there any more powerful words in the English language? Each year, 6 million women in the United States hear those life-altering words. Not all of them end up with a baby, of course. In fact, of the 6 million women who become pregnant each year, only 4 million give birth. The remainder of the pregnancies—more than one-third—end in an abortion or miscarriage.[14] Regardless of the outcomes, for the 6 million women whose pregnancy test reads positive, emotions run high. How high? Read on.

Every few years, the federal government's National Survey of Family Growth probes the sexual behavior, fertility, and childbearing of women under age 45. One of the survey questions asks women to rate their happiness, on a scale of 1 to 10, with any pregnancy during the past three years. Excluded are pregnancies ending in abortion because, by definition, women who have abortions were not happy with the pregnancy. The results show women's feelings toward pregnancy range from despair to euphoria. Specifically, older women are happier to be pregnant than younger women, and married women are happier than single women.

Behind these differing levels of happiness is choice. Women who wanted to become pregnant are much happier (9.2 on the scale) than those who did not want to become pregnant (4.2).[15] Not surprisingly, older women are most likely to have wanted to become pregnant (77 percent say their pregnancy was wanted), and the youngest women least likely (24 percent). Married women, too, are most likely to have wanted the pregnancy (77 percent), and single women least likely (39 percent).

Fortunately, many women who are unhappy when they hear the words "you're pregnant," change their minds by the time they get to the delivery room. Unfortunately, some women give birth to children they do not want.

Factoid source: National Center for Health Statistics, *Fertility, Family Planning, and Reproductive Health of U.S. Women: Data from the 2002 National Survey of Family Growth,* Vital and Health Statistics, Series 23, No. 25, 2005, p. 60.

PERCENTAGE OF BIRTHS
THAT ARE UNWANTED: 14

Usually, but not always, having a baby is a happy occasion. Most children are wanted and eagerly anticipated. Among babies born to women in the past five years, 65 percent were wanted at the time of conception, according to the National Survey of Family Growth.[16] For these lucky children, names have been chosen with care, nurseries lovingly decorated, and grandparents anxiously hover nearby.

Some babies are a surprise, wanted but conceived too soon. Over the five-year period of the study, a substantial 21 percent of births were mistimed. These are the children whose parents must make hurried preparations and financial adjustments, whose siblings are told to move over to make room for one more. The parents might have been dismayed when they realized a baby was on the way already, but they soldier on.

An unlucky 14 percent of children were not wanted at the time they were conceived. It is more than likely tears were shed when the pregnancy test came back positive. Sleepless nights ensued, followed by hard decisions and grudging acceptance. The 14-percent figure translates into more than half a million children born each year who were unwanted when they were conceived.

Who is most likely to have an unwanted birth? The very same women who have babies out of wedlock: the young, the uneducated, and the unmarried—in other words, the disadvantaged. Another factor also plays a surprising role in the likelihood that a woman will have an unwanted child—her religion. Among the women most likely to have an unwanted child are fundamentalist Protestants, 20 percent of whom had an unwanted child in the past five years, higher than the rate for any other religious group. Not surprisingly, fundamentalist Protestants are also among the women least likely to use birth control.[17]

Factoid source: National Center for Health Statistics, *Fertility, Family Planning, and Reproductive Health of U.S. Women: Data from the 2002 National Survey of Family Growth,* Vital and Health Statistics, Series 23, No. 25, 2005, p. 56.

PERCENTAGE OF WOMEN
WHO HAVE HAD TWO CHILDREN: 35

Two. For most couples, that is the lucky number. When asked to name the ideal number of children, the 49 percent plurality of the public says just two, according to the General Social Survey.[18] The two child ideal has appealed to the largest share of Americans for several decades.

In this arena at least, Americans are living up to their ideals. Demographers have been trained to calculate the exact number of children women will have in their lifetime, based on age-specific fertility rates. In fact, they get paid to do this. The answer is just over two—or 2.101 to be exact.[19] But real life is a lot messier than statistics, with some women having more than two children and others fewer. Among women aged 40 to 44—most of them unlikely to have more children—only 35 percent have had two children.[20] A substantial 19 percent have not had any children (only 1 percent of the public thinks no children is ideal). Seventeen percent have had only one child (an ideal number for just 2 percent). And 29 percent of women in the age group have had three or more children (less than the 36 percent who think three or more is ideal). The percentage of women who have had three or more children has fallen sharply over the past few decades as the two child ideal took hold. Three decades ago, the 59 percent majority of women aged 40 to 44 had given birth to three or more children.

With the average woman having just two children, you might think the fertility rate of Americans is low by worldwide standards. But you would be wrong. At two each, women in the United States have more children than women in 43 percent of the world's countries including most of Western Europe, Canada, China, Brazil, Iran, Turkey, and Vietnam.[21]

Factoid source: Bureau of the Census, Fertility of American Women, http://www.census.gov/population/www/socdemo/fertility.html (accessed March 19, 2007).

PERCENTAGE OF WOMEN
WHO HAVE ADOPTED A CHILD: 1

Madonna has done it. So have Angelina Jolie, Nicole Kidman, and Sheryl Crow. Adoption has become the "it" way to have a baby—but mainly among globetrotting celebrities. For all the talk about adoption, few women have committed themselves to the lifelong project of raising another woman's biological child. Although one in three women aged 18 to 44 has considered adopting, only one in one hundred has actually done so.[22] Even among women struggling to have a baby—using fertility services to try to become pregnant—just 5 percent ultimately adopt a child, according to the federal government's National Survey of Family Growth.

What prevents the average woman from doing what so many celebrities have done? Are their standards too high? Not according to them. Women who want to adopt are not looking for the perfect child, according to government statistics.[23] They would accept a boy or a girl. They would accept a black or white child. Most would welcome a child with a mild disability, although only 30 percent would accept one with a severe disability. The majority would take siblings, and most would accept children up to the age of 12. Teenagers are another matter—only 31 percent would adopt a teen. If picky is not the problem, what keeps more women from adopting? It could be the financial and legal barriers to adoption are too high for all to scale but the rich and famous. Or, more likely, many of the women who say they have considered adopting are simply having a Hallmark moment. Sweetly stated, but not necessarily sincere.

With adoption such a rare event, only a tiny fraction of the nation's children—slightly more than 2 percent—are adopted.[24] Even less common are foreign-born adopted children. Only 258,000 of the nation's 2 million adopted children were born outside the United States.

Factoid source: National Center for Health Statistics, *Fertility, Family Planning, and Reproductive Health of U.S. Women: Data from the 2002 National Survey of Family Growth,* Vital and Health Statistics, Series 23, No. 25, 2005, p. 122.

PART II

YOUR STATUS

Chapter 6
SCHOOL

PERCENTAGE OF AMERICANS WITH
A HIGH SCHOOL DIPLOMA IN 1950: 34

Twin Peaks, The Sopranos, Lost—television dramas come and go, with fans reveling in each episode until the finale brings it to a close. Social scientists, too, have their dramas. Their plot lines revolve around rapidly changing socioeconomic statistics. These do not occur often because most demographic change is slow and steady. But every now and then an indicator will take off and become a hit series. Such is the case with education. For those of you who missed it, here is a recap of the episodes.

Episode One: This sets the stage for the story about how millions of penniless immigrants became the most highly educated people on earth. Between 1950 and 2007 the percentage of Americans aged 25 or older with a high school diploma climbed 52 percentage points—from 34 to 86 percent—as young adults stayed in school.[1] Social scientists were stunned.

Episode Two: Generational conflict is the focus here. As the decades progressed, the high school diploma gap between older and younger adults grew, peaking at a yawning 39 percentage points. The year was 1974. Social scientists now think they can explain the Seventies.

Episode Three: Romance rears its head as women rush onto college campuses, surpassing men in educational attainment. Among young adults today, 33 percent of women but only 26 percent of men have a college diploma.[2] Some fret about how this will affect the divorce rate.

Episode Four: Race is often an issue, but never a bigger one than in this story. For every 100 Asians, 52 are college graduates. For every 100 Hispanics, only 13 have a degree.[3] Evidently, some children are being left behind.

Final Episode: Will the numbers continue to climb, or will the next generation fall behind its parents in educational attainment? The final episode has yet to be aired. Stay tuned for details.

Factoid source: Bureau of the Census, Educational Attainment, historical tables, http://www.census.gov/population/www/socdemo/educ-attn.htm (accessed June 10, 2008).

PERCENTAGE OF 3- AND 4-YEAR-OLDS
ENROLLED IN SCHOOL: 56

Maybe going to school is addictive. That would explain why the education industry has grown to such mammoth proportions. It would explain why the educated can't seem to get enough of going to school, always going back for more.

Not only do we spend billions on education, but millions of us spend our day either teaching or learning. Education is the fourth largest industry in the United States, employing one in twelve Americans—more workers than all but the healthcare, retail trade, and manufacturing industries. These workers include 796,000 educational administrators, 942,000 teaching assistants, and 6,789,000 teachers, plus all the cafeteria ladies.[4] They serve 75 million students from nursery school through graduate school. Overall, 27 percent of Americans aged 3 or older are enrolled in school.

School enrollment is starting earlier and lasting forever. Once it started with kindergarten. Now it begins with preschool. Thanks to working mothers, most 3- and 4-year-olds are in school today, up from only 10 percent a few decades ago.[5] The percentage of children enrolled in school rises above 95 percent among 6-year-olds and remains at that level through age 16, when compulsory school requirements end. Most choose to remain in school. Among 20-year-olds, half are still enrolled; among 22- to 24-year-olds, the figure is more than one in four; even among 25- to 29-year-olds, a substantial 12 percent are in school.

At some point, the training has to end and the real work begins, right? Wrong. The more schooling Americans have, the more likely they are to go back for more. The percentage of people who have taken an adult education course in the past year rises with education, from just 33 percent of high school graduates to fully 66 percent of those with a graduate degree.[6]

Factoid source: Bureau of the Census, Current Population Surveys, School Enrollment—Historical Tables, http://www.census.gov/population/www/socdemo/school.html (accessed June 10, 2008).

PERCENTAGE OF TEENAGERS FROM SINGLE-PARENT FAMILIES WHO HAVE REPEATED A GRADE IN SCHOOL: 23

Finger-waggers, take your positions. It is time to play the blame game again. This time the target is parents and their unwillingness to become more involved in their children's education. "The importance of parent involvement in children's education has long been established," states the National Center for Education Statistics.[7] "Schools nationwide are being called upon to develop policies and practices that encourage parents to become more involved."

So say the experts. But what if they have it backwards? Maybe it's not the kids with the involved parents who do better, but the kids with the less involved parents who do worse. As schools emphasize parental involvement, making it one of the keys to academic success, some children are being left behind. Invariably, the stragglers are the kids living in single-parent families. According to the Census Bureau, 23 percent of teenagers from single-parent families have repeated a grade compared with only 8 percent of teens in two-parent families.[8] Just 13 percent of the one-parent children are in gifted classes versus 28 percent of the two-parent kids.

Most single parents make a valiant effort to shepherd their children through school. But many do not have time to assume the duties of the public education system. Most single parents have full-time jobs. Many do not have a car and must depend on public transportation. Yet the National Center for Education Statistics thinks the problem is one of motivation, "Schools need to work harder . . . to let parents know the importance of being involved in their children's education."[9] Oh, really?

This disconnect between the public schools and the parents who need them most has consequences, and they are playing out in the classroom, on test scores, and in college admissions. Remove parents from the equation for academic success, and they might begin to level the playing field.

Factoid source: Bureau of the Census, A Child's Day: 2004 (Selected Indicators of Child Well-Being), Survey Income and Program Participation, Detailed Tables, http://www.census.gov/population/www/socdemo/2004_detailed tables.html (accessed October 31, 2007).

PERCENTAGE OF AMERICANS WHO GIVE THE NATION'S PUBLIC SCHOOLS A GRADE OF A OR B: 16

Americans are concerned about the nation's public schools. So what else is new? Over the years, the public has consistently given low marks to the public schools. In the latest report card, 80 percent give the public schools a grade of C or lower, according to the 2007 Phi Delta Kappa/Gallup poll. Only 16 percent give the schools an A or B.

The Phi Delta Kappa/Gallup poll has been taken each year for nearly four decades, and in all of those years most have given the public schools low marks. But zoom in for a closer look and the picture improves. Ask Americans to grade their local schools, and a much larger 45 percent give them a B or higher.[10] Get closer still and ask parents to grade the school their oldest child attends, and fully 67 percent give the school an A or B.

One social scientist calls this the "local advantage," and other surveys on a variety of topics uncover a similar preference for the local over the national. "The local advantage prevails in all topical areas," says Tom W. Smith, director of the General Social Survey, writing in *Public Perspective*.[11] What accounts for the local advantage? Smith explains: "Knowledge of conditions in the neighborhood primarily comes from personal observation and direct communication among family members, neighbors, and other friends and acquaintances. Little information at this level probably comes from the mass media."[12] Bottom line: When we evaluate our neighborhood, we know what we are talking about. When we evaluate the nation, we don't. Our knowledge of far-flung cities and towns too often has its roots in sensational headlines.

So are the nation's public schools in trouble or not? Clearly, some schools are troubled. But with 67 percent of parents giving their child's school an A or B, the nation's schools might be doing a better job than we think.

Factoid source: Lowell C. Rose and Alec M. Gallup, *The 39th Annual Phi Delta Kappa/Gallup Poll of the Public's Attitudes Toward the Public Schools*, September 2007, p. 40.

PERCENTAGE OF CHILDREN
WHO ATTEND A PRIVATE SCHOOL: 9

Public or private: This is a decision most parents must make, and the over-whelming majority of parents choose to send their children to public school. In fact, over the decades—despite all the supposed discontent with the public schools—the percentage of children attending private elementary or secondary school has remained virtually unchanged.

Money explains why, of course. How many parents can afford to spend thousands of dollars a year on private school when their children can receive a public education for free? About 3 million parents can afford to do so—that's the number of families in the United States with children in private school, according to the American Housing Survey.[13] Two kinds of families send their children to private school: those who can afford the luxury, and those whose beliefs motivate them to invest in a private school education. The latter category may be the larger one. Fully 82 percent of children enrolled in private school attend a Roman Catholic or other type of religious school.[14] Even among the religious, however, money rules: the children most likely to attend a religious private school are from the highest income groups.

Would more parents send their children to private school if they could afford to do so? The public has long opposed allowing parents to send their children to private school at the public's expense, according to the Phi Delta Kappa/Gallup Poll. In the latest survey, 60 percent were against it.[15] But if public school parents were handed a full-tuition voucher and told they could send their children to any school, public or private, 59 percent say they would send their children to a private school.[16]

Factoid source: Bureau of the Census, Current Population Surveys, School Enrollment—Historical Tables, http://www.census.gov/population/www/socdemo/school.html (accessed June 10, 2008).

PERCENTAGE OF STUDENTS
BEING HOMESCHOOLED: 2

American families have all the enthusiasm for home schooling that American workers have for working at home, which is to say not much. Human beings are social creatures, and most balk at the idea of staying home when everyone else is passing notes behind the teacher's back or gossiping at the water cooler. Homeschoolers, it turns out, are more of a virtual than a real community, a movement made possible by the Internet. But they have been noisy enough to convince the government to collect statistics about them.

At last count, about 1 million children were being homeschooled, according to the National Center for Education Statistics.[17] One million sounds like a lot, but it accounts for only 2 percent of the 50 million students aged 5 to 17 in the United States. Even the definition of homeschooling stretches it a bit. The government defines homeschooled students as those whose parents say they homeschool their children and whose enrollment in a public or private school does not exceed 25 hours per week.

It is easy to guess the characteristics of homeschooled students without the expense of a government study, but on second thought it is always good to know the facts. Homeschooled students are more likely than the average student to be non-Hispanic white, live in a rural area, and hail from the South. The 54 percent majority lives in a two-parent family with a stay-at-home mom. Someone has to do the teaching.

When asked why they homeschool, the 31 percent plurality of parents say the most important reason is concern over the school environment.[18] Close behind, another 30 percent say it is to provide religious or moral instruction. Note passing is not allowed.

Factoid source: D. Princiotta and S. Bielick, *Home-schooling in the United States: 2003*, National Center for Education Statistics 2006-042 (Washington, DC: US Department of Education, 2005), p. 5.

MINORITY SHARE OF STUDENTS
IN CALIFORNIA'S PUBLIC SCHOOLS: 68

Are non-Hispanic whites willing to pay to educate black and Hispanic children? The jury is still out, but the signs do not look good. Many of the nation's property owners—a group dominated by non-Hispanic whites—are having a fit about rising property taxes, which are one of the main sources of funding for the public schools. Since non-Hispanic whites pay most of the property tax, their protests have a way of turning into political movements with empowering names such as School Choice and Taxpayer Relief. No matter the name, the results are the same: reducing the dollars available for the education of minority children.

OK, maybe property taxes are not the best way to fund public education. But why do the rebels focus only on taxes and not on education? Maybe it is not fair to call them racially motivated, but it is well documented that the modern-day school choice movement had its roots in the public school desegregation battles of the 1950s and 1960s. A comparison of the demographics of school children and taxpayers makes the charge even more plausible. According to the National Center for Education Statistics, 42 percent of public school students are black, Hispanic, or Asian.[19] In ten states, minorities are the majority. Non-Hispanic whites, meanwhile, pay more than 80 percent of property taxes.[20]

It is no coincidence that the property tax revolt started in California, one of the most diverse states. Proposition 13, passed by California's (mostly non-Hispanic white) voters in 1978, capped property taxes and gutted funding for the public schools. In the years since, other states have followed suit in an effort to appease homeowners—also known as voters.

This is a phase. Eventually, the younger, more diverse generations will become homeowners, taxpayers, and voters, and the argument over how to fund public education will lose its racial undercurrent. But this will happen only if the black and Hispanic children of today can get enough of an education to join the ranks of the middle class.

Factoid Source: National Center for Education Statistics, Digest of Education Statistics: 2007, http://nces.ed .gov/programs/digest/d07/tables_2.asp (accessed June 10, 2008).

PERCENTAGE OF ADULTS WITH A COLLEGE DEGREE IN 1950: 6

As a college graduate in 1950, how pleasant it must have been to apply for a job. Your credentials made you an elite job-seeker, with doors opening faster than you could walk through them. Today, college graduates are a dime a dozen, with 29 percent of Americans aged 25 or older having a college degree.[21] In the past half century, no other characteristic of the American population has changed as much as our educational attainment.

What is behind this rocket-propelled growth in education? The fuel is the power of parental aspirations. By accident of birth, the young adults of the 1950s were riding a postwar wave of expansion and prosperity. But they knew success would not be as easy to come by for their children, competing with millions of others in the largest cohort ever born in the United States—the baby-boom generation. Getting a college education, they thought, would guarantee their children's success. Parents encouraged—even demanded—that their children go to college, which explains why the percentage of Americans with a college degree has more than quadrupled since 1950.

Here's the catch: the bandwagon rolling toward college is dangerously overcrowded. Rather than being a mark of distinction, a college degree now carries the same status as a high school diploma in 1950. It is the minimum credential required for admittance into the American middle class. Has this turn of events dampened parental enthusiasm for their children's enrollment in an institution of higher education? Not in the slightest. In fact, it has added to the frenzy, making parents even more focused on their children's college plans. According to the Census Bureau, 85 percent of today's parents expect their children to graduate from college.[22]

Factoid source: Bureau of the Census, Educational Attainment, Historical Tables, http://www.census.gov/population/www/socdemo/educ-attn.html (accessed April 8, 2007).

PERCENTAGE OF COLLEGE FRESHMEN ATTENDING SCHOOL WITHIN 100 MILES OF HOME: 53

Ah, independence! There's nothing like turning 18 and stretching your wings a bit. Or not. The nation's college students seem more concerned with staying close to the nest rather than learning how to fly. At least that's what the University of California's annual survey of college freshmen reveals. Most college freshmen at four-year institutions attend a school within a few hours drive from home, according to the survey. Since the question was first asked in 1969, the percentage of students attending a school close to home has barely changed, with 52 percent of freshmen within 100 miles of home nearly forty years ago.[23] This is one of the few areas of stability in the rapidly evolving industry of higher education.

Since 1969, the number of four-year colleges has grown by more than 50 percent.[24] The number of students at four-year schools has expanded by 85 percent.[25] Most students now apply to at least four schools.[26] Despite all these changes, the proportion of students who end up at a school close to home has remained virtually unchanged.

Two factors account for this stability: cost and comfort. Let's start with cost. Chances are, schools within 100 miles of a student's home are in state, with lower tuition than out-of-state schools farther away. And many states offer financial incentives for in-state students. In fact, 37 percent of college freshmen say they chose their school because of its cost, which includes an even larger 46 percent of students attending a public school. But cost is not the only factor in the decision to stay close to mom and dad. Comfort is also important. Nearly one in five college freshmen say they chose their school because they wanted to be near home. After all, someone has to do the laundry.

Factoid source: John H. Pryor et al., *The American Freshman: National Norms for Fall 2007* (Los Angeles: Cooperative Institutional Research Program, Higher Education Research Institute, University of California, December 2007), p. 31.

WOMEN'S SHARE OF STUDENTS
AT FOUR-YEAR COLLEGES: 56

Each year the nation's colleges and universities award more than 1 million bachelor's degrees, and women outnumber men among the recipients by more than 200,000.[27] Women account for the growing majority of students on college campuses, and they earn most college degrees. The educational differences between young men and women are becoming stark: among adults aged 25 to 29, a substantial 33 percent of women have a bachelor's degree compared with a smaller 26 percent of men.[28]

Until the late 1970s, men dominated college campuses. Now the gender gap has reversed—and it is growing each year. The gap is wreaking havoc on the dating scene, and it is bad for college admissions. Most college applicants want to attend a school where men and women are about equal in number. Yet enrollment is growing increasingly lopsided—not only in the United States but in developed countries all over the world, according to researchers at the National Bureau of Economic Research. The reason for the gender gap is all too familiar to the anxious parents of sons—boys mature more slowly than girls. Or, as the NBER researchers put it: "Because college preparation and applications must be done by teenagers, small differences in development can lead to large disparities in college outcomes."[29]

Traditional sex roles, the researchers theorize, had long suppressed women's college enrollment. But in recent decades the playing field has leveled, and girls—who have always done better than boys in school—are eager to go to college, enrolling at a higher rate than boys, according to the National Center for Education Statistics.[30] On paper at least, girls look better than boys, giving college admissions officers a headache as they try to balance the numbers.

Factoid source: Bureau of the Census, School Enrollment—Social and Economic Characteristics of Students: October 2006, Detailed Tables, http://www.census.gov/population/www/socdemo/school/cps2006.html (accessed June 10, 2008).

PERCENTAGE OF STUDENTS GRADUATING FROM COLLEGE WHO BORROWED TO PAY FOR THEIR EDUCATION: 65

$50,000-plus. That's the cost of one year of college at a growing number of the nation's private, four-year schools. Few families can afford to pay such a hefty sum, which is why the college loan business has exploded over the past few years, attracting more than a few unsavory characters.

A little more than a decade ago, fewer than half of college students borrowed to pay for school. Today, two out of three go into debt to get educated, personally owing an average of $24,000 on graduation day—60 percent more than their counterparts owed in 1992–93 after adjusting for inflation, according to the National Center for Education Statistics.[31] Before they get their first job, these freshly minted graduates are responsible for a loan payment of nearly $300 a month.

College loans are a lucrative business. You can tell the big guys are involved if your mailbox is full of loan offers, college Web sites provide easy access to lenders, and *60 Minutes* profiles those pocketing the profits. Students and their families have become eager customers of these borrowed dollars because a college education has become a must. Unfortunately, family incomes have not kept pace with college costs. Since the early 1990s, the cost of one year of college has grown three times faster than median family income.[32]

Students (and their parents) are feeling the pain. In a survey of student borrowers, the Nellie Mae Corporation found the 56 percent majority burdened by college debt.[33] Most of the borrowers still believe the benefits of college outweigh the cost, however. One statement in the report sums up the sorry situation for too many students today: "A consistent majority of students who borrow to pay for their higher education believe they could not have gone to college without student loans."[34] Welcome, college graduates, to indentured servitude.

Factoid source: National Center for Education Statistics, "The Condition of Education," http://nces.ed.gov/ programs/coe/2004/section5/indicator38.asp#info (accessed April 7, 2007).

PERCENTAGE OF PARENTS WHO CAN CORRECTLY ESTIMATE THE COST OF ONE YEAR OF COLLEGE: 22

Have parents simply given up on paying for college? Have college costs soared to such stratospheric levels that parents no longer even bother to put much money aside, figuring that other kids have found a way to pay the bills and so will theirs? That may be the most logical explanation for the strange behavior of families whose children are about to embark on one of life's most expensive endeavors.

Among parents with household incomes of $50,000 or more and children likely to attend college, 95 percent say they intend to pay some or all of their child's college expenses, according to a survey by AllianceBerstein Investments.[35] But only 41 percent expect to pay the entire cost. Eighty-seven percent say they are counting on scholarships or grants to help out. They may be counting on too much. Fully 97 percent of college financial aid administrators say parents have a false sense of security about how much help colleges can offer, according to another AllianceBerstein Investments survey.[36] Two-thirds of administrators say scholarships and grants are less available today than in the past.

Only about half of parents with children under age 17 have started saving for college, reports a Vanguard/Upromise survey.[37] Even worse, the savers have accumulated only $4,700—an amount that will barely cover one year of tuition (never mind room and board) at a public university. But wait—maybe the parents have a plan. A John Hancock survey found 43 percent of parents counting on others to help them pay the college bills.[38] Are they hoping for a corporate or even heavenly benefactor? Actually, they are counting on somebody much more down to earth—their own parents. A MetLife poll finds that 55 percent of grandparents with grandchildren aged 21 or younger are contributing funds toward their grandchildren's education.[39]

Factoid source: Laura J. Horn, Xianglei Chen, and Chris Chapman, *Getting Ready to Pay for College—What Students and Their Parents Know about the Cost of College Tuition and What They Are Doing to Find Out*, National Center for Education Statistics Statistical Analysis Report, September 2003, p. 80.

LIFETIME EARNINGS DIFFERENCE BETWEEN MALE HIGH SCHOOL AND COLLEGE GRADUATES: $1.3 MILLION

Most college graduates are in debt. Most will spend years paying off their loans. Is getting a college degree worth the extraordinary cost? In a word, yes. College graduates still earn more over their lifetime than the cost of college, including interest on student loans. Think of it as a deadly serious game of Chutes and Ladders. It pays to graduate from college not so much because it puts you on the ladder of success, but because those without a college degree are likely to land on the chute of downward mobility.

For decades men with a college education have enjoyed rising incomes. Consequently, a college diploma now separates the nation's haves from the have-nots. College graduates head the majority of households with incomes of $100,000 or more. These affluent households spend much more than the average household on things such as travel, entertainment, and even college tuition itself. The college-educated are far more likely to send their children to college than those with less education. In fact, the parents of most college freshmen are themselves college graduates.[40] A college degree will even lengthen your life. According to a study by the National Bureau of Economic Research, rates of sickness and death tumble with each additional year of education.[41]

Between 1970 and 2000, the median income of men with only a high school diploma fell 18 percent, after adjusting for inflation.[42] In contrast, the median income of men with a college degree climbed 10 percent during those years—more proof that it still pays to go to college. But this tale of effort rewarded has a disturbing ending. The immunity against economic hardship granted by a college degree may be wearing off. Between 2000 and 2006, the median income of male college graduates fell 2 percent, after adjusting for inflation.

Factoid source: Author's calculations based on Bureau of the Census, 2007 Current Population Survey Annual Social and Economic Supplement, http://pubdb3.census .gov/macro/032007/perinc/toc.htm (accessed November 27, 2007).

PERCENTAGE OF AMERICANS TAKING WORK-RELATED ADULT EDUCATION CLASSES: 27

For more than a generation, getting an education has been the ticket into the middle class. That explains why most high school students enroll in college within a few months of graduation. It explains why more than one in four adults are taking work-related courses, upgrading their job skills.

But getting an education isn't enough anymore. With the Internet rapidly globalizing what is called the "conceptual economy"—the economy of ideas, which supports many college graduates—getting an education is still necessary but no longer sufficient for prosperity. The good news is that the Internet is leveling living standards around the world. The bad news is that many Americans are going to be cut off at the knees, toppling from the middle class into the struggling class despite their college education.

The erosion in our standard of living is the elephant in the room that few are willing to acknowledge. Most experts still exhort anxious Americans to go back to school and get reeducated to keep up. But it is not that simple anymore. "Do you need to be re-educated?" asks Paul Kasriel, chief economist at Northern Trust in Chicago and one of the few analysts bold enough to acknowledge the elephant.[43] "Maybe you just need to accept a lower wage rate," he says.

The paradigm shift caused by the Internet's globalization of economies will be a boon to some. The survivors will live in a consumer's paradise of falling prices. But others will see their standard of living fall. They will not go down without a fight, and the battle lines are being drawn. The percentage of Americans who think free trade has hurt the United States climbed from 30 to 46 percent between 1999 and 2007, according to an NBC News/*Wall Street Journal* poll.[44] When asked how the global economy is affecting them, 27 percent say they have been helped. A larger 31 percent say they have been hurt.

Factoid source: National Center for Education Statistics, "Adult Education Survey of the 2005 National Household Education Surveys Program," http://nces.ed.gov/pubs2006/adulted/01.asp (accessed June 11, 2007).

Chapter 7
WORK

AVERAGE LENGTH OF TIME IT TAKES
TO GET TO WORK: 25 MINUTES

Road rage. If you have ever wondered why people get so upset, this is where it comes from: on an average weekday, more than 100 million Americans travel between their home and their workplace. This twice-daily migration is the reason we have so many automobiles, with nearly one vehicle for every American of driving age. All those cars on the road at once (most of us leave for work between 6:00 and 8:30 AM) create traffic congestion, frustration, and outright anger. We get all worked up over a relatively short eleven-mile journey—the median length of our commute to work, according to the Census Bureau.[1] It seems a lot longer because congestion slows the journey to a crawl.

We know these facts because the federal government keeps close tabs on how people get to work. A lot of money rides on the findings. Commuting patterns determine each county's metropolitan status, which directs the flow of federal funds. Commuting is the foundation of urban planning and the principal guide to business location decisions. The government data prove what we all suspected—the commute to work is trapping us in our cars for a growing length of time, but the increase is not as great as urban sprawl might suggest. Between 1990 and 2005, the length of the average commute grew by just 2 minutes.[2]

There is an alternative to sitting in traffic, but most people ignore it. A tiny 5 percent of workers take public transportation to work. Fully 76 percent drive to work alone.[3] Is there a good reason for shunning buses, trains, and other forms of mass transit? Maybe. According to researchers at the University of Southern California, the average length of the commute to work by public transit is 57 minutes—34 minutes longer than the commute by car.[4]

Factoid source: Bureau of the Census, 2006 American Community Survey, http://www.census.gov/acs/www/ (accessed October 10, 2007).

PERCENTAGE OF WORKERS WHO ARE SATISFIED WITH THEIR JOB: 89

"Take this job and shove it" is not something you are likely to tell your boss any time soon. Most workers are satisfied with their job. That explains why a substantial 69 percent say it is somewhat or very likely they will work for their current employer for the rest of their lives, according to a Pew Research Center survey.[5] But data from the Bureau of Labor Statistics call into question this complacence. Long-term employment has fallen sharply—especially among men—over the past decade.

The tension is palpable. Fifty-nine percent of the public says workers today must work harder to earn a decent living than workers did in the past. Most also think employers and employees are less loyal to one another.[6] The government statistics confirm these feelings. The percentage of men who have worked for their current employer for ten or more years fell in every age group between 1996 and 2006. Among men aged 45 to 49, the figure plummeted from 51 to 43 percent over the decade.[7] Women's long-term employment is also down. Dare we say the sky is falling?

Not so fast, says economist Ann Huff Stevens in a report for the National Bureau of Economic Research.[8] Job stability for individual workers may not have eroded as much as the aggregate statistics suggest. She bases her findings on an analysis of employment history data over different time periods. In 1969, she says, men aged 58 to 62 reported spending 21.9 years at their longest job. In 2002, men in the same age group reported spending an almost identical 21.4 years at their longest job. Will today's workers look back on equally lengthy careers or do recent declines in long-term employment point to profound change ahead? The jury is still out.

Factoid source: Pew Research Center, *Public Says American Work Life Is Worsening, but Most Workers Remain Satisfied with Their Jobs,* August 30, 2006, p. 9.

PERCENTAGE OF MARRIED MOTHERS
WHO WORK: 69

Women are being watched. Pundits, politicians, and the media closely monitor women's labor force participation rates. Like clockwork every few years, one of the talking heads gets excited because the rate dipped oh so very slightly. They dissect and debate the meaning of the bobble, many of them hoping for a return to the good old days of the stay-at-home mom. They are delusional.

The percentage of American women who have a job or are looking for one stood at 59 percent in 2007, according to the Bureau of Labor Statistics.[9] A half-century ago, generally considered the epicenter of the good old days, the figure was just 37 percent. But even the 59 percent figure understates the degree to which working women have become the norm. A better gauge is the percentage of married women with children under age 18 who are in the labor force. The 69 percent figure of today is up from just 28 percent in 1960.[10]

The enormous 41-percentage-point increase in the labor force participation rate of married mothers says it all. It says men no longer earn enough to maintain a middle-class lifestyle, and it says women must work to support their families. Most Americans have gracefully accepted this change and do not hunger for a return to the good old days. When the Pew Research Center asked the public recently whether it agreed or disagreed with the statement, "Women should return to their traditional roles in society," the 51 percent majority "completely" disagreed.[11] Among the youngest adults, those raised by working mothers, an even larger 63 percent completely disagreed. The old folks—those born before 1946—are the only ones who aren't so sure. Only 38 percent completely disagreed with the notion that women should return to the home. They still get excited about the bobbles.

Factoid source: Bureau of Labor Statistics, *Employment Characteristics of Families in 2007,* May 30, 2008, p. 11.

PERCENTAGE OF MEN IN THE LABOR FORCE: 73

While the nation's busybodies have been wagging their fingers at the working woman, they have largely ignored the shenanigans of the working man. Over the past half-century, men have deserted the workplace in droves. Today, only 73 percent of men aged 16 or older are in the labor force, down from 86 percent in 1950.

There is no single explanation for why men today are so much less likely to work than their counterparts in the past. Men's labor force participation rates have fallen in every age group. Among men under age 25, more are going to school, reducing their participation. Among men aged 55 or older, early retirement is the culprit. But labor force participation is down even among men of prime working age. Between 1950 and 2007, the labor force participation rate of men aged 25 to 54 fell from 96 to 91 percent.[12] Nearly 6 million men in the age group are neither working nor job hunting. What are they doing?

Let's find out. According to the Census Bureau, few of the missing 6 million are playing Mr. Mom. Only about 200,000 husbands are not in the labor force because they are caring for their family.[13] Could they be enhancing their educational credentials? About 2 million men aged 25 to 54 are in school, but three out of four are also employed, so most of the missing millions are not in classrooms.[14] A look at the disability rolls, however, may reveal the answer. Among men aged 25 to 54, more than 5 million have a work disability and most of the disabled do not work. In fact, disabled men account for 65 percent of the missing 6 million.[15] Over the past half century, the average age of men receiving Social Security disability payments has fallen from 59 to 52, as growing numbers of younger men drop out of the labor force because of health problems.[16]

Factoid source: Bureau of Labor Statistics, Labor Force Statistics from the Current Population Survey, Custom Tables, http://data.bls.gov/PDQ/outside.jsp?survey=ln (accessed June 10, 2008).

PERCENTAGE OF TEENAGE BOYS
IN THE LABOR FORCE: 29

Get a job. That's what parents once told their teenagers, and most teens did what they were told. Three decades ago, half of boys aged 16 to 17 were in the labor force. Not anymore. Today's parents no longer push their children to get a job. In 2007, only 29 percent of boys aged 16 to 17 had a job or were looking for one. The pattern is the same for girls. Even during the summer, the percentage of teens with jobs is well below 50 percent.[17]

What keeps today's teens out of the labor force? Here is a surprise: mom and dad are keeping them out. More than nine out of ten parents want their children to get a college degree.[18] With that goal in mind, today's teens have no time for flipping hamburgers. Their hours are filled with extracurricular activities, volunteer work, and school—even during the summer—as teens pad their resumes in preparation for college applications. The percentage of 16- to 19-year-olds enrolled in school in the month of July has more than tripled since 1985, rising to 38 percent, according to the Congressional Budget Office.[19]

There is another reason for the labor force decline among teens, according to researchers at the Federal Reserve Bank of Chicago.[20] State-funded merit scholarship programs have made it more important for students to hit the books rather than the streets. In many states, students with good academic records receive sizable grants that greatly ease the pain of college expenses. The scholarships are awarded to students with good academic records. Rather than urging their children to find a job, parents are pushing them to study harder. Teen labor force participation, the researchers report, has fallen the most in states with merit scholarship programs.

Factoid source: Bureau of Labor Statistics, Labor Force Statistics from the Current Population Survey, Custom Tables, http://data.bls.gov/PDQ/outside.jsp?survey=ln (accessed June 10, 2008).

PERCENTAGE WHO THINK RETIREMENT BENEFITS ARE NOT AS GOOD AS THEY ONCE WERE: 51

Many Americans think work life is not as rewarding as it used to be, and one reason for the downfall is the erosion of job benefits. The majority of the public thinks retirement benefits are worse than they used to be, and 44 percent say health and other benefits are worse, according to a Pew Research Center survey.[21]

Many are tempted to blame big business for abandoning the nation's workers. But blaming Congress may be more appropriate. The substitution of defined-contribution for defined-benefit pension plans (shifting retirement income risk from employers to employees) occurred after Congress tinkered with the tax code in 1978. By creating the 401(k) provision as a tax shelter for executives at Kodak and Xerox, Congress opened the barn door and allowed businesses to escape from the costly defined-benefit pension system.[22] Businesses can hardly be blamed for galloping with gusto through the open door. Well, maybe they deserve some blame for the gusto part.

Many businesses have tried valiantly to maintain their workers' health insurance. It hasn't been easy. Fully 98 percent of employers with 200 or more employees offer health insurance—a figure that has remained virtually unchanged for years despite steeply rising costs. Smaller employers, however, have been unable to keep up, and their benefits are disappearing. Among businesses with fewer than 200 workers, only 60 percent offered health insurance to employees in 2006, down from 68 percent five years earlier according to a GAO report.[23]

Workers themselves are also partially to blame, according to another study. The percentage of workers participating in their employer's healthcare plan fell from 88 to 84 percent between 1988 and 2005, according to a study by the Employee Benefit Research Institute.[24] When asked why they do not participate in their employer's plan, nearly one in four said it was too expensive.

Factoid source: Pew Research Center, *Public Says American Work Life Is Worsening, but Most Workers Remain Satisfied with Their Jobs,* August 30, 2006, p. 2.

PERCENTAGE OF AMERICANS
WHO ARE SELF-EMPLOYED: 6.6

This is laughable: only 6.6 percent of American workers report self-employment as their primary job. Each year, the figure shrinks a little more. Today, it is below the level found in most other developed countries including Australia, Canada, Denmark, Germany, Italy, New Zealand, Sweden, and the United Kingdom, according to a study by economist David G. Blanchflower of Dartmouth College.[25] Even the corporate-oriented Japanese are more likely to be self-employed than we are.

Horatio Alger must be spinning in his grave. His rags-to-riches stories are increasingly hard to find outside of Silicon Valley. The entrepreneurial spirit is all but dead in the United States because of our cumbersome employer-provided health insurance system. The cost of buying private health insurance has become an unbearable burden for those who want to start a business, forcing would-be entrepreneurs into the wage-and-salary work force. Many of those who have taken the leap and are running their own business are only a divorce away from the hunt for a job with health insurance benefits. The statistics bear this out. The 52 percent majority of the nation's self-employed either have no health insurance at all or they are covered through their spouse's employer-provided plan, according to an analysis by the Employee Benefit Research Institute.[26]

The health insurance problem explains a peculiar pattern in our self-employment statistics—a spike in self-employment among people aged 65 or older. A substantial 15 percent of workers aged 65 or older work for themselves, according to the Bureau of Labor Statistics, more than double the average rate. The enthusiasm among older workers for self-employment is explained by one thing: Medicare. The government's health insurance program for the elderly allows people aged 65 or older to start their own businesses without worrying about health insurance.

Factoid source: Bureau of Labor Statistics, Labor Force Statistics from the Current Population Survey, http://www .bls.gov/cps/home.htm (accessed February 14, 2008).

PERCENTAGE OF WORKERS
WHO WORK AT HOME: 4

In futuristic fantasies it was once predicted that American workers would embrace working at home. And why not? By working at home they could avoid the morning commute, lounge in their slippers, and care for their preschoolers while earning a living. But things did not turn out that way. Most people enjoy getting together with colleagues. The distractions of home are many, and children have a habit of getting in the way. Consequently, few Americans work primarily from home. Only 5 million people worked primarily at home last week, according to Census Bureau estimates, or just 4 percent of the labor force.[27]

But more than 5 million people work at home at least occasionally. The Bureau of Labor Statistics uses a broader question to determine the size of the work-at-home population, classifying respondents as "work-at-homers" if they usually work at home even once a week as part of their primary job. This broader definition boosts the pajama-clad workforce to 21 million, or 15 percent of the total.[28] But nearly half of those workers (49 percent) are not paid for toiling in the den. Another 34 percent are self-employed. Only 16 percent are paid by their employer to work at home.

The percentage of workers who work at home is not growing, according to the Bureau of Labor Statistics—despite predictions to the contrary. When those who work at home are asked to list the reasons for choosing home over office, most say it is because they are catching up with their work or it is in the nature of their job (such as school teachers). Only 7 percent say they work at home for the reasons the futurists once envisioned—to avoid the commute or to care for their children.

Factoid source: Bureau of the Census, 2006 American Community Survey, http://www.census.gov/acs/www/ (accessed October 11, 2007).

MEDIAN AGE OF LIBRARIANS: 51

In the geology of occupations, librarians inhabit one of the oldest strata. Found deep in the sedimentary layers, librarians and other occupations dominated by older workers are often the product of the passions and economic incentives of decades past. Librarians are not the oldest layer, however. Near the bottom are farmers, with a median age of 56.

The average American worker has a median age of 41—meaning half are older and half are younger. But workers in some occupations are much older.[29] Studying the age structure of occupations is like examining sedimentary rock, each layer telling something about the environment in which it formed. Some of the occupations filled by older workers sparked the imagination of youth decades ago—such as psychologists, with a relatively old median age of 49. Many psychologists were young adults in the heady days of navel gazing, when *Psychology Today* rivaled *Rolling Stone* in popularity and *Primal Scream* was on the best-seller list. Older workers fill other occupations because younger workers deserted the profession in search of better opportunities. The occupations made old by attrition include farmers, tool grinders, and tailors. A few of the oldest occupations require decades of experience before workers can claim the title. Legislators have a median age of 54 and judges 51.

The youngest occupations are found in the top sedimentary layer, typically jobs filled by entry-level workers. The list of occupations with a median age below 30 offers few surprises and includes fast-food workers, cashiers, motion picture projectionists, lifeguards, and gas station attendants. More interesting is the layer just below the youngest. This is the one filled with ambitious young adults pursuing the next big thing. The nation's computer software engineers—who brought us Google Earth, YouTube, the iPhone, and other life-transforming inventions—have a median age of just 39.

Factoid source: Bureau of Labor Statistics, Employed Persons by Detailed Occupation, Sex, and Age, Annual Average 2007, unpublished table from the 2007 Current Population Survey.

PERCENTAGE WHO VOLUNTEER: 26

What happened to America's can-do spirit? The terrorist attacks of 9/11 were supposed to give rise to a nation of volunteers. But in fact, the percentage of Americans who volunteer has stalled, according to the Bureau of Labor Statistics. And while today's rate is higher than the rate of the 1970s and 1980s, the reasons for the rise might not win any community spirit awards.

Teenagers are one segment of the population volunteering more today than in the past. The percentage of 16- to 19-year-olds who volunteer climbed from a low of 13 percent in 1989 to the 25 percent of today, according to a report by the Corporation for National & Community Service.[30] But before you pat your teen on the back for his good deeds, take a look at the college application form on his computer screen. Volunteering is almost a requirement for getting into college these days.

Volunteering has climbed among the middle-aged as well over the past few decades. Today, 30 percent of 35- to 54-year-olds are volunteers—a higher rate than in any other age group.[31] But many, if not most, are "helicopter parents" hovering over their offspring. Among women with children under age 18 who volunteer, fully 46 percent are donating their time to an educational organization. What do you want to bet they are helping out at their child's school?

Older Americans are also more likely to volunteer than in decades past, with 24 percent doing so in 2007. But as is true with the middle-aged, many are working for an organization that benefits them personally. Among volunteers aged 65 or older, 47 percent donate their time to a religious organization—most likely their own church.

Maybe selfish motives need to be recognized and used as a tool to boost volunteering. That is the idea behind the book *Volunteering as Leisure/ Leisure as Volunteering*, which instructs charitable organizations to attract more volunteers by marketing their activities as leisure pursuits—a win-win situation for everyone.[32]

Factoid source: Bureau of Labor Statistics, *Volunteering in the United States, 2007*, January 23, 2008, p. 2.

Chapter 8
MONEY

YEAR IN WHICH MEDIAN
HOUSEHOLD INCOME PEAKED: 1999

It has been a good run: nearly forty years of rising incomes for American households. But all good things must come to an end, and this one is drawing to a close.

Between 1967 and 2006, median household income grew by a substantial 32 percent, after adjusting for inflation—rising to $48,201. It sounds great, until you take a closer look. The 2006 figure is below the peak of $49,209 reached in 1999, after adjusting for inflation. The average American household makes $1,000 less today than it did a few years ago, yet costs continue to rise.

It gets worse. Between 1967 and 2006, the earnings of men working full-time grew 15 percent after adjusting for inflation. It sounds impressive, but there's a catch. Men's earnings peaked decades ago in 1986.[1] Today, men's earnings are 5 percent below the peak, after adjusting for inflation. Only one thing explains the continued rise in household incomes until 1999: working women.

Women's paychecks not only padded household incomes, but those paychecks were getting bigger as women became better educated. Between 1967 and 2006, the median earnings of women who worked full-time grew by a hefty 53 percent, after adjusting for inflation. Those dollars allowed families to buy houses, SUVs, and other goodies. The flush times have come to an end, however. The median earnings of women who work full-time peaked a few years ago, in 2002, and have fallen 4 percent since then. Unless we put our children to work, we can no longer hide the erosion in our standard of living.

Many of us sense that something is wrong. According to the Pew Research Center, only 45 percent of Americans think they rank among the "haves" today, down from a much larger 59 percent who felt that way in 1988.[2]

Factoid source: Bureau of the Census, Current Population Survey, Historical Income Tables—Households, http://www.census.gov/hhes/www/income/histinc/inchhtoc.html (accessed September 20, 2007).

PERCENTAGE OF YOUNG ADULTS
WHO THINK THEY WILL BE RICH: 51

We are the victims of a disease: Hollywood Syndrome. We caught the disease from the media, which exposed us to the infectious lifestyles of the rich and famous—their Beverly Hills mansions, luxury cars, and designer clothes. We want what they have, and many of us are convinced we will get it. The majority of 18- to 24-year-olds think they will be rich someday, according to a Gallup poll.

Alas, we might ache to be rich but most of us are decidedly middle class and will be for the duration. That's not to say we haven't made progress. Median household income today is close to $50,000, a full 32 percent higher than it was four decades ago, after adjusting for inflation.[3] For some reason, however, our rising incomes have done nothing to quell our lust for wealth. Nor have they made us any happier. The percentage of Americans who say they are "very happy" has barely budged over the years, according to the General Social Survey.[4]

If we are richer, why aren't we happier? Because, as your mother once said, money does not buy happiness. Social scientists agree with mom, and they have proof. In one of many studies probing what makes people happy, researchers asked respondents how they felt at twenty-five-minute intervals throughout their workday.[5] Then they compared each person's happiness with their income, finding almost no correlation between income and average happiness during the day.

Evidently, your bank account does not determine your happiness. Surprisingly, however, your neighbor's bank account does. One of the keys to happiness, say social scientists, is having as much money as your peers. According to a National Bureau of Economic Research study, the less money people have compared to their neighbors, the less happy they are.[6] *Homo sapiens*, it turns out, are finely tuned to their relative economic standing, which is why knowing too much about our Hollywood neighbors is hazardous to our health.

Factoid source: David W. Moore, "Half of Young People Expect to Strike It Rich," Gallup Poll, March 11, 2003, http://www.galluppoll.com/content/?ci=7981&pg=1 (accessed September 29, 2007).

RANK OF 55- TO 64-YEAR-OLDS
IN HOUSEHOLD INCOME GROWTH: 1

Loser's wind: that's what sailors call the wind that fills the sails of the trailing boat on the downwind leg of a race. As the wind fills in, the loser appears to make headway—but the gains are short lived. Such is the plight of today's middle-aged Americans. The government statistics show their sails filling. The pundits applaud their gains. But few have recognized the loser's wind propelling them along.

Here is the evidence. Every three years the Federal Reserve Board surveys American households to determine how wealthy they are. It tallies household assets (such as homes, cars, stock, and retirement accounts) and subtracts household debts (such as mortgages, credit cards, and car loans). The remainder is called net worth—or wealth. The 2004 survey (the latest available) found the median net worth of the average household barely growing, inching up just 1.5 percent over the three-year period, after adjusting for inflation.[7] But one age group did remarkably well. The net worth of householders aged 55 to 64 grew 29 percent during the three years.

There's more. Among households, those headed by 55- to 64-year-olds saw their median income increase the most between 2000 and 2006, while younger householders lost ground.[8] Among men and women, the median income of those aged 55 to 64 climbed substantially during those years, while the incomes of younger men and women either fell or barely grew at all.

A loser's wind explains these anomalies. The net worth and median income of householders aged 55 to 64 is growing not because they are savvy investors, but because fewer can afford to retire. The median income of men and women aged 55 to 64 is rising not because they are valued employees, but because more are employed. The labor force participation rate of men aged 55 to 64 has reached 70 percent—the highest level in more than twenty years.[9]

Factoid source: Bureau of the Census, Historical Income Data, Current Population Survey tables, http://www.census.gov/hhes/www/income/histinc/h10ar.html (accessed September 28, 2007).

AMOUNT TRANSFERRED IN TAXES EACH YEAR FROM THE MIDDLE-AGED TO THE YOUNG AND OLD: $376 BILLION

What is it with some people and taxes? A large group of supposedly intelligent people has lost sight of what life is all about, and they have been given free rein to promote their shortsighted views. Take the ludicrous report issued by the Tax Foundation, which analyzes generational equity in governmental taxation and spending and finds that "the nation's fiscal system is clearly designed to benefit some age groups much more on a dollar-for-dollar basis than others."[10] Not to be rude, but "Duh."

"Many large government spending programs are specifically targeted at the nation's youngest and oldest households," says the Tax Foundation.[11] Has it really come to this? Is it now acceptable to begrudge the tax dollars spent to educate children, care for the sick, and support the elderly? Apparently so, since a vocal faction of Americans is hard at work trying to convince the rest of us that selfishness is a virtue. Have they forgotten everything they learned in kindergarten?

That young and old get more than the middle-aged are "spending priorities established by lawmakers," states the Tax Foundation.[12] True only if by "lawmaker" they mean the Big Lawmaker in the sky. Biology is more like it. The middle-aged are in the biological weeds, caring for children and elderly parents. Government spending helps them do that. Does the Tax Foundation think the middle-aged would prefer to have their children underfoot rather than in school, their parents in the guestroom rather than living on their own?

Maybe the kindergarten lesson on sharing should be repeated. Even better, how about a little evolutionary biology? According to economist C. Y. Cyrus Chu and demographer Ronald D. Lee, transfers between generations are the way long-lived species bestow higher survival rates on their progeny.[13] Could it be that the people who do not believe in taxes also do not believe in evolution?

Factoid source: Andrew Chamberlain and Gerald Prante, "Generational Equity: Which Age Groups Pay More Tax, and Which Receive More Government Spending?" *Tax Foundation Special Report* 156 (Washington, DC: Tax Foundation, June 2007), p. 1.

MEDIAN INCOME OF DUAL-EARNER
MARRIED COUPLES: $95,018

OK, admit it. You are desperate to keep up with the Joneses. In fact, keeping up with the neighbors—whether their last name is Jones or not—is the very key to your happiness, according to social science research. How do you play the game? Get married. Never has marriage been more essential to a high income than it is today. Sure, a college education is a good idea if you have your heart set on parking a BMW in your driveway. But getting married is even better. That's because, over the past few decades, the little woman has become a big money maker, turning dual-earner couples into the nation's income elite. The $95,018 median income of couples in which both husband and wife work full-time is nearly twice the $48,201 median income of the average household. Among households with incomes of $100,000 or more, dual-earner couples head the 61 percent majority.[14]

The fraternity boys are on to this get-rich-quick scheme. The percentage of men in their first year of college who think women should stay home rather than work has fallen from two out of three in the late 1960s to just one in four today.[15] Most of today's young men know where to find their meal ticket. They just have to convince the young women to marry them. Fortunately, their potential mates are not averse to this arrangement, either. Less than one in five college freshman women think they should stay home rather than go to work.[16] Young women want to play the game as well.

Before most women worked, marriage wasn't as necessary for getting ahead. Now that most women have jobs, it is almost the only way to keep up. The median income of dual-earner couples exceeds that of single-earners by an eye-popping $34,000.[17] Although most working wives still earn less than their husbands, one in four now earns more.[18]

Factoid source: Bureau of the Census, 2007 Current Population Survey Annual Social and Economic Supplement, http://pubdb3.census.gov/macro/032007/faminc/ toc.htm (accessed November 21, 2007).

MEDIAN WEEKLY EARNINGS OF THE AVERAGE FULL-TIME WORKER: $695

Multiply $695 by the 52 weeks in a year, and you get a modest $36,140 in median annual earnings, before taxes, for the average full-time worker in the United States, according to the Bureau of Labor Statistics. If this is not enough for you, then scan the BLS list of occupations by earnings and find something better. The usual suspects crowd the top of the list—CEO, engineer, lawyer, pharmacist—all with median weekly earnings of $1,500 or more. Familiar faces also crowd the bottom of the list—day care provider, cashier, and fast-food worker—all with median weekly earnings of less than $400. How do you make sure you end up at the top rather than the bottom of the list? Follow the Three Rules of Success.

Rule Number One: Do not go to the college you want. Go to the college that wants you. Colleges that want you will pay you to sit in their classrooms. This will allow you to graduate from college debt free, already well ahead of the pack. (If you're lucky, your mom and dad will cover college expenses and you can skip this rule entirely.)

Rule Number Two: Do not follow your bliss. That might have been good advice for your parents, back in the days when a college diploma itself was a mark of distinction. College graduates are a dime a dozen today, making your career choice a strategic financial decision. So pick something that pays a lot, regardless of how much you like it.

Rule Number Three: Do not let yourself be outsourced. Choose a career in which jobs will expand rather than contract. Every two years the federal government publishes the list of likely winners and losers.[19] The winners include almost anything having to do with computer software, as well as medical assistants of all types, and veterinarians. The losers include almost anything with a blue collar, as well as typists and telemarketers.

If you follow the three rules, you have almost guaranteed yourself a comfortable, middle-class lifestyle. Just one more step: marry someone who also followed the rules.

Factoid source: Bureau of Labor Statistics, Labor Force Statistics from the Current Population Survey, http://www.bls.gov/cps/home.htm (access June 10, 2008).

AVERAGE AMOUNT OF DISCRETIONARY INCOME PER HOUSEHOLD: $11,000

It is the end of the month. Your bills are paid. Food is on the table. If you are like most households in the United States, you have money left over to do something fun just for the heck of it. Discretionary income, sometimes known as "fun money," is what is left over in your paycheck after taxes are deducted and the bills are paid. The average household has $11,000 a year in uncommitted dollars to hide under the mattress or spend on a Caribbean cruise, according to an analysis by New Strategist Publications.

You might scoff at the notion that you have even one dollar left over after paying for necessities, and some households have little or no discretionary income. Those with incomes below $30,000 a year, for example, typically have none. Nor do single parents. But the average married couple has nearly $17,000 a year in discretionary dollars.[20]

Of course, it's not like you have a stack of bills in your dresser drawer ready to peel off and spend as you please. In fact, most of our extra dollars disappear in dribs and drabs for movie rentals, a bottle of wine, a bag of dog food, and the cable bill. Although your dog might think that dog food is a necessity, pets and pet food are considered discretionary expenses.

Which brings us to this point: determining what is discretionary and what is necessary is more art than science. Some things qualify wholeheartedly as discretionary—such as a six-pack of beer. But how do you classify a restaurant meal? To produce the $11,000 discretionary income average, for example, the researchers considered fast food to be a necessity and full-service restaurant meals to be discretionary. One man's toy is another's lifeline, however. The researchers placed cable television in the discretionary column, for example, despite the fact that half of people aged 65 or older say cable TV is a necessity.[21]

Factoid source: New Strategist Publications, *American Incomes: Demographics of Who Has Money*, 6th ed. (Ithaca, NY: New Strategist, 2007), pp. 275–90.

PERCENTAGE OF AMERICANS WHO THINK
THE MINIMUM WAGE SHOULD BE RAISED: 84

The American people disagree with economists. Economists do not like the minimum wage, fearing each up-tick in the wage adds to the unemployment rate—particularly among low-skilled workers. The American people do not care what economists think. They overwhelmingly support raising the minimum wage. When the Pew Research Center asked the public in March 2007 whether it supported increasing the minimum wage, fully 84 percent said yes. The minimum wage had not been raised in ten years, and the public wanted something done about it. They were willing to risk an increase in unemployment.

The politicians did as they were told, sort of. They scheduled three increases in the federal minimum wage, which is now slated to rise to $7.25 an hour by July 2009. Even so, the minimum wage will remain well below its 1968 peak of $10 an hour, after adjusting for inflation.[22] Why are Americans so concerned about the minimum wage? Only 2 percent of the nation's workers who are paid hourly rates earn minimum wage or less. Most minimum wage workers are under age 25, work only part-time, and are employed by restaurants.[23] Why do we care what McDonalds pays its workers?

We care because a growing number of Americans are upset about an economy they think is out of whack. Congress enjoys a pay raise every year. So do Social Security recipients. Why not the nation's lowest-paid workers? The public's demand for an increase in the minimum wage is a symptom of its dissatisfaction with the status quo. Survey questions probing the issue have exposed the anger as well. Like this Pew Research Center question: "Is America divided into 'haves' and 'have-nots'?" The proportion seeing such a split has grown from 26 to 48 percent over the past two decades.[24] And this question, asked by Gallup: "Do you think our government should redistribute wealth by heavy taxes on the rich?" Fifty-one percent of the public says yes—the highest proportion ever.[25]

Factoid source: Pew Research Center, *Trends in Political Values and Core Attitudes: 1987–2007,* March 22, 2007, p. 70.

NET WORTH REQUIRED TO BE ONE OF THE RICHEST 400 AMERICANS: $1.3 BILLION

America needs a good dose of Prozac. Most of us are dissatisfied with the state of the nation, we think the country is headed down the wrong track, and we have little confidence in the economy. Why all the gloom and doom? One reason is that every September, *Forbes* magazine subjects us to the 400 richest Americans list, reminding us of our shortcomings. According to psychologists, our happiness depends on how much money we have relative to our peers.[26] The more we have the merrier. That's why *Forbes'* list of the rich is destroying our peace of mind. Let's end it here, ditch the rich and make a different kind of list, one guaranteed to make us feel better—giddy even. Coming to a newsstand near you: The Poorest 400 Americans.

Crass? Maybe, but a look down the ladder will cure you of that stiff neck—the one you got from craning your neck to look up the ladder for so many years. It takes at least $1.3 billion in net worth to be included in the Forbes 400 list of richest Americans.[27] They are not your peers. With half of American households having an income of less than $50,000, and half having a net worth of less than $100,000, most of us are much closer to the poorest than the richest 400. So let's get to work and draw up our list. It's not hard to do. Just head to Allen, South Dakota, with clipboard in hand. Allen is the poorest place in the United States, according to rankings of the Census Bureau's per capita income estimates.[28] With a population of 419, Allen is the ideal location for rearranging our priorities. Fully 96 percent of Allen's residents are poor. Their median household income is just $8,300. Sixty-one percent of adults are unemployed. No one there has a college degree. School bus driver is the most common occupation for men. Feeling better yet?

Factoid source: Matthew Miller, "The Forbes 400," September 20, 2007, http://www.forbes.com/2007/09/19/richest-americans-forbes-lists-richlist07-cx_mm_0920rich_land.html (accessed November 28, 2007).

NET WORTH OF THE AVERAGE
AMERICAN HOUSEHOLD: $93,100

How much money do you have in your checking account? How about your 401(k)? What is the outstanding balance on your credit card bill? The government wants to know. Every three years the Federal Reserve Board fields the Survey of Consumer Finances to determine how much you save and how much you owe. You might think some Americans would object to being asked detailed questions about their finances. In fact, 30 percent of those contacted to take part in the survey tell the government to go to hell. But 70 percent of us are willing to spill the beans, allowing the number crunchers to calculate our wealth.

And the grand total is . . . only $93,100. That is the median net worth (or wealth) of the average American household—the difference between everything we own (our assets) and everything we owe (our debts). It's not a lot, and it increased by only 1.5 percent between 2001 and 2004, after adjusting for inflation.[29] This anemic growth is surprising, considering how the population is aging. With more Americans saving for retirement, our net worth should be doing the 100-meter freestyle, not treading water.

The fickle stock market has something to do with our stagnant net worth. The ups and downs of the Dow have sent stock portfolios into a tailspin. But the biggest drag on our net worth is growing mortgage debt. Not only are homebuyers taking on bigger mortgages than ever, but it is taking them longer to pay them off—sometimes well into the Golden Years. The percentage of householders aged 65 or older who still write a check for the mortgage each month has doubled in the past twenty years, climbing from 17 to 32 percent between 1985 and 2005, according to the American Housing Survey.[30] Many will be making those payments until they go to their grave, leaving their grieving spouse to pay off the bill. Among people aged 65 or older with a mortgage, on average sixteen more years of payments remain.

Factoid source: Brian K. Bucks, Arthur B. Kennickell, and Kevin B. Moore, "Recent Changes in U.S. Family Finances: Evidence from the 2001 and 2004 Survey of Consumer Finances," *Federal Reserve Bulletin* 92 (February 2006): A8.

PERCENTAGE OF HOUSEHOLDS
THAT SAVE MONEY: 56

It is hard to save money. Almost everyone agrees. Because it is so hard to save, we do very little of it. The personal saving rate has been falling for the past two decades, and it finally dipped into negative territory in 2005, according to the Bureau of Economic Analysis. Only 56 percent of households spend less than they make, which is how the Federal Reserve Board defines household saving. Is something wrong with us, or is something happening to us?

Most people think there is something wrong with them. Americans are wracked with guilt about their inability to save. Sixty-three percent of the public says it should be saving more, according to a Pew Research Center survey.[31] But the struggle to save is not a battle against our personal demons, but a fight to remain in the middle class. The people who have the hardest time saving are parents, 73 percent of whom say they should be saving more, according to Pew. But it is not their fault that the cost of a middle-class lifestyle has soared and they are left with the bills—day care, car payments, mortgages, health insurance, college expenses, not to mention the 401(k) contribution. The most amazing statistic is that *only* 41 percent of parents say they sometimes spend more than they can afford, according to Pew.[32]

Who is most satisfied with their ability to save? Those with the fewest bills—people aged 65 or older. Only 34 percent think they should be saving more. Just 19 percent say they sometimes spend more than they can afford.[33] The elderly live in comfort not because they are thrifty, however, but because their children and grandchildren are helping them pay their bills. The single biggest expense for the average American household—even bigger than the mortgage interest payment—is Social Security tax.

Factoid source: Brian K. Bucks, Arthur B. Kennickell, and Kevin B. Moore, "Recent Changes in U.S. Family Finances: Evidence from the 2001 and 2004 Survey of Consumer Finances," *Federal Reserve Bulletin* 92 (February 2006): A5.

MEDIAN DEBT OF THE
AVERAGE AMERICAN HOUSEHOLD: $55,300

The federal government might not be able to balance its budget, but American households are more disciplined. The median amount of debt carried by the average household is a surprisingly modest $55,300—including mortgage debt. While most of us are in debt, only a few are in trouble.

Every three years the Federal Reserve Board takes a long, hard look at the finances of American households. The latest data from the Survey of Consumer Finances shows that 76 percent of households are in debt and that debt levels are rising rapidly. Between 2001 and 2004, median household debt grew 34 percent, after adjusting for inflation.[34] This might sound like a big increase, but we are not out of control—not even close. The rise in debt can be explained almost entirely by homeownership. Debt is growing because more of us own a home. Seventy percent of the money we owe is mortgage debt.[35]

Don't believe what you read about credit card debt either—except for the next few sentences. Yes, many of us carry a balance on our credit cards. But the Federal Reserve Board says the median balance is just $2,200 per household.[36] Numbers from a Pew Research Center survey look even better: only 31 percent of adults are making payments on credit card bills, while 24 percent pay card balances in full each month.[37] The rest either don't have credit cards or don't use them regularly.

Some people are in trouble, and they know it. Thirty-six percent of adults have felt like their finances are out of control, according to Pew.[38] But most find a way to tame their spending and pay the bills. According to the Federal Reserve Board, in the past year only 9 percent of households with debt have been more than 60 days late paying a bill.[39]

Factoid source: Brian K. Bucks, Arthur B. Kennickell, and Kevin B. Moore, "Recent Changes in U.S. Family Finances: Evidence from the 2001 and 2004 Survey of Consumer Finances," *Federal Reserve Bulletin* 92 (February 2006): A29.

PERCENTAGE OF HOUSEHOLDS EXPECTING
TO RECEIVE AN INHERITANCE: 14

Will she or won't she? Will your Aunt Sue leave you a fortune or a fortune cookie? Welcome to another installment of Get Rich Quick. The saga began back in 1993 when a mild-mannered economist and professor, Robert B. Avery, and his colleague, Michael S. Rendall, presented the first inheritance calculations at a Cornell University Philanthropy Roundtable. They estimated, based on data from the Federal Reserve Board's 1989 Survey of Consumer Finances, that the older generation would leave its children $10 trillion (in 1990 dollars) over the next fifty years.[40] It was a bombshell. Every media outlet trumpeted the good news: Someday you will be rich!

We're still waiting. So far, the windfall has not materialized, and more than a few economists have revisited the inheritance calculations to figure out where the money went. Here are the reasons Aunt Sue is likely to disappoint, according to a Federal Reserve study:[41]

1. Today's older Americans are less inclined to leave anything to their children. The percentage of people aged 65 or older who believe it is important to leave an estate has fallen from 56 to 47 percent.

2. Much of the wealth of today's elderly is annuitized—such as Social Security benefits—which disappear with a poof upon death. Meanwhile, the older generation's savings—or bequeathable assets—are being spent on their increasingly long lives.

3. You will have to fight with your many siblings for the leftovers. Because the middle-aged population is so much larger than the elderly population, the amount you will inherit is not likely to raise any eyebrows.

The inheritance bombshell turned out to be a dud. So far, only 20 percent of households have gotten an inheritance, receiving a median of just $49,902, according to the AARP.[42] Another 14 percent of households are still waiting, filled with hope, for Aunt Sue to come through.

Factoid source: John Gist and Carlos Figueiredo, *In Their Dreams: What Will Boomers Inherit,* AARP Public Policy Institute, June 2006, p. 4.

POVERTY THRESHOLD FOR
A FAMILY OF FOUR: $20,444

Mollie Orshansky may be the Patron Saint of Best Intentions. As an employee of the Social Security Administration, she meant well when she created the first poverty threshold calculations in 1963. Little did she know that her measuring stick was on fire, turning the poverty threshold into a hot potato. No politician has been willing to touch it for more than forty years.

Here's how it happened. In the early 1960s, Orshansky was charged with the task of determining the minimum amount of money American families needed to make ends meet. She came up with a great idea—start with how much money a family required to purchase enough food for an economical but nutritionally adequate diet.[43] She multiplied the food figure by three to create the poverty thresholds. Why three? At the time, the average American family spent about one-third of its after-tax income on food. To this day, the poverty threshold remains the same, with the government simply adjusting the figures for inflation each year.

The Social Security Administration never intended the measurement of poverty to be cast in stone. Orshansky and her colleagues assumed her calculations would be updated every few years to account for rising living standards and changing spending patterns. No update has ever occurred. Meanwhile, our standard of living has grown and our spending patterns have changed. The average family today devotes just 13 percent of its budget to food, down from the one-third share required when the poverty lines were drawn. We spend less on clothes, alcohol, and tobacco, but more on housing, cars, health care, and education.

It is not for lack of trying that the methodology has not been updated. Over the years various organizations—including the National Academy of Sciences—have studied the issue and recommended changes. None has been enacted. The public has lost interest in the War on Poverty, and the politicians will not touch this hot potato.

Factoid source: Bureau of the Census, Poverty Thresholds 2006, http://www.census.gov/hhes/www/ overty/ threshld/thresh06.html (accessed August 30, 2007).

PERCENTAGE OF THE POOR OWNING A COLOR TELEVISION: 97

What does it mean to be poor? In the United States today, it means your income is below the level required to purchase what was deemed a nutritionally adequate diet more than forty years ago multiplied by three and adjusted for inflation. It does not mean you do not own a house, a car, a television, a microwave, or even a cell phone. Poverty is relative, Adam Smith once cautioned. When living standards rise, the meaning of poverty changes—or it should. Many do not see it that way, however, which is why we have failed to update the poverty yardstick since its creation in the 1960s.

Enter the words "poverty" and "color television" into Google's search engine and you will unearth outrage. The *National Review* calls it "the luxury of American poverty" because 97 percent of the poor own a color television.[44] The rumors are true. Most of the poor do own a color TV. Most also own a microwave (89 percent) and have air conditioning (80 percent).[45] These one-time luxuries are universally owned today and most Americans consider them necessities, according to the Pew Research Center.[46] Begrudging the poor these twenty-first-century necessities makes no more sense than begrudging them twentieth-century basics such as refrigerators, running water, and indoor plumbing. The definitions of both poverty and wealth should reflect rising standards of living. An income of $50,000 is no longer a mark of wealth. Neither is a color television.

The good news is that living standards have improved for the poor and everyone else. The bad news is that, because poverty is relative, the poor will never go away. The War on Poverty is a war we can never win.

Factoid source: Bureau of the Census, Extended Measures of Well-being: Living Conditions in the United States, 2003, Detailed Tables, http://www.census.gov/population/ www/socdemo/p70-110.html (accessed July 11, 2007).

PERCENTAGE OF AMERICANS
AGED 15 OR OLDER WHO RECEIVE INCOME
FROM PUBLIC ASSISTANCE: 1

The "Welfare Queen" rules a very small kingdom. With less than 1 percent of Americans aged 15 or older receiving income from public assistance, the United States is in no danger of becoming a welfare state. In fact, Americans are just as inclined to push the needy off a cliff as to lend them a helping hand.

Twelve percent of Americans are poor, but even among the poor dependence on welfare is uncommon. An astonishingly small 6 percent of the poor receive public assistance income from the government. Fifteen percent of the poor live in subsidized housing, 32 percent receive food stamps, and 40 percent are on Medicaid.[47] Yet even these tokens of generosity are too much for a surprisingly large number of Americans. We begrudge the poor these meager handouts because a large share of the public thinks the poor themselves are wholly or partly to blame for their troubles.

This antipathy toward the poor separates us from our counterparts in Europe, and it explains why welfare benefits in the United States are so much smaller than those across the Atlantic, according to a study by researchers at the National Bureau of Economic Research. Europeans are sympathetic toward the poor, with 60 percent believing the poor are trapped by circumstances. Americans are contemptuous of the poor, with 60 percent believing the poor are lazy.[48] What explains our contempt? Skin color. "Hostility to welfare comes in part from the fact that welfare spending in the U.S. goes disproportionately to minorities," say the NBER researchers.[49] Social science research shows repeatedly that people are more altruistic toward members of their own group. In the United States, the dividing line between the in-group and the out-group has always been race: "It is clear that racial heterogeneity within the U.S. is one of the most important reasons why the welfare state in America is small," the researchers conclude.[50]

Factoid source: Bureau of the Census, 2007 Current Population Survey Annual Social and Economic Supplement, http://pubdb3.census.gov/macro/032007/perinc/ toc.htm (accessed August 31, 2007).

Chapter 9
RETIREMENT

PERCENTAGE OF WORKERS WHO ARE 'VERY CONFIDENT' IN HAVING ENOUGH MONEY FOR A COMFORTABLE RETIREMENT: 18

Eighteen percent is not much. But add to that number the 43 percent who are "somewhat confident," and an astounding 61 percent of the public feels at least somewhat confident in its ability to afford a comfortable retirement, according to the Retirement Confidence Survey (RCS). This annual check-up of our attitudes toward retirement finds only 37 percent of workers feeling "not too" or "not at all" confident in their retirement finances. How could our confidence be so high when the experts never miss an opportunity to tell us how bad we are at saving? There are only three possibilities:

1. We are idiots. It might boil down to this. Analysts for the National Bureau of Economic Research have hypothesized that retirement savings behavior is less rational than commonly believed, with many workers experiencing a "surprise" when they retire and discover they have not saved enough.[1] The RCS suggests many workers could fall into this category. Only 47 percent have calculated how much money they will need in retirement.[2]

2. We are not idiots, because we *are* saving enough. Some academics take this point of view. An analysis of longitudinal data from the Health and Retirement Survey concludes that only 20 percent of households nearing retirement have not saved enough.[3] Another contrarian, economist Laurence Kotlikoff of Boston University, claims financial service firms overstate how much Americans need to save because they are trolling for customers.[4]

3. We have lowered our expectations. The percentage of workers who expect to retire at age 66 or older climbed from 18 to 36 percent in the past decade, according to the RCS. The labor force participation rate of men aged 65 or older is rising and is now at 21 percent, the highest level in two decades. We may be more confident about retirement because we have no plans to retire anytime soon.

Factoid source: Employee Benefit Research Institute, Retirement Confidence Survey, http://www.ebri.org/ surveys/rcs/ (accessed April 16, 2008).

PERCENTAGE OF WORKERS WITH
A DEFINED-BENEFIT PENSION PLAN: 21

If someone swipes your wallet, it is a crime. If someone steals your retirement income, it is much harder to point a finger at the perp. Most victims won't even know what happened to them. Such is the case with today's workers, whose retirement savings accounts have been plundered by the long fingers of politics.

This is about a fundamental change in job benefits—the shift from defined-benefit pension plans (a guaranteed monthly benefit for life paid by your employer) to defined-contribution retirement accounts (a lump sum received at retirement, largely funded by you). That's a complicated way of saying, "Hand over your money." Defined-contribution plans are a poor substitute for defined-benefit plans. Since Congress tinkered with the tax code in 1978, businesses have been swapping one for the other, stripping tens of thousands of dollars from workers' future income in retirement.

Here are the facts. Among all private-sector workers, only 21 percent now have a defined-benefit pension plan. Among workers participating in any type of retirement plan, the percentage with a defined-benefit plan has plunged from 84 percent in 1979 to just 37 percent today, according to the Employee Benefit Research Institute.[5] Most workers with retirement plans now participate in defined-contribution accounts instead. But the two are not the same. Helpfully, an economist at the Bureau of Labor Statistics has calculated just how different they are, projecting the income generated by each type of plan at age 62 for workers born between 1946 and 1960. With a defined-benefit plan, retirees would receive $777 per month for life.[6] With a defined-contribution plan, workers would have accumulated $128,000 in their accounts by age 62. At a 5 percent withdrawal rate, this would generate only $533 per month, far less than their peers with a defined-benefit plan. As they pinch pennies in retirement, they won't even know they were robbed. Maybe it's better that way.

Factoid source: Bureau of Labor Statistics, *National Compensation Survey: Employee Benefits in Private Industry in the United States, March 2007,* August 2007, p. 9.

PERCENTAGE OF WORKERS
WITH A 401(K) RETIREMENT PLAN: 36

In an ideal world, American workers would save dutifully for retirement and we would not be having this little talk. In the real world, there are a thousand and one reasons not to save—starting with the cappuccino you bought this morning.

The problem with asking people to voluntarily save for retirement is that many don't. That is why the government created the Social Security system in the first place—to force people to save for retirement. The same kind of paternalistic attitude was behind the defined-benefit pension plan. These days, paternalism is all but dead. "Choice" is now the watchword. Employers can choose whether or not to offer retirement benefits. Workers can choose whether or not to participate in their employer's plan. Choice is why so few workers have a 401(k) and why, among those who do, 401(k) balances are pitifully small.

The way the media gush about 401(k)s, you would think everyone had one—like a car or a cell phone. But in fact, only 36 percent of all wage and salary workers participate in a defined-contribution retirement plan, according to the Employee Benefit Research Institute (EBRI).[7] The figure is low in part because most employers choose not to offer them—only 44 percent of private-sector companies offer defined-contribution retirement plans, according to the National Compensation Survey.[8] Even when an employer offers a plan, many employees choose not to participate. Among workers whose employers offer a plan, only 77 percent participate. Then there is the matter of contributions. Many workers choose to contribute a little rather than a lot. The median balance of 401(k) accounts open continuously since 1999 was just $66,650 in 2006, according to EBRI.[9]

Those who choose not to save will see their choices narrow in retirement. They will have just one option left: Social Security, the seventy-year-old, paternalistic, involuntary retirement program is all that will keep many Americans afloat in old age.

Factoid source: Author's calculations based on Craig Copeland, "Retirement Plan Participation and Retirees' Perception of Their Standard of Living," Employee Benefit Research Institute, *Issue Brief* 289, January 2006, p. 6.

PERCENTAGE OF THE ELDERLY IN POVERTY WITHOUT SOCIAL SECURITY: 38

How much money will you need to live comfortably in retirement? Would an annual income of $5,500 do it for you? Without their monthly Social Security check, that paltry figure would be the median income of Americans aged 65 or older.[10] Without Social Security, the poverty rate among the elderly would climb from a lowly 9 percent to a heart stopping 38 percent.

Like it or not, older Americans are dependent on Social Security, which is their single largest source of income. Social Security accounts for 40 percent of the income of people aged 65 or older, according to the Employee Benefit Research Institute.[11] Younger Americans think it will be different when they retire. Only 31 percent of today's workers expect Social Security to be a major source of income in retirement, according to the Retirement Confidence Survey (RCS).[12]

One reason workers downplay the importance of Social Security is that they have been told too many times that Social Security may not be there for them. Seventy-one percent of workers are not confident the system will provide them with benefits equal to those received by today's retirees, according to the RCS. But savings are not likely to make up the difference. Among all households, only half have any retirement savings, according to the Survey of Consumer Finances. Those with retirement savings have stashed away a median of just $35,200.[13] Not even close: to generate the kind of income Social Security provides for a twenty-year retirement would require $189,000 in retirement savings—per person.[14]

Even those who have saved a lot would suffer without Social Security. According to a study by the National Bureau of Economic Research, the richest households—with more than $2 million in assets—would see their standard of living fall by 36 percent if the Social Security program were abolished the day they retired.[15]

Factoid source: Bureau of the Census, "The Effects of Government Taxes and Transfers on Income and Poverty," http://pubdb3.census.gov/macro/032007/altpov/newpov01 _000.htm (accessed April 16, 2008).

YEAR THE SOCIAL SECURITY TRUST FUND
WILL EXHAUST ITS SURPLUS: 2041

Don't jump. Contemplating the elimination of Social Security because of the aging of the baby-boom generation is like considering suicide because you have a few wrinkles. You might want to consider a Botox treatment, but you will soldier on with or without the injections. The same is true with Social Security.

Social Security is the most important source of income for the nation's elderly. Nine out of ten people aged 65 or older receive a Social Security check each month, which accounts for 40 percent of their income. These statistics are not likely to change much as younger generations enter the program. Their track record in saving for retirement is not impressive, and the decline in defined-benefit pension plans means Social Security could be even more significant for future generations than it is today.

But not to worry. At the current rate, the trust fund's surplus will not be drained until 2041, according to the Social Security Board of Trustees (or 2046, according to the Congressional Budget Office). Even so, the money paid into the fund each year will allow the program to provide benefits not too radically different from today. If no changes are made to the Social Security system and benefits must be cut to match revenues beginning in 2041, then payments to retirees will fall by 25 percent.[16] Ouch, but not the end. The fix for this shortfall is a nip here and a tuck there, not Dr. Kevorkian. The long-term prognosis is not so dire either. According to projections by the Congressional Budget Office, the Social Security benefits paid to future retirees will exceed the benefits paid to today's retirees—even after the hypothetical benefit cut.[17] Workers retiring today will receive a median of $151,000 in lifetime benefits from Social Security (in 2006 dollars). Future retirees being born today will receive a much larger $228,000 (in 2006 dollars) in their old age.

Factoid source: Social Security and Medicare Board of Trustees, "The 2008 Annual Report of the Board of Trustees of the Federal Old-Age and Survivors Insurance and Federal Disability Insurance Trust Funds," http://www .socialsecurity.gov/OACT/TR/TR08 (accessed March 25, 2008).

WOMEN'S SHARE OF THOSE
RECEIVING SOCIAL SECURITY: 58

Watch what you say—your mother might be listening. At least, that's what you should keep in mind before you complain too much about the nation's burgeoning entitlement programs. What many seem to overlook in the heated discussions about the future of Medicare and Social Security is that we are talking about your mother. Among those receiving Medicare and Social Security benefits, women far outnumber men. They account for the 58 percent majority of both Medicare enrollees and Social Security recipients.[18]

It is all because of the sex ratio—or the number of males per 100 females. For some biological mystery, the sex ratio is tipped in favor of males at birth, with 105 boys born for every 100 girls. No one knows why the sex ratio at birth is lopsided, but it turns out to be a good thing. If boys and girls were born in equal numbers, then boys would be in short supply by prom night. The mortality rate of males exceeds that of females at every age.

The higher death rate of males pares down their excess numbers and pretty well equals things out just in time for love, marriage, and the baby carriage. Women begin to outnumber men in the forty-something age group. The difference starts out small—just 57,000 among those aged 40 to 44—but grows with every birthday. Among people in their late sixties, women outnumber men by more than 700,000. Among those aged 85 or older, women outnumber men by nearly 2 million.[19] This explains why 75 percent of women aged 85 or older are widows and most live alone.[20] Which brings the discussion back to Social Security and Medicare. Without them, your mother would be living in your guest room, and you would be paying her healthcare bills on top of your own. All those in favor of dismantling Social Security and Medicare, raise your hand.

Factoid source: Bureau of the Census, 2007 Current Population Survey, Personal Income Tables, http://pubdb3.census.gov/macro/032007/perinc/toc.htm (accessed September 3, 2007).

PERCENTAGE OF WORKERS WHO
PLAN TO WORK IN RETIREMENT: 63

Isn't the idea of working in retirement an oxymoron? Apparently not, since respondents do not burst out laughing when asked this question by survey researchers. When interviewed, nearly two out of three workers say (with a straight face) that they plan to work in retirement, according to the Retirement Confidence Survey. And they appear to be doing just that. The labor force participation rate of men aged 65 or older is on the rise, reaching 20 percent in 2006—the highest level in two decades.

An entire generation of Americans—the Greatest Generation, in fact—transformed retirement into a leisure industry. It was their good fortune to grow old during a time when corporate generosity in the form of defined-benefit pensions was at a peak, when the government bit the bullet and created Medicare (in 1965), and to top it off indexed Social Security to inflation (in 1972). No wonder the labor force participation rate of men aged 65 or older plummeted from nearly 50 percent in 1950 to an all-time low of 16 percent by the mid-1990s. Why work in old age when pensions, Social Security, and Medicare guaranteed financial security?

The Greatest Generation is a hard act to follow, especially when their upstanding character gets the credit for their good fortune. But dumb luck, not character, insulated the generation from the struggle for economic security in old age. Now the luck has run out, and the younger generations that follow—a sorry lot (or so the story goes), who cannot pay for their children's college education let alone save for retirement—are already feeling the pinch. According to the Retirement Confidence Survey, 78 percent of those who plan to work in retirement say they will need the money to make ends meet.[21]

Factoid source: Employee Benefit Research Institute, Retirement Confidence Survey, http://www.ebri.org/surveys/rcs/ (accessed April 16, 2008).

PERCENTAGE OF OLDER AMERICANS WHO COULD NOT GET MEDICAL CARE IN THE PAST YEAR DUE TO COST: 2

How's this for a nightmare: imagine growing old without health insurance. This nightmare was reality for most of the nation's elderly until Medicare's enactment in 1965. Medicare is the government's health insurance program for people aged 65 or older. Until Medicare, few of the elderly had any meaningful health insurance, according to MIT economist Amy Finkelstein.[22] When they became ill, they were forced to spend down their savings to pay medical bills, driving many into poverty. In the years just before Medicare was enacted, the poverty rate of the elderly stood at 35 percent. After Medicare, the poverty rate of the elderly fell, skidding to 25 percent by 1970.[23] (The indexing of Social Security to inflation in 1972 was the knockout punch, reducing poverty among the elderly to just 9 percent today.)

No one can deny the financial challenges Medicare faces as its ranks expand with the aging of the population. But before we throw out the baby with the bathwater in our zeal to reform the system, it is important to note that no one is happier with their healthcare than people aged 65 or older. When Americans are asked to rate the quality of the healthcare they receive on a scale from zero to ten, the 62 percent majority of people aged 65 or older rate it a nine or ten, according to the Medical Expenditure Panel Survey.[24] Only 45 percent of younger adults rate their healthcare that highly. The elderly are most likely to get a doctor's appointment when they need one and least likely to have problems receiving medical care because of cost.

Are Americans of all ages ready for the same type of universal coverage? Maybe so: when asked whether they prefer the current employer-based health insurance system or universal health insurance through a program such as Medicare, the 56 percent majority of the public chooses Medicare.[25]

Factoid source: National Center for Health Statistics, Early Release of Selected Estimates Based on Data from the National Health Interview Survey, Obtaining Needed Medical Care, http://www.cdc.gov/nchs/about/major/nhis/released200706.htm#3 (accessed July 2, 2007).

Chapter 10
TROUBLES

PERCENTAGE WHO WERE
SLEEPLESS LAST NIGHT: 5

Five percent might not look like a lot, but looks can be deceiving. Millions of Americans do not get enough sleep. This diagnosis is brought to you by the National Sleep Foundation, a nonprofit organization that promotes sleep as a vital public health issue. In annual surveys, the National Sleep Foundation tracks how much sleep Americans get and what keeps them from getting more. Thanks to those surveys, we know more about patterns of sleep among young and old, men and women, drivers and coffee drinkers. Its surveys have discovered, for example, that high school seniors get only 6.9 hours of sleep on school nights; half of women wake up feeling unrefreshed at least a few mornings a week; only 11 percent of people aged 55 or older (compared with 30 percent of people under age 55) stay up past midnight on weekends.[1]

The National Sleep Foundation is not alone in tracking the sleep patterns of Americans. The federal government also records the time people spend in bed (some of it sleeping) through the American Time Use Survey. The survey collects data on the amount of time people spend doing everything from feeding their dogs to shopping for groceries by asking them to account for their activities minute-by-minute during the past 24 hours. The survey results show that the average person sleeps 8.63 hours a night, but that figure includes the time people spend trying to get to sleep.[2]

Sleeplessness is a big problem for many people, according to the American Time Use Survey. The number who struggle to sleep rises with age to a peak of 11 percent among people aged 75 or older. A few keystrokes on a calculator reveal 12 million people of all ages counting sheep on an average night. That's a lot of sheep.

Factoid source: Bureau of Labor Statistics, unpublished tables from the 2006 American Time Use Survey.

PERCENTAGE OF AMERICANS EXPERIENCING A PROBLEM IN THE PAST YEAR: 92

Every now and then someone nails it, describing with precision the changing nature of the human condition. This is what Tom W. Smith, director of the General Social Survey, has succeeded in doing. Using data from the General Social Survey, Smith explored how many of 58 different problems a representative sample of Americans experienced in 2004. He then compared the problems experienced by the average person in 2004 with those experienced by the average person in 1991. It is not a pretty picture.

"Americans on average are worse-off now than in the past," says Smith.[3] He came to this conclusion after comparing the 2004 data with the 1991 results. In both years, survey respondents were asked to identify the frequency with which they encountered a variety of problems ranging from the death of a spouse to a pay cut. The percentage of Americans experiencing at least one problem during the past 12 months increased over those years from 89 to 92 percent. The number of problems experienced by the average person grew from 3.8 to 4.3.[4] Smith reports significant increases in problems such as being unemployed, being pressured to pay bills, being unable to afford food, going without health insurance, and being hospitalized.

What factors might explain this erosion in our quality of life? One might be the aging of the population, which leads to more health problems. Another might be technological change and the outsourcing of jobs. Smith's study sheds some light on why things may be turning south. He examined the demographic segments with the most and least troubles. The biggest change in the distribution of trouble is by education. In 1991, the least educated experienced 1.33 problems for every 1 problem experienced by the most educated, reports Smith.[5] By 2004, the ratio was a higher 1.79 to 1. Education is playing an ever-larger role in sorting out the haves from the have-nots.

Factoid source: Tom W. Smith, *Troubles in America: A Study of Negative Life Events across Time and Sub-Groups*, GSS Topical Report 40 (Chicago: National Opinion Research Center, 2005), p. 11.

PERCENTAGE EXPERIENCING THE DEATH OF A CLOSE FRIEND IN THE PAST YEAR: 23

Most of us escape life's biggest problems during an average year, but almost no one escapes every problem. According to an analysis of General Social Survey results by director Tom W. Smith, fully 92 percent of people aged 18 or older experience at least one of 58 "negative life events" during a year's time.[6]

Negative life events run the gamut from poor health to being accused of a crime, from money troubles to not getting along with the boss. The number one problem, experienced by the largest share of Americans, is going to the doctor. The 58 percent majority of people aged 18 or older visited a doctor because of illness during the past 12 months. This may not be a big problem for most, but problem number two is a whopper for everyone. The second most common problem is the death of a close friend. During an average year, nearly one in four adults lose a friend, making it far more common than being unemployed for a month or more (15 percent), having serious trouble with a spouse (9 percent), or having a child with a drug or drinking problem (3 percent). Going without health insurance is the third most common problem, with 18 percent not having health insurance during the past year.[7]

It gets worse. The list of problems is long and includes a decline in financial status (15 percent), not having a car (9 percent), the death of a parent (3 percent), and going bankrupt (1 percent). The problems range from the relatively mundane—such as being passed over for a promotion (5 percent), to the profound—such as being homeless (4 percent). If you are ever tempted to feel sorry for yourself because of some misfortune, just think of the trouble others are having. Or, as the old-timers used to say, if all of our problems were hung on a line, you would take yours and I would take mine.

Factoid source: Survey Documentation and Analysis, Computer-Assisted Survey Methods Program, University of California, Berkeley, General Social Surveys, 1972–2006 Cumulative Data Files, GSS Topical Module: Troubles, http://sda.berkeley.edu/cgi-bin32/hsda?harcsda+gss06 (accessed October 9, 2007).

PERCENTAGE WHO THINK MOST PEOPLE
CAN BE TRUSTED: 33

Whoever said the grass is greener on the other side of the fence was wrong. The grass is much greener right here. Just ask Americans how they feel about any issue, and you will hear the same story—it's a big problem for the nation as a whole, but not as big a problem here at home.

Take the issue of crime. When people are asked in surveys whether they think crime is getting worse, a larger proportion sees crime getting worse in the nation as a whole than in their local area. Fully 71 percent of the public think crime is getting worse in the nation. But a smaller (although still significant) 51 percent believe it is getting worse in their local area, according to a Gallup poll.[8]

Or take the issue of schools. When the public is asked to grade the nation's public schools, only 16 percent give them an A or a B, according to the Phi Delta Kappa/Gallup Poll.[9] But when asked to grade the public schools in their community, a larger 45 percent give them high marks. When parents are asked to grade the school their oldest child attends, the figure rises to 67 percent.

Even on the issue of trust in government, local is better. Only 47 percent of the public has a "fair" to a "great deal of trust" in the federal government to do what is right in handling domestic problems, according to Gallup.[10] A much larger 69 percent trust their local government to handle problems the right way.

People fear the unfamiliar, which might explain why trust rises with education. The best-educated Americans, who know the most about the world and the way it works, are the most trusting. The 56 percent majority of Americans with a graduate degree say most people can be trusted. Among those who went no further than high school, the figure is just 28 percent.[11]

Factoid source: Survey Documentation and Analysis, Computer-Assisted Survey Methods Program, University of California, Berkeley, General Social Surveys, 1972–2006 Cumulative Data Files, GSS Variable TRUST, http://sda .berkeley.edu/cgi-bin32/hsda?harcsda+gss06 (accessed September 29, 2007).

RANK OF TERRORISM AMONG THE CRIMES AMERICANS FEAR THE MOST: 3

If the goal of terrorism is to strike fear in the heart of the enemy, then Osama bin Laden has been successful. Americans are afraid. A large percentage of us now worry at least occasionally about being the victim of a terrorist attack. In the list of crimes Americans fear the most, terrorism ranks third, with 44 percent saying they frequently or occasionally worry about becoming a victim of terrorism, according to a Gallup survey.[12] Americans' fear of terrorism is behind only two other fears—the fear of having their cars stolen (47 percent) and the fear of having their homes burglarized (50 percent).

The terrorist attacks of September 11, 2001, sent a shock wave through the nation, including the statistical community—in particular health officials charged with classifying causes of death. Until 2001, there was no category—or code—for deaths caused by terrorism. All of a sudden, they needed one. As the National Center for Health Statistics (NCHS) explains: "Without these additional codes, injuries and deaths associated with terrorism cannot be separately identified, making statistical assessment extremely difficult."[13] So the government came up with new codes for terrorism: U01, U02, and U03, along with numerous detailed subcategories such as U01.1, terrorism involving destruction of aircraft; U01.6, terrorism involving biological weapons; and U03, the suicide of terrorists.[14]

Since 2001, there have been few deaths by terrorism in the United States. In fact, among the millions of deaths recorded in the general mortality tables kept by the NCHS, there has been only one American who died due to terrorism in the years since 2001.[15] But this has not assuaged our fear, which is stoked by ambitious politicians and the enormously profitable antiterrorism industry. Their efforts have worked. Americans worry much more about becoming the victim of a terrorist attack than about the far more common crimes of murder (18,000 a year),[16] rape (272,000 a year), or robbery (712,000 a year).[17]

Factoid source: Joseph Carroll, "Americans' Crime Worries," Gallup Poll, October 19, 2006, http://www.gallup .com/poll/25081/Americans-Crime-Worries.aspx (accessed November 30, 2007).

PERCENTAGE OF AMERICANS WHO SUPPORT REQUIRING A POLICE PERMIT BEFORE PURCHASING A GUN: 80

In the list of controversial issues in the United States, gun control ranks close to the top. For most Americans, however, no such controversy exists because the great majority supports gun control. Survey after survey reveals strong public support for a variety of gun control measures. The latest findings from the General Social Survey show 80 percent of the public supporting the need for a police permit before buying a gun, as well as overwhelming support for limiting the sale of semiautomatic assault weapons (85 percent), criminal background checks for private gun sales (80 percent), and stricter gun control after the terrorist attacks (82 percent).[18]

Gun control is controversial only among politicians. Academics in the field call this the "gun control paradox."[19] The paradox is this: despite widespread public support for gun control, our elected representatives have yet to pass comprehensive gun control legislation. Many academics have tried to explain the paradox, but so far there has been no "aha" moment of enlightenment. One theory is that the power of the NRA is so great that no politician dares cross the organization. Another theory is that those fighting gun control form a block of single-issue voters that can make or break a political campaign. A third theory is that gun control is a clash of urban versus rural culture, and rural wins despite the fact that most Americans live in urban areas.[20] Behind the power of the rural block are the eccentricities of our political system, with each state allotted two senators regardless of population size. This gives disproportionate power to rural areas and allows policy to be overly influenced by a small fraction of the population.[21]

Will the politicians ever give the public what it wants? If gun ownership is any measure, that day may be coming. The percentage of Americans with a gun in their home has fallen from nearly half three decades ago to just one-third today.[22]

Factoid source: Survey Documentation and Analysis, Computer-Assisted Survey Methods Program, University of California, Berkeley, General Social Surveys, 1972–2006 Cumulative Data Files, GSS Variable GUNLAW, http://sda .berkeley.edu/cgi-bin32/hsda?harcsda+gss06 (accessed October 9, 2007).

AMONG THE WORLD'S COUNTRIES, RANK OF THE UNITED STATES IN PRISONERS PER CAPITA: 1

We are not just number one. We are number one by a huge margin. The rate at which we imprison people dwarfs the rate in every other country. Our 738 prisoners per 100,000 US residents is 21 percent higher than the 611 per 100,000 in the number two country, Russia. It is more than twice the rate of South Africa, nearly four times the rate of Mexico, and nearly seven times the rate of Canada. The United States is home to just 5 percent of the world's population but almost one-fourth of the world's prisoners.[23] Is there something in the air that explains our swollen prison population?

The explanation lies not in the air, but in the attitude. No one can accuse us of being bleeding hearts when it comes to putting people away. Thanks to the War on Drugs, more people are being sentenced to prison terms. Thanks to tougher sentencing laws and lower parole rates, they are behind bars longer than ever. The number of people imprisoned in the United States is growing by 2.8 percent a year and reached 2.4 million in 2006.[24] The rapid growth of our prison population is projected to continue, according to one study. The incarcerated population will grow three times faster than the total population during the next five years, reports the Pew Charitable Trusts.[25] Feeding, clothing, and housing these prisoners is not cheap, costing the nation $62 billion a year. Pew sees this figure expanding by another $27 billion during the next five years.

Today there are as many Americans in prison as there are in college dormitories.[26] Interestingly, it costs about as much to keep someone in prison as it does to send someone to a public university—about $24,000 a year, according to Pew.[27]

Factoid source: Roy Walmsley, *World Prison Population List*, 7th ed., International Centre for Prison Studies, King's College London School of Law, undated, p. 1.

PERCENTAGE OF AMERICANS WHO OPPOSE THE DEATH PENALTY FOR MURDER: 33

Americans espouse a biblical sense of justice: if you kill someone, you deserve to die. End of story. Sixty-seven percent of the public favors the death penalty for murder, according to the General Social Survey.[28] This figure is down from a peak of nearly 80 percent two decades ago, but the death penalty remains an issue about which most Americans agree. Support for the death penalty is strong in almost every segment of the population, including women (66 percent), college graduates (62 percent), and self-described liberals (55 percent). Blacks are the only holdouts, with just 45 percent favoring the death penalty.

The United States is finding itself increasingly alone in demanding an eye for an eye. We are one of only 60 countries in the world still practicing the death penalty. A much larger 137 countries have abolished the death penalty entirely or no longer carry it out, according to Amnesty International.[29] Our compatriots in support of the death penalty include China, Cuba, Iran, Pakistan, Saudi Arabia, and Uganda.

In 1972, the death penalty hit a legal bump when the Supreme Court ruled it unconstitutional in practice. For the next few years, executions came to a halt until, in 1976, the justices relented after the states rewrote their death penalty statutes. We were back in business. In the years since, tougher sentencing laws and the complicated legal process of actually putting people to death has inflated the number of prisoners on death row from 420 to more than 3,000.[30]

All told, more than 1,000 people have been executed in the United States since the Supreme Court gave the death penalty the thumbs up in 1976.[31] Also since that year, 119 death row inmates have been found innocent and set free.[32]

Factoid source: Survey Documentation and Analysis, Computer-Assisted Survey Methods Program, University of California, Berkeley, General Social Surveys, 1972–2006 Cumulative Data Files, GSS Variable CAPPUN, http://sda .berkeley.edu/cgi-bin32/hsda?harcsda+gss06 (accessed October 9, 2007).

PERCENTAGE OF PEOPLE AGED 45 TO 49
WHO HAVE SMOKED MARIJUANA: 57

Today's parents may worry about their teenagers experimenting with marijuana, but their children are less likely to have tried the drug than the parents
themselves. The biggest users of marijuana are graying at the temples. Most
Americans aged 45 to 49 have smoked marijuana in their lifetime, surpassing the rate in every other five-year age group.

But some age groups are not far behind. Most people from the youthful
age of 20 to the decidedly older age of 54 have smoked marijuana at some
point in their life.[33] Despite their experience with marijuana—or perhaps
because of it—Americans do not favor legalizing the drug. Sixty-three percent of the public is against the legalization of marijuana, according to the
National Opinion Research Center's General Social Survey.[34]

Few middle-aged Americans still smoke marijuana. Among 45- to 49-
year-olds, only 5 percent have used marijuana in the past month. The urge to
get to work on time and the pressing need to lose a few pounds keep many
middle-aged adults away from the weed. Those most likely to have used
marijuana recently are young adults. "Past month use" peaks among people
aged 20—many of them college kids. Even for this typically rowdy bunch,
only one in five has smoked marijuana in the past month. Alcohol is another
matter.

Marijuana is also losing popularity among teenagers. The percentage of
high school students who have ever smoked marijuana fell from 47 to 38
percent between 1999 and 2007, according to the Youth Risk Behavioral
Surveillance System—a government survey that monitors the behavior of
the nation's 9th through 12th graders.[35] The percentage who used marijuana
in the past month dropped from 27 to 20 percent during those years. What is
behind the decline in marijuana use among teens? Maybe it is the advice of
their parents, who speak from experience.

Factoid source: SAMHSA, Office of Applied Studies,
Results from the 2006 National Survey on Drug Use and
Health: Detailed Tables, Table 1-12B, http://www.oas
.samhsa.gov/nsduh/2k6nsduh/tabs/Sect1peTabs11to18.pdf
(accessed November 30, 2007).

PERCENTAGE USING METHAMPHETAMINES IN THE PAST MONTH: 0.3

No, the decimal is not in the wrong place. Only 0.3 percent of Americans aged 12 or older have used methamphetamines in the past month. Maybe we should declare the War on Drugs over and give ourselves a medal for a job well done.

Not so fast, many would argue. Drug use is rampant in the United States. True, but only sort of. Many Americans have, at some point, experimented with illicit drugs—which the federal government defines as marijuana, cocaine, heroin, hallucinogens, inhalants, or the nonmedical use of prescription drugs such as pain relievers, tranquilizers, or stimulants. Among the population aged 12 or older, 45 percent—nearly half—have ever used an illicit drug, according to the government's National Survey of Drug Use and Health.[36] But a better gauge of drug use is the percentage of people who have used illicit drugs more recently, say in the past month. By that measure, only 8 percent are drug users. Subtract marijuana from the figure—a drug considered by some to be less harmful than alcohol or tobacco—and the percentage falls to just 4 percent, most accounted for by the nonmedical use of pain relievers.

By any reasonable measure, drug use in the United States has been pushed to the margins. It is so low, in fact, that federal researchers became concerned that their drug survey was understating the use of methamphetamines due to the way in which the questions were presented to respondents. The media had spotted a meth epidemic, but the government was having a hard time coming up with the numbers to support the headlines. The feds changed the questions on the survey to better pinpoint meth use.[37] The new approach did the job, finding more meth users. It boosted the proportion of the population using meth in the past month from 0.2 to 0.3 percent.

Factoid source: SAMHSA, Office of Applied Studies, National Survey on Drug Use and Health, 2006, Appendix B: Statistical Methods and Measurement, Table B-6, http://www.oas.samhsa.gov/nsduh/2k6nsduh/AppB.htm# (accessed October 9, 2007).

PERCENTAGE WHO SMOKE CIGARETTES: 21

It has been a tough fight, and it is not over yet. Despite years of antismoking campaigns, a substantial percentage of the population still smokes cigarettes. But the percentage of people who smoke has dropped by half over the past few decades.

This scenario would have been hard to imagine in 1965, when 42 percent of Americans aged 18 or older smoked cigarettes.[38] Among men at that time, the 52 percent majority smoked (as did 34 percent of women). The figure peaked at 61 percent among men aged 25 to 34. Today, a much smaller 26 percent of men aged 25 to 34 smoke cigarettes—above average, but well below the rate of 1965.

Smoking has become less popular for a number of reasons. The overwhelming scientific evidence linking smoking to cancer, the increased cost of cigarettes through taxes, and legislation making it difficult to smoke at work sites and in public places have had a pronounced effect. These efforts discouraged people from smoking and encouraged them to quit. They also transformed the demographics of smokers.

The typical smoker today is decidedly downscale, with little money or education. Smoking declines as income rises, despite the steep cost of a pack of cigarettes. Among people with household incomes below $20,000, fully 28 percent are cigarette smokers. Among those with household incomes of $75,000 or more, just 14 percent smoke.[39] Education, more than any other factor, differentiates those who smoke from those who do not. Among high school dropouts, 26 percent smoke cigarettes. Among college graduates, only 8 percent smoke.

Even teenagers are getting the message. More than 80 percent of high school seniors disapprove of smoking, according to the University of Michigan's Institute for Social Research.[40] Smoking is still cool in only one place: cigarette company advertising.

Factoid source: National Center for Health Statistics, *Summary Health Statistics for U.S. Adults: National Health Interview Survey, 2006,* Provisional Report, Vital and Health Statistics, Series 10, No. 235, 2007, Table 24.

PERCENTAGE OF WOMEN WHO CONSUME MORE THAN ONE ALCOHOLIC DRINK A DAY: 4

People lie. This is a fact of life in survey research. They lie about their height, their weight, their sexual orientation, and their drinking. According to how much people say they drink, Americans are practically teetotalers, but according to volume sales of wine, beer, and hard liquor, not so much.

Data collected by the USDA's Economic Research Service show that each American drinks 25 gallons of beer, wine, and distilled spirits each year, on average.[41] But not everyone drinks alcoholic beverages. In fact, only 61 percent of people aged 18 or older report drinking any alcohol at all in the past year.[42] That leaves more for the drinkers, each of whom consumes 372 cans of beer, 126 glasses of wine, and 147 cocktails a year—or about two drinks a day, on average.

That seems about right. Two drinks a day is a reasonable figure for the nation's drinkers. But there is a problem—few Americans admit that they drink two drinks a day. Among women, 55 percent say they drink, but just 4 percent say they have more than one drink a day (defined as "heavy" drinking for women, according to the straitlaced folks in the federal government). Among men, 68 percent say they drink, but only 28 percent say they drink more than one drink a day. If you subtract the nondrinkers from volume sales and adjust for those who claim to drink only lightly, an awful lot of alcohol is being poured down the drain. Someone isn't telling the truth.

The fact that Americans lie about how much they drink is not out of the ordinary. It happens all over the world. An international study comparing alcohol consumption by country finds survey respondents reporting the consumption of only 40 to 60 percent of the retail volume of alcohol sold.[43] Does bald-faced lying account for the difference? Not entirely. Another reason for the shortfall, say the researchers, is "poor recall."

Factoid source: National Institute on Alcohol Abuse and Alcoholism, Self-Reported Amounts and Patterns of Alcohol Consumption, http://www.niaaa.nih.gov/Resources/ DatabaseResources/QuickFacts/AlcoholConsumption/ dkpat25.htm (accessed October 9, 2007).

PART III

YOUR COUNTRY

Chapter 11
GEOGRAPHY

PERCENTAGE OF 18- TO 24-YEAR-OLDS WHO CAN LOCATE OHIO ON A MAP: 43

Westward ho! The pioneer spirit is a fundamental American trait. Exploring and expanding into the frontier is a defining element of our history and provides us with a deeply rooted sense of who we are even today. But we are only kidding ourselves. Americans no longer venture far from home and seemingly have little interest in the world outside their suburban homestead unless it shows up on twenty-four-hour cable news.

Ask young adults to identify 7 states on a map of the United States, and they can correctly name only 3.4. Most cannot locate Ohio, and just half can find New York, according to a National Geographic–Roper survey.[1] The nation's young adults don't know much about geography because few have explored the country, let alone the world. Two-thirds of native-born Americans still live in the state in which they were born, according to the American Community Survey.[2] Only 34 percent of us own a passport.[3] Even the nation's supposedly adventurous 18- to 24-year-olds are homebodies at heart. Only 30 percent have traveled outside the United States in the past three years.[4]

Hold on: 30 percent sounds like a substantial number. Not compared to the wanderlust of young adults from other countries. Among the world's 18- to 24-year-olds, the Swedes are the most outgoing—92 percent have visited a foreign country in the past three years, according to National Geographic–Roper.[5] Young adults from Germany, Great Britain, Canada and even Japan are far more likely than we are to leave familiar surroundings. Of course, the Europeans have a good reason for going elsewhere, because elsewhere is only a stone's throw away. But there is another reason Americans are less likely than others to leave home. We have The Beach, and they don't. Specifically, we have warm, sunny beaches. In January. And the beach, according to a MasterCard survey, is America's number-one vacation choice.[6]

Factoid source: National Geographic and Roper Public Affairs, National Geographic–Roper Public Affairs 2006 Geographic Literacy Study, May 2006, http://www .nationalgeographic.com/roper2006/findings.html (accessed April 19, 2007).

PERCENTAGE OF AMERICANS
WHO LIVE IN A COASTAL COUNTY
1970: 54
2005: 52

You might think everyone wants to live on the beach, but in fact they only want to vacation there. It may be hard to believe, but our coastal counties are growing more slowly than their landlocked counterparts. Consequently, the proportion of Americans who live in a coastal county is slowly declining—and the decline began before most of us had ever heard of global warming.

One of the many statistical projects of the federal government is defining and identifying coastal counties. The National Oceanic and Atmospheric Administration is charged with this task, and it defines a coastal county as one with at least 15 percent of its land area either in or between a coastal watershed. By this definition, 673 of the nation's 3,143 counties are coastal, and those counties are home to 155 million people.[7] Our coastal geography includes not only the east and west coasts, but also the counties along the Great Lakes. In fact, the Great Lakes are second only to the Atlantic in the number of counties bordered by their waters. The Atlantic Ocean laps 285 counties, the Great Lakes 158, the Gulf of Mexico 142, and the Pacific just 88.

The term *coastal* has a great ring to it. It brings to mind beaches, palm trees, and vacations. The reality is not as idyllic. The nation's coastal counties include eight of the ten largest metropolitan areas: New York; Los Angeles; Chicago; Philadelphia; Miami; Houston; Washington, DC; and Detroit. In fact, the rapid growth of the inland suburban counties surrounding these metropolitan areas explains why landlocked areas are growing faster than the coast.

Some places are stereotypically coastal—like Hawaii, where 100 percent of the population lives in a coastal county. Other states are more of a surprise—like Ohio, where 38 percent of the population lives in a coastal county, exceeding the percentage in Georgia or North Carolina.

Factoid source: Bureau of the Census, *Statistical Abstract of the United States: 2007* (Washington, DC: US Government Printing Office, 2007), p. 33.

PERCENTAGE WHO MOVED TO A
DIFFERENT STATE IN THE PAST YEAR: 2

Allied Van Lines and U-Haul take notice: Americans are moving a lot less than they once did. And when they move, they don't go very far. In a year's time, only 14 percent of people move from one house to another. In 1950, the figure was a much larger 21 percent.[8]

What has calmed American "mobility," as demographers call the arduous process of packing and hauling boxes of belongings from one address to another? While no one has been able to identify precisely the reason for the decline, common sense suggests several things. One, the homeownership rate is higher today than in the past, and homeowners move much less often than renters. The process of selling and buying a home is simply too expensive and time consuming to undertake very often, which is why economists consider houses to be "illiquid" assets—not easily converted into cash. Two, there are more dual-income couples than ever before, making moves more complicated when a spouse must hunt for a job. The third reason for the decline in mobility is the aging of the population. Older people are much less likely to move than young adults. The mobility rate peaks, in fact, among 20- to 24-year-olds, with 29 percent moving in a year's time—many having just graduated from college. Among people aged 70 or older, the mobility rate is only 4 percent.

Although the mobility rate has sagged since 1950, the number of people moving in a year's time has grown along with the US population. A substantial 40 million people move annually, supplying Allied Van Lines and U-Haul with plenty of customers. Most aren't going very far, however. The 62 percent majority of movers do not cross a county line.

Factoid source: Bureau of the Census, Geographic Mobility: 2005 to 2006, Detailed Tables, http://www.census .gov/population/www/socdemo/migrate/cps2006.html (accessed October 16, 2007).

PERCENTAGE OF RURAL AMERICANS
WHO LIVE IN A METROPOLITAN AREA: 51

More than 3,500 statisticians are hard at work in the federal government. They spend their days staring at the voluminous data collected by their employer, laboring in the nation's darkroom, so to speak, developing portraits that show us who we are.

One of the most iconic series of portraits is of the rural population. The stereotypical rural character of rugged individualism lies at the core of the American identity. Yet these portraits are fading as farm life recedes, small towns stagnate, and urban populations grow. In 2000, only 21 percent of Americans still lived in a rural area—defined as open countryside and settlements with fewer than 2,500 people.[9]

Even the "rural" and "urban" concepts are under siege, being overtaken by the more user-friendly metropolitan area classification system. "Urban" and "rural" are defined by population density at the geographic level of a "census block"—literally an area the size of a city block. This kind of precision makes tracking rural and urban populations cumbersome. Enter the metropolitan area concept. Metropolitan areas are, conveniently, entire counties. Their all-important demographic and socioeconomic data are updated annually. Since they are so user-friendly, it was inevitable that "metropolitan" would replace "urban" and "nonmetropolitan" would replace "rural" in the minds of Americans.

But there is a problem. Metropolitan does not necessarily mean urban. Metropolitan areas are defined as a county with a population of 50,000 or more and any surrounding counties with strong commuting ties to the central county. Many surrounding counties are, in fact, more rural than urban in character. Thanks to overlapping definitions, most rural residents now live in metropolitan areas, and more than one-third of metropolitan counties are mostly or completely rural. It looks like we need a better way to differentiate country from city. How about distance to the nearest Starbucks?

Factoid source: USDA, "Economic Research Service, Briefing Rooms, Rural Population and Migration: Trend I— Harder to Define 'Rural,'" http://www.ers.usda.gov/ Briefing/Population/Rural.htm (accessed April 20, 2007).

CHANGE IN THE NEW ORLEANS METROPOLITAN AREA POPULATION AFTER HURRICANE KATRINA: DOWN 39 PERCENT

Watching paint dry—that is how some describe the study of demographic change. Usually, it happens at a glacial pace. But not always. Case in point: New Orleans. Every year millions of people move from one place to another. But never before in the history of the United States have so many people moved away from one place as fast as they abandoned New Orleans after Hurricane Katrina struck on August 29, 2005. The levees did not hold, the floodwaters came, and the people fled for their lives.

Thanks to the efforts of the Census Bureau's survey researchers, we know just how many people left New Orleans. The bureau was in the field both before and after Katrina, collecting information for its American Community Survey. Realizing the importance of capturing the demographic dimensions of the event, the bureau divided the 2005 data it was collecting into two parts—the eight months before Katrina and the four months following Katrina. The before-and-after profiles show the New Orleans metropolitan population falling by a catastrophic 39 percent in a matter of weeks. The Census Bureau estimated the population of New Orleans pre-Katrina to be 1,191,000. The bureau's post-Katrina estimate was just 724,000—a loss of nearly half a million people.[10] The before-and-after profiles also show the number of housing units falling by 24 percent, the number of workers by 43 percent, and the number of students by 46 percent.

Where did everybody go? Hundreds died, and the rest scattered to all fifty states. Nobody knows where they are today. According to the Greater New Orleans Community Data Center, the best source of information on the location of the displaced is FEMA, but when the displaced stop receiving government assistance, FEMA no longer updates their addresses.[11] Evidently, some are returning to New Orleans. According to the Census Bureau's July 2007 estimate, the New Orleans metropolitan area population had rebounded to just over 1 million.

Factoid source: Bureau of the Census, 2005 American Community Survey Gulf Coast Area Data Profiles, New Orleans–Metairie–Kenner, LA Metropolitan Statistical Area, http://www.census.gov/acs/www/Products/Profiles/gulf_coast/tables/tab1_katrinaK0100US2203v.htm (accessed September 19, 2007).

RANK OF NORTH DAKOTA AMONG THE STATES IN VIOLENT CRIMES PER 100,000 POPULATION: 50

It's all the same—from one end of the country to the other, the United States has become an unchanging landscape of interstates, Wal-Marts, and McDonalds. Only it hasn't. Step outside the interstate swath, and you're back in the realm of the local, where you can have a different kind of life. So go for it. Find your nirvana—in North Dakota.

North Dakota has a lot to offer, like the lowest crime rate among the fifty states. With only 98 violent crimes each year per 100,000 population, North Dakota's crime rate is far below the 761 of South Carolina—the state with the highest crime rate in the nation.[12] Yet North Dakota is shrinking because people are moving out of the state, and South Carolina is growing because people are moving into the state.[13] Apparently, safety is not the most important factor when people decide on a place to live.

Another plus for North Dakota—the shortest commute. The state's workers spend only 16 minutes getting to work compared with an average of 25 minutes nationally.[14] Traffic is not an issue in North Dakota, with only 9.2 people per square mile. Only Montana, Wyoming, and Alaska are less densely populated.

Looking for an affordable home? North Dakota has them in abundance. The state ranks fifth from the bottom in the median price of housing, at just $99,700. Contrast that with what you would pay in California, where the median house costs $535,700.[15] Yet North Dakota is losing population, and California is gaining. Maybe affordable housing is not such a big deal either.

North Dakota has another claim to fame. Among the states, it has the largest percentage of very old people in its population. Why? Because younger people have moved away. As it turns out, most of us do not want a different kind of life. We would rather take our chances along with everyone else in the overcrowded, high-priced, diverse, and bustling American metropolis.

Factoid source: Bureau of the Census, The 2007 Statistical Abstract, Statistical Abstract State Rankings, http://www.census.gov/compendia/statab/rankings.html (accessed September 2, 2007).

SQUARE MILES OF SELF-STORAGE SPACE IN THE UNITED STATES: 78

Seventy-eight square miles is more than three times the size of Manhattan. That's how much rentable self-storage space is available to Americans who have run out of room in the garage to store all their stuff. According to the Self Storage Association (yes, there is an association), every man, woman, and child in the United States could fit inside the nation's self-storage units. The association estimates there are 2.2 billion square feet of rentable self-storage space in the United States.[16]

Self-storage has grown into a mammoth industry over the past couple of decades for two reasons. One, the sheer size of the United States makes space itself so inexpensive that it is cost effective for us to rent more space rather than edit our belongings. Two, our affluence has turned shopping into a popular pastime, and we have gotten into the habit of buying more than we are willing to throw out. Ten percent of American households now rent space in a self-storage facility, according to the association.

This accumulation of stuff is not uniquely American, but a function of our vast geography. If Europeans had as much space per capita, they too would be filling self-storage lockers. Many of us bemoan our crowded closets, cluttered desktops, and garages with no room for cars. But only one thing will bring an end to the ever-growing piles: the price of land must rise to the point where we can no longer afford to rent space just to store our belongings. With the US population passing the 300 million mark, you may think we are nearing that point. But we have a long way to go before our population density reaches European levels and accumulation is curtailed. How many Americans would it take for our population density to equal that of, say, Germany? Two billion.

Factoid source: Self Storage Association, Self Storage Industry Fact Sheet, http://www.selfstorage.org/pdf/FactSheet.pdf (accessed June 11, 2008).

Chapter 12
IMMIGRANTS

PERCENTAGE OF US RESIDENTS BORN
IN ANOTHER COUNTRY: 13

The United States is being overrun by foreigners—that's what many people think. When asked to estimate the percentage of the US population born in another country, the majority of Americans guess 25 percent or more, according to a Pew Research Center survey.[1] They are way off. Even if you include second-generation Americans in the count, the figure still does not reach the 25 percent level. Only 22 percent of US residents are first- or second-generation Americans—meaning they or at least one of their parents was born outside the United States.[2]

Those who think the huddled masses are overrunning the country are right about one thing—the United States does attract a disproportionate share of the world's immigrants. We are, in fact, the number-one destination for those on the move. According to the United Nations, 191 million people live outside their country of birth, and fully 38 million (or 20 percent) are in the United States.[3] In second place is Russia, home to a much smaller 12 million (or 6 percent) of the total. The foreign-born are a small percentage of the US population only because our population is enormous—the third largest in the world.

The US government might not be very good at controlling immigration, but it is good at counting immigrants. According to Census Bureau estimates, immigration (both legal and illegal) accounts for 40 percent of our population growth.[4] The Department of Homeland Security reports that about 1 million legal immigrants are granted permanent residence each year in the United States.[5] The numbers are large, but we have seen the percentages before. The foreign-born share of the US population was even larger than it is today from 1860 until things turned sour in the Great Depression of the 1930s.[6]

Factoid Source: Bureau of the Census, 2006 American Community Survey, http://factfinder.census.gov/servlet/ DatasetMainPageServlet?_program=ACS&_submenuId=& _lang=en&_ts= (accessed September 22, 2007).

NUMBER OF AMERICANS WHO SPEAK A LANGUAGE OTHER THAN ENGLISH AT HOME: 55 MILLION

Americans are upset about the number of immigrants coming to the United States, and language is one of their concerns. Because millions of immigrants do not speak English at home, the public fears they do not speak English at all and have no interest in doing so. Wrong on both counts.

One in five Americans aged 5 or older speaks a language other than English at home, according to the Census Bureau.[7] This is enough to raise eyebrows, but it is no cause for alarm. Most of those who speak other languages at home are also fluent in English. Only 9 percent of the 300 million people in the United States report that they cannot speak English "very well."

This does not stop the public from wanting to see English made the official language. More than 80 percent of US residents believe English should be official, according to a Rasmussen survey.[8] Thirty states have adopted official English legislation, according to U.S. English, Inc.[9] Attitudes are hardening toward bilingual education as well, with a shrinking share of the public supporting native-language instruction in the public schools for children who do not speak English. Nevertheless, the 61 percent majority of the public still thinks schools should help children learn English, according to a Phi Delta Kappa/Gallup survey.[10]

Those so wrought up about the use of the English language are tilting at windmills, however. Even most Hispanics—the nation's largest group of non-English speakers—believe the ability to speak English is important. When asked whether immigrants must speak English to be part of American society, the majority of Hispanics agree, according to a Pew Hispanic Center survey.[11] And when asked how important it is for the children of immigrants to learn English, a nearly universal 92 percent of Hispanics say it is "very important." In fact, Hispanics are more likely than whites or blacks, Republicans or Democrats, to believe it is very important to learn English.

Factoid source: Bureau of the Census, 2006 American Community Survey, http://factfinder.census.gov/servlet/DatasetMainPageServlet?_program=ACS&_submenuId=&_lang=en&_ts= (accessed September 13, 2007).

PERCENTAGE OF THE FOREIGN-BORN
WHO ARE NATURALIZED CITIZENS: 42

Fewer than half the nation's foreign-born are naturalized citizens, meaning they have successfully navigated the increasingly cumbersome process of becoming a US citizen. But this figure is deceptive because the Census Bureau's count of the foreign-born includes both legal immigrants and the undocumented, who are not eligible to become citizens. The Census Bureau's surveys include both legal and illegal immigrants because the bureau does not ask respondents to prove their legal status. If it did, survey response rates would plummet, and we would know a lot less about the US population.

A study by the Pew Hispanic Center estimates that most (52 percent) legal foreign-born residents of the United States are naturalized citizens—14 percentage points greater than in 1990 and the highest level in a quarter century.[12] What is behind the growing tendency of the foreign-born to become citizens? The Pew study suggests a number of reasons, and fear is one of them. Some of the foreign-born may be afraid of being targeted or even deported by ambitious politicians and their agitated constituents. To avoid the wrath of the American electorate, a growing number of foreign-born are taking the citizenship oath.

It is not easy to become a citizen, however. Not only do the foreign-born have to speak, read, write, and understand English, but they must submit to a background check and pass a test most native-born Americans would find a challenge, to say the least.[13] "When was the Constitution written?" "How many amendments does the Constitution have?" "Who was president during World War I?" "What are two rights only for United States citizens?" Those are a sampling of the questions on the test, and just another reason to be thankful you were born in the United States.

Factoid source: Bureau of the Census, 2006 American Community Survey, http://factfinder.census.gov/servlet/ DatasetMainPageServlet?_program=ACS&_submenuId=& _lang=en&_ts= (accessed September 23, 2007).

PERCENTAGE OF LEGAL IMMIGRANTS
WHO SETTLE IN CALIFORNIA, NEW YORK,
FLORIDA, OR TEXAS: 54

Anyone who makes the pilgrimage across the United States by car knows how different one state is from another geographically. The demographic differences are just as extreme, and immigration is the reason.

One million legal immigrants come to the United States each year, and most of them make a beeline to just four states.[14] Not surprisingly, those states are the nation's most populous, but they are home to only 32 percent of the total population—well below their 54 percent share of annual immigrants. This imbalance makes California, New York, Florida, and Texas fundamentally different from, say, New Hampshire, Kansas, Idaho, or Tennessee. The states' residents not only look and sound different, but they have different wants and needs. Those differences must be thrashed out—or not—in the nation's capital, where the politicians are deadlocked on what to do about many things, such as immigration.

If our government could bring immigration to a halt, life would continue on undisturbed in most of the 50 states. But it would be thrown into turmoil in the states receiving the most immigrants. New York would begin to shrink because the state is losing residents faster than its maternity wards can replace them.[15] In California, the state's growth (and vitality) would slow to a crawl because it is losing hundreds of thousands of residents to Arizona, Nevada, and other states in the domestic migration sweepstakes. Florida would become even older than it is today because immigrants of working age would no longer counterbalance its aging retirees. In contrast, children would overwhelm the population of Texas because most of its growth would shift to its burgeoning birthing centers. In short, be careful what you wish for because you might get it—and you might not like the results.

Factoid source: Department of Homeland Security, 2007 Yearbook of Immigration Statistics, http://www.dhs.gov/ximgtn/statistics/publications/LPR07.shtm (accessed June 11, 2008).

NUMBER OF ILLEGAL IMMIGRANTS
IN THE UNITED STATES: 11.6 MILLION

Where there's smoke, there's fire. That might be why the four states most popular among legal immigrants are also the prized destinations of undocumented immigrants—or illegals. Fifty-two percent of illegal immigrants live in California, New York, Florida, and Texas, according to government estimates.[16]

The government estimates come from the Department of Homeland Security, which is quite interested in the nation's immigrants—both legal and illegal. The DHS is so interested, in fact, that it took over the Immigration and Naturalization Service a few years back. The government may not be able to stem the tide of illegals, but it can tell us how many there are, where they live, and where they came from.

How do you determine whether someone is in the country illegally? You can't just ask them, obviously, which is why government surveys do not force the foreign-born to show proof of legal residence. (As noted earlier, no one would respond to their surveys if they did.) To get around this problem, the government produces estimates of the size of the illegal population by what is called the "residual method." In other words, the statisticians work backwards. First, they estimate the size of the legally resident foreign-born population from immigration documents. Then they subtract the legal residents from the total foreign-born figures from the Census Bureau's American Community Survey. The remainder is the illegal population.

In 2006, the remainder was 11.6 million, up from 8.5 million in 2000—a 37 percent increase over the six years. Most (57 percent) illegal immigrants are from Mexico. And although the majority live in California, Texas, Florida, and New York, the number is growing the fastest in Georgia, where the illegal immigrant population more than doubled between 2000 and 2006.

Factoid source: Michael Hoefer, Nancy Rytina, and Christopher Campbell, *Estimates of the Unauthorized Immigrant Population Residing in the United States: January 2006*, Office of Immigration Statistics, Department of Homeland Security, August 2007, p. 1.

PERCENTAGE OF AMERICANS WHO THINK IMMIGRATION IS A "VERY BIG" PROBLEM: 42

No wonder the politicians can't agree on what to do about immigration. Neither can their constituents. If politicians seem befuddled about whether to build a wall or issue an invitation to the world's huddled masses, it is because they are channeling the confusion of the voters. Americans are of many minds about immigration. When asked what we should do about illegal immigrants, for example, the public splits into three almost equal factions: 27 percent want the undocumented sent home; 32 percent want to grant them temporary worker status; another 32 percent want to allow them to stay here permanently, according to a joint survey by the Pew Research Center and the Pew Hispanic Center.[17]

In the past few years, Americans have become increasingly agitated about immigrants, seeing them as a cost rather than a benefit. The percentage of the public calling immigrants a burden grew from 38 to 52 percent between 2000 and 2006, according to the Pew survey. It is no coincidence that our concern about immigration has grown along with our economic problems. Immigrants are not the cause of these problems, however. Our anger toward immigrants is just a symptom of the erosion of the middle class resulting from the loss of manufacturing jobs and the decline in men's wages.

The Pew survey finds compelling evidence of this: among people whose parents were born in the United States, fully 65 percent of those living in areas with the fewest immigrants say immigrants are a burden. In contrast, a smaller 47 percent of those living in areas with the highest concentration of immigrants call them a burden.[18] In other words, the people most affected by immigration are least concerned about it, evidence that fantasy—not reality—is driving the narrative and stoking the immigration debate.

Factoid source: Pew Research Center for the People & the Press and Pew Hispanic Center, *America's Immigration Quandary*, March 30, 2006, p. 12.

AMOUNT ILLEGAL IMMIGRANTS CONTRIBUTE EACH YEAR TO THE SOCIAL SECURITY TRUST FUND: $7 BILLION

They will never collect it. Those billions end up in what the Social Security Administration calls the "earnings suspense file," paid into the system by individuals whose names and Social Security numbers do not match the government's records. Many are undocumented workers using fake IDs and paying Social Security taxes with no chance of ever collecting benefits. Without this hefty sum sitting in the trust fund—it has grown to more than $500 billion—our nation would be even deeper in debt.[19]

Illegal immigrants pay billions of dollars in taxes, but they also use public services. Who comes out ahead—the illegals or the American taxpayer? The answer depends on where you stand in the immigration debate, because each side has data to bolster its argument. One side argues that the children of immigrants must be educated, draining tax dollars. But a study in Florida shows that immigrants pay their fair share of taxes.[20] Some say immigrants take jobs away from native-born Americans. But a study in California shows immigrants boosting jobs for the native-born by increasing the demand for products and services.[21] A study by the Center for Immigration Studies estimates that households headed by illegal immigrants pay $4,212 a year in taxes. But the same study shows illegals using an even larger $6,949 in services.[22]

The experts will argue forever—that's their job. What do the people think? On the issue of jobs, they do not see much of a problem. Only 24 percent of the public think immigrants take jobs away from Americans, and people living in areas with high concentrations of immigrants are least likely to feel that way.[23] On the issue of taxes there is more controversy. The majority believe immigrants are the winners in the tax game, with 56 percent saying immigrants do not pay their fair share of taxes. But this drain does not seem to be a problem. Sixty-two percent of the public say immigrants have had no effect on the quality of local services in their area.

Factoid source: Steven A. Camarota, *The High Cost of Cheap Labor: Illegal Immigration and the Federal Budget,* Center for Immigration Studies, August 2004, p. 6.

Chapter 13
POLITICS

PERCENTAGE OF AMERICANS WHO THINK
THE UNITED STATES IS BETTER
THAN MOST OTHER COUNTRIES: 79

Americans are proud of their country. How proud? That is precisely what a group of social scientists wanted to measure—the degree of national pride felt by citizens around the world. To measure pride, the International Social Survey Program—a collaboration of social scientists from dozens of countries—fielded a national identity survey. Respondents in 33 different countries were asked a battery of questions measuring national pride, such as, "Is your country better than most other countries?"

Americans, it turns out, are number one in pride. No surprise there. More surprising is that we are not alone in the top spot, tying with Venezuela. What accounts for the upwelling of pride in some countries but not others? The countries with the most national pride, according to an analysis of the survey results, are those united by a history of conflict—such as the former colonies of England and Spain.[1] More recent conflict also boosts pride. Comparing the 2004 survey results with those from a similar study undertaken in the mid-1990s, the analysts note a marked increase in national pride in the United States—probably due to the 2001 terrorist attacks.

A little pride goes a long way. Too much pride can lead to trouble (think Germany in the 1930s). The survey results show respondents with the most national pride are least tolerant of globalization and immigration. In almost every country, national pride is much greater among older than younger generations. In the United States, fully 52 percent of people aged 65 or older "strongly" agree that America is a better country. Among adults under age 30, the figure is a much smaller 26 percent.[2] Since the younger generations will have to cope with the global culture inevitably resulting from technological change, their more moderate attitude may work to their advantage.

Factoid source: Survey Documentation and Analysis, Computer-Assisted Survey Methods Program, University of California, Berkeley, General Social Surveys, 1972–2006 Cumulative Data Files, GSS Variable AMBETTER, http://sda.berkeley.edu/cgi-bin32/hsda?harcsda+gss06 (accessed September 30, 2007).

PEOPLE MOST LIKELY TO VOTE:
65- TO 74-YEAR-OLDS

Americans puff up with pride over their democracy, but they are famous for not exercising their most important right. In the last presidential election, less than two-thirds of those eligible to vote cast a ballot. If the average voter and the average American were alike, then the low voter participation rate would not matter. But voters are different, and it matters a lot. This is what voters are like:

Old. If you wonder why politicians are so often clueless about the Internet (one famously describing it a "series of tubes"), it is because most of them belong to the generation that cannot seem to wrap its mind around computer technology. Politicians are old because voters are old, and voters—like it or not—tend to elect their own kind. Fewer than half of 18- to 24-year-old citizens cast a ballot in the last presidential election.[3] Voting rates rise with age, peaking at more than 73 percent among 65- to 74-year-olds.

White. The nation's politicians do not reflect the diversity of the United States because voters are not diverse. Non-Hispanic whites account for only 66 percent of Americans but for nearly 80 percent of voters. Non-Hispanic whites overwhelm elections because they are most likely to vote, proving again that voters elect politicians very much like themselves.

Rich. The average voter is considerably more affluent than the average American. Despite the fact that many voters are retirees, their median family income greatly exceeds the median income of the average family.[4] Terrorism, wars, hurricanes, and global warming loom, but the politicians obsess about tax cuts, sheltering their real constituents—the rich.

What motivates old, white, rich people to go to the polls? They vote to protect the status quo, of course. Our low voter participation rate explains why the nation's politics are decades behind the nation's demographics. And those who stay home on Election Day have no one to blame but themselves.

Factoid source: Bureau of the Census, *Voting and Registration in the Election of November 2004*, Current Population Reports, P20-556, March 2006, p. 4.

PERCENTAGE OF 18-YEAR-OLDS WHO VOTED IN THE LAST PRESIDENTIAL ELECTION: 39

Why won't they vote? The indifference of young adults to the electoral process has frustrated political activists for decades. The youngest voters have always been least likely to cast a ballot, and the apathy of the young only deepened when 18- and 19-year-olds were permitted to join the electorate in 1972. Some wonder why the young have so little interest in politics, but there is a simple explanation for their indifference: they are still children. It takes the maturity of an adult to register to vote and get to the polling place on Election Day. It also takes the maturity of an adult to be willing to compromise on issues and candidates. As the road to adulthood has lengthened, voter participation in the younger generations has fallen.

A look at voting rates by single year of age reveals the gradual awakening to adult responsibility that occurs as people age. Voting rates rise slowly, from the rock bottom 39 percent of 18-year-olds to a slightly higher but still abysmal 45 percent among 30-year-olds. Between the ages of 30 and 34, however, the voter participation rate finally tops 50 percent.[5] It continues to rise with age, frequently surpassing 70 percent among people aged 55 or older.

If you want to blame the apathy of the young on something, blame modern times. With more schooling, delayed marriage, and postponed childbearing, people under age 30 are more like children than adults. The modern age of adulthood is not 18, when people gain the right to vote, or 21 when they can legally drink. Instead, it lies between the ages of 30 and 34. That is when the percentage of people who are married, have children, and own a home finally passes the 50 percent mark—and so does their voting rate. These adult commitments give people a stake in society. To protect and expand their stake, they vote.

Factoid source: Bureau of the Census, Voting and Registration in the Election of November 2004, Detailed Tables, http://www.census.gov/population/www/socdemo/voting/cps2004.html (accessed May 31, 2007).

HISPANICS AS A PERCENTAGE OF VOTERS IN THE PRESIDENTIAL ELECTION: 6

What a disappointment: Hispanics are the nation's largest minority, but their abysmal voting record is preventing them from grabbing hold of the political power bestowed by such numbers. Only a handful of Hispanics are in the Senate or House of Representatives, which may explain why the United States is busy building a wall at the Mexican border and discussing at the highest levels of government how to make life more difficult for millions of Hispanic immigrants.

When we elect a president every four years, few Hispanics turn out at the polls. Only about one in four Hispanics vote in presidential elections. One reason for their poor showing is that many are not citizens and are ineligible to vote. But even among the citizens, fewer than half cast a ballot.[6] The younger age of the Hispanic population does not explain it either because the voting rate is well below average even among older Hispanics. No wonder non-Hispanic whites remain firmly in control of both houses of Congress and the debate over what to do about immigration. Two out of three non-Hispanic whites vote. Blacks have long struggled to make their vote count, and they are succeeding. Black voter turnout is close to that of non-Hispanic whites. Asians have an even worse voting record than Hispanics. But Asians account for only 5 percent of the US population, so not much is expected of them—and, as expected, they don't deliver.

So what keeps Hispanics from flexing their political muscle? The Census Bureau is trying to find out. In post-election surveys, it asks people why they did not register to vote and, if registered, why they did not go to the polls. The excuses for not voting are the same regardless of race or Hispanic origin—too busy, not interested, ill, out of town, and even "I forgot." But no group is hurt more by its own indifference than Hispanics.

Factoid source: Bureau of the Census, Voting and Registration in the Election of November 2004, Detailed Tables, http://www.census.gov/population/www/socdemo/voting/cps2004.html (accessed May 15, 2007).

PERCENTAGE WHO WOULD NOT VOTE FOR A WOMAN FOR PRESIDENT: 6

Americans are nearly unanimous in their willingness to vote for a woman for president of the United States. When asked, fully 94 percent of the public says it would vote for a qualified female candidate. So unanimous is the response, in fact, that the General Social Survey hasn't asked the question since 1998. It wasn't always this way. Back in 1972, the first time the question appeared on the General Social Survey, a substantial 26 percent of Americans said they would not vote for a female candidate for president no matter how qualified.

A century ago, women were fighting for their right to vote. Today, they are fighting for the Congress, the Senate, and the White House. Women have come a long way since the Nineteenth Amendment was enacted in 1920, giving them the right to vote. Today, women account for the 54 percent majority of the nation's voters.[7] Not only do women outnumber men in the voting booth, but they are more likely than men to cast a ballot. That line was crossed in the 1980 presidential election when 59.4 percent of women and a slightly smaller 59.1 percent of men cast a ballot.[8] The gap has widened since then.

Still, doubts persist about women's political skills. When asked whether men are better suited emotionally for politics, 23 percent of the public still agrees. While this is down from nearly half the public in the mid-1970s, it is still a large enough fraction of the population that the General Social Survey continues to probe the issue.[9] Those who harbor the greatest doubts about women's governing skills are the oldest Americans. One-third of Americans aged 65 or older—the age group most likely to vote—think women are not suited for politics.

Factoid source: Survey Documentation and Analysis, Computer-Assisted Survey Methods Program, University of California, Berkeley, General Social Surveys, 1972–2006 Cumulative Data Files, GSS Variable FEPRES, http://sda .berkeley.edu/cgi-bin32/hsda?harcsda+gss06 (accessed September 30, 2007).

PERCENTAGE OF AMERICANS
WHO ARE POLITICAL MODERATES: 65

The jury system works. It works because it forces a group of strangers to sit down together, focus on specifics, examine facts, and reach a consensus. Too bad our political system does not work that way. If it did, the red and the blue, Democrat and Republican, conservative and liberal divisions would soon disappear.

Too much has been made of the ideological divide among Americans. The nation has been split ideologically since it was founded, and today's divide is neither unique nor large. Only about one-third of Americans place themselves at either end of the political spectrum—15 percent call themselves liberal or extremely liberal and 20 percent say they are conservative or extremely conservative. A much larger 65 percent consider themselves moderate or only slightly inclined one way or the other.[10] This is nothing new. What is new is the role of the media in reporting and analyzing the issues. Rather than bridging the gaps, the media have widened our small differences into chasms by diverting the discussion away from facts, specifics, and consensus instead toward spin, generalization, and argument. He-said/she-said journalism is a lucrative arrangement for everyone but the majority of Americans. The media get their ratings, the pundits get their fees, the politicians get their votes, and we get a dysfunctional political system. There is no doubt the moderate public could arrive at a consensus on most of the "wedge" issues said to divide us if we were encouraged to act more like a jury and less like gamecocks.

There are signs that Americans are getting fed up with their role as the audience in this media-sponsored cockfight. According to the General Social Survey, over the past few decades the percentage of the public with "hardly any" confidence in television or the press has grown from just a handful to nearly half the population.[11]

Factoid source: Survey Documentation and Analysis, Computer-Assisted Survey Methods Program, University of California, Berkeley, General Social Surveys, 1972–2006 Cumulative Data Files, GSS Variable POLVIEWS, http://sda .berkeley.edu/cgi-bin32/hsda?harcsda+gss06 (accessed September 30, 2007).

Chapter 14
RELIGION

PERCENTAGE OF AMERICANS WHO
BELIEVE IN GOD WITHOUT A DOUBT: 63

Americans have a reputation for being deeply religious, and a casual glance at the numbers would seem to confirm the claim. Survey after survey finds a small number of people admitting to survey researchers that they do not believe in God. But a closer look reveals doubt to be more widespread. Although only 2 percent of the public flatly states that it does not believe in God, all those with misgivings should also count among the nonbelievers. Apparently, many Americans like to hedge their bets—such as the 4 percent who say they do not know whether God exists and there is no way to find out. And the 10 percent who do not believe in a personal God but believe in a "higher power" of some kind. Throw in the doubters—the 20 percent of Americans who believe in God only when it is convenient—and the ranks of nonbelievers swell to a substantial 37 percent of the population.[1]

Even after winnowing out the wafflers, however, Americans are still more religious than their European counterparts. Eighteen percent of Europeans say they do not believe in a God of any kind. Another 27 percent believe in a spirit or life force rather than God and cannot count as true believers. That leaves only 52 percent of Europeans who believe in God, much less than the comparable figure of 63 percent in the United States.[2] Peer pressure might well explain the difference. In the United States, it is considered impolite in some circles to profess disbelief in God. In any society, those who want to get along go along, which is what drives up the American numbers. In Europe, atheism is far more acceptable, resulting in more atheists.

On the other hand, maybe we know something the Europeans do not. Americans believe they are special. We believe we live in the greatest country on earth. What were the chances we would be so lucky? Ergo, there must be a God.

Factoid source: Survey Documentation and Analysis, Computer-Assisted Survey Methods Program, University of California, Berkeley, General Social Surveys, 1972–2006 Cumulative Data Files, GSS Variable GOD, http://sda .berkeley.edu/cgi-bin32/hsda?harcsda+gss06 (accessed October 4, 2007)

PERCENTAGE OF AMERICANS WHO THINK IT IS NECESSARY TO BELIEVE IN GOD TO BE MORAL AND HAVE GOOD VALUES: 57

Which country does not belong on this list: Argentina, Britain, Canada, Italy, Japan, Poland, Spain, and the United States. If you said the United States, you are correct. In every other country on the list, the majority of the public believes it is possible for people to be moral without believing in God, according to the Pew Global Attitudes Project. Not so in the United States. Here, the majority believes faith in God is a prerequisite for morality.

Americans embrace religion with as much fervor as the citizens of Mexico, Venezuela, and Lebanon, according to the Pew survey, and this makes us unique among nations in the developed world.[3] To prove it, just grab a piece of graph paper and a pencil. Plot per capita GDP on one axis and religiosity on the other, and most countries fall close to the curve—the more economically developed the country, the lower the level of religiosity. The United States, however, is the "outlier"—the point positioned far above the rest. We are the richest country on earth, yet also one of the most religious. What gives?

No one can answer the question, although many have tried. The reasons posited range from our genes to our history to the Constitution itself. Did early immigrants carry a gene for religiosity, depleting it from the European nations they left behind and making those countries more secular? Did our history of slavery encourage religiosity as a way to justify oppression? Some think the separation of church and state, written into the Constitution, caused religion to flourish. Since Americans are not force-fed belief, many different religions have been allowed to take root and grow.

Whatever the reason, the consequences have been profound—not only for us, but for the rest of the world as well. We are not only more religious than the citizens of most other developed countries, but also more militaristic. Perhaps because we think God is on our side, fully 77 percent of Americans believe it is sometimes necessary to use military force to maintain order in the world.[4]

Factoid source: Pew Global Attitudes Project, *World Publics Welcome Global Trade—But Not Immigration*, October 4, 2007, p. 33.

PERCENTAGE WHO PRAY
AT LEAST ONCE A DAY: 60

Praying is like dental flossing—something we are supposed to do every day. Most Americans are dutiful about praying. Sixty percent say they pray at least once a day, according to the General Social Survey. The manufacturers of dental floss should be so lucky.

Because prayer is of such importance to so many, most Americans were unhappy with the 1963 Supreme Court ruling banning Bible readings and prayer from the public schools. They still are. More than forty years later, only 42 percent of the public approves of the Supreme Court decision, according to the General Social Survey—a figure that has remained essentially unchanged for decades despite a Constitution that specifically separates church and state.[5] Three out of four Americans favor a constitutional amendment to allow voluntary prayer in the public schools, a Gallup survey finds, although most favor a moment of silence rather than spoken prayer.[6]

There are many reasons people pray. One is to ask for God's help—nearly half the public admits asking for God's help at least once a day, according to the General Social Survey.[7] Another reason is to make things right with God, ensuring entry into heaven. Americans believe wholeheartedly in heaven, with most saying it will be "like life on earth only better." Most also describe it as a "life of peace and tranquility," "a paradise of pleasures and delights," and a place where they will enjoy a "reunion with loved ones," according to the General Social Survey

Being optimists at heart, most Americans think they are on their way to heaven. According to an ABC poll, 75 percent of the public believes the pearly gates will open for them.[8] What about the rest? Ten percent do not believe in heaven, which—according to the believers—may damn them to hell. Nine percent believe in heaven but don't know which way they will go. A feisty 5 percent believe in heaven but know they're going to hell.

Factoid source: Survey Documentation and Analysis, Computer-Assisted Survey Methods Program, University of California, Berkeley, General Social Surveys, 1972–2006 Cumulative Data Files, GSS Variable PRAY, http://sda .berkeley.edu/cgi-bin32/hsda?harcsda+gss06 (accessed October 4, 2007).

PERCENTAGE WHO THINK THE UNITED STATES IS A CHRISTIAN NATION: 67

If the majority ruled in the United States, we would be a Christian nation. Most Americans already think we are, according to a Pew Research Center survey. Consequently, the politicians wager that the only way to get elected is to parade their Christian credentials, signaling that they belong to the club. They got that one right.

Among a list of traits that make a presidential candidate more appealing to voters, being a Christian ranks second only to military service, according to Pew.[9] Forty-eight percent of the public says military service is a plus. Second is Christianity, with 39 percent saying being a Christian adds to a candidate's appeal. The 2004 presidential election shows, however, that military service may not be as significant in the voting booth as people claim. In that year, the presidential candidate with little military experience defeated the decorated war veteran. Religion, however, may be even more important than people claim. Survey after survey finds a large proportion of Americans unwilling to vote for a candidate with "questionable" Christian credentials—such as Mormons. Many also would not vote for a candidate outside the Christian faith, such as Muslims or atheists.

How do candidates advertise their Christian credentials? They, like so many other Americans, belong to a church and attend religious services regularly. But unlike the rest of us, politicians go to church while the cameras are rolling. Sixty-one percent of the US public belongs to a church or synagogue, according to a 2007 Gallup survey, and 41 percent say they have been to church in the past week, a figure that has held steady since Gallup first asked the question as far back as 1939.[10] Some scholars dispute the 41 percent figure, according to Gallup, arguing that only about half that number show up in church on a given Sunday.[11] Why would people lie about how often they go to church? Because in a nation that believes itself to be Christian, it is important to show you belong to the club.

Factoid source: Pew Research Center for the People & the Press, *Many Americans Uneasy with Mix of Religion and Politics,* August 24, 2006, p. 5.

INFORMATION COLLECTED BY THE CENSUS ABOUT OUR RELIGIOUS IDENTITY: 0

If we were Canadian, our government would provide us with a detailed look at our nation's religious identity every five years. We would know the median age of Baptists. We could get a state-by-state breakdown of Roman Catholics and calculate the growth of the Mormon religion. Because we live in the United States, however, we do not have this kind of data.

Thanks to Public Law 94–521, the Census Bureau is prohibited from requiring us to report our religion on the decennial census. It is not exactly a "don't ask, don't tell" situation, since the government can, and occasionally does, ask people to volunteer their religion on surveys. But the consequence of the census ban is a dearth of information about religious trends in the United States. This is ironic, to say the least, since Americans rank among the most religious in the world.

Nature abhors a vacuum. Others have stepped in to provide faith-based numbers—such as the American Religious Identification Survey taken in 1990 and 2001, the Gallup Poll, and the General Social Survey. Gallup has been probing Americans' religious beliefs for almost seventy years. These surveys cannot provide the kind of reliable, comparative, and detailed information of a census, but they are all we've got.

And what do they tell us? They tell us that our religious identity is changing rapidly. Only 49 percent of Americans are Protestant today, down from more than 60 percent just a few decades ago, according to Gallup.[12] Catholics have held steady at about 23 percent. Only 2 percent of Americans are Jewish, another 1 percent are Mormon, and 12 percent have no religion. Most of the remainder—another 12 percent—follows "other" religious beliefs such as Islam, Hinduism, and Buddhism. Thanks to immigration, this group has grown from less than 1 in 100 Americans several decades ago to 1 in 8 today. Not only is the diversity of our population growing, but also the diversity of our beliefs.

Factoid source: Bureau of the Census, "Does the Census Bureau Have Data for Religion?" Question & Answer Center, https://ask.census.gov/cgi-bin/askcensus.cfg/php/enduser/std_adp.php?p_faqid=29 (accessed March 29, 2007).

AVERAGE AGE OF FIRST SEXUAL INTERCOURSE FOR FUNDAMENTALIST PROTESTANTS: 16.9 YEARS

Does religious belief dictate behavior, or do people behave pretty much the same regardless of religion? Data from a federal survey suggest religion may determine where you sit on Sunday morning, but not what you did on Saturday night. In fact, women with the most conservative religious upbringing, raised as fundamentalist Protestants, lose their virginity at a younger age than the average woman—a tender 16.9 years for the fundamentalists compared with 17.3 years for the average woman.

They probably feel guilty about it, too. When it comes to sex, religion determines what you think but not what you do. Among women under age 45, fundamentalist Protestants are least likely to approve of premarital sex— only 29 percent think it is all right for unmarried 18-year-olds to have sex.[13] This is well below the 51 percent of all women in the age group who approve of premarital sex. Despite their disapproval of premarital sex, few fundamentalist Protestants manage to uphold the vow of chastity before marriage. Only 17 percent of women raised as fundamentalists are virgins on their wedding day, not much different than the 15 percent of all women who wait for marriage.[14]

Fundamentalist Protestants also disapprove of out-of-wedlock childbearing. But that doesn't prevent them from having children outside of marriage. Among women under age 45, only 49 percent of fundamentalists think it is all right for a woman to have a child out of wedlock. This is well below the 70 percent of all women in the age group who think out-of-wedlock childbearing is acceptable.[15] Although they disapprove of out-of-wedlock childbearing, fundamentalists are more likely than the average woman to have given birth outside of marriage. Among all women in the under-45 age group, 42 percent have had an out-of-wedlock birth.[16] Among fundamentalists, the figure is an even larger 47 percent.

Factoid source: National Center for Health Statistics, *Fertility, Family Planning, and Reproductive Health of U.S. Women: Data from the 2002 National Survey of Family Growth,* Vital and Health Statistics, Series 23, No. 25, 2005, p. 73.

AMOUNT OF MONEY DONATED BY
THE AVERAGE HOUSEHOLD TO
RELIGIOUS ORGANIZATIONS EACH YEAR: $753

Americans give away billions of dollars every year. Most of our generosity is directed at only one place—the collection plate at church. Of the $1,000-plus a year the average household donates to charities and nonprofit organizations, we give 70 percent of it to religious organizations. Religious groups collect four times more money from us than all the charities combined, including the United Way and the American Red Cross. They collect seven times more from us than do universities and other educational organizations. They collect 34 times more from us than political candidates and organizations.

Where does all this money go? It pays for the salaries of religious leaders and for the upkeep of houses of worship. It is used to supply food and clothing for the poor, summer camps for children, international relief efforts, and, in some cases, it lines the pockets of those in charge of the collection plate. The *National Catholic Reporter* calls the lack of financial account-ability the "worst kept secret in church financial circles."[17] It has some people so upset they have created their own nonprofits to fight for more transparency in the finances of religious groups. One such group, Ministry Watch, rates more than 500 Christian ministries by their financial account-ability, according to *Forbes* magazine.[18] Ministry Watch's "Donor Alert" puts potential contributors on notice about religious organizations whose leaders are more likely to use their donations for luxurious houses, cars, and even private jets—rather than for charitable causes.

Of course, whenever you have nearly $90 billion in play—which is how much Americans give to religious organizations each year—you attract crooks and invite corruption. But a little less faith and a little more doubt about where the money goes might direct more of those dollars to doing good work.

Factoid source: Bureau of Labor Statistics, unpublished tables from the 2006 Consumer Expenditure Survey.

PERCENTAGE OF AMERICANS
WHO BELIEVE IN EVOLUTION: 49.6

The decimal is there to make a point: the percentage of Americans who believe in evolution is surpassed by the 50.4 percent who do not, according to the General Social Survey.[19] The US population has never been better educated, and scientific information has never been more widely disseminated. Nevertheless, the percentage of adults who believe in evolution hovers below 50 percent in most surveys. Evidently, humans are not evolving.

Or maybe we are. Younger adults are more likely than older adults to believe in evolution. And the General Social survey finds belief in evolution rising strongly with education. Those with the lowest levels of education are the ones least likely to believe in evolution—only 42 percent of adults with a high school diploma or less education believe humans developed from other life forms. Among college graduates, the figure is a much larger 69 percent.[20]

Religion also determines attitudes toward evolution, with the religious least likely to believe humans evolved from other life forms. Only 32 percent of people who attend church at least once a week believe in evolution. Among those who seldom or never go to church, the figure is twice as high— 64 percent, according to a Gallup survey.[21] The churchgoers may have a different attitude toward evolution because it is a frequent topic of Sunday sermons, according to a Pew Research Center survey.[22] Forty percent of regular churchgoers say their clergy have talked about evolution.

Religion and science have clashed throughout history. In the United States—one of the most religious countries in the world—the sparks are flying. When asked whether we believe too often in science and not enough in faith, the 54 percent of Americans agree.[23]

Factoid source: Survey Documentation and Analysis, Computer-Assisted Survey Methods Program, University of California, Berkeley, General Social Surveys, 1972–2006 Cumulative Data Files, GSS Variable EVOLVED, http://sda .berkeley.edu/cgi-bin32/hsda?harcsda+gss06 (accessed October 4, 2007).

Chapter 15
RACE

NUMBER OF RACIAL GROUPS COUNTED BY THE 2000 CENSUS: 63

OK, we admit it: We are hung up about race. Because of our hang-ups, the 2000 census divided us into 63 racial groups—a figure that doesn't even include Hispanics, who are an ethnic group rather than a race.

The 2000 census was the first in modern times to allow respondents to identify themselves as being of more than one race. Oh, what a Pandora's box that turned out to be. By dropping the requirement that Americans categorize themselves in only one racial group, the government created the most complex and confusing system of racial accounting imaginable. It began with the 2000 census and by law has been incorporated into most other government surveys since then. We are stuck with this pointillistic vision of ourselves for the foreseeable future.

So, here's what you need to know. The 2000 census asked Americans to identify themselves as belonging to one *or more* of six racial groups. Key words: or more. By allowing people to identify themselves as multiracial, 63 different combinations resulted, ranging from the largest (white only—211 million people) to the smallest (white *and* black *and* American Indian *and* Native Hawaiian *and* "other"—68 people).[1]

How do you even begin to talk about this many races? To start the discussion, the Census Bureau created three new terms to distinguish one group from another: the race-alone population (people of only one race); the race-in-combination population (people of more than one race); and the race-alone-or-in-combination population (the two groups combined). If you are wondering whether the numbers add up, they don't.

Maybe the craziness of 63 racial categories has served one useful purpose. It is forcing us to accept the fact that we are obsessed with race, and acceptance is the first step toward recovery.

Factoid source: Bureau of the Census, *Overview of Race and Hispanic Origin*, Census 2000 Brief, March 2001, pp. 3–5.

PERCENTAGE OF HISPANICS WHO ARE WHITE: 52

Here is the weirdest thing about race in the United States: Hispanics or Latinos are not a part of the discussion—at least officially. If you have ever glanced at a government document on race and Hispanic origin, you will have bumped into the lengthy explanation of what Hispanics are and are not. The government considers them an ethnic group with origins in Spain, the Spanish-speaking countries of Central or South America, or any other Spanish-speaking nation. Interestingly, this definition excludes anyone from Brazil because they speak Portuguese.

Most decidedly, according to the federal government, Hispanic is not a race. In fact, Hispanics may be of any race. This is where things get complicated: There are white Hispanics (such as New Mexico's Governor Bill Richardson), black Hispanics (such as baseball player Sammy Sosa), Asian Hispanics (think Filipinos), and even American Indian Hispanics (many live in the American Southwest). This parsing of race and Hispanic origin results from two different questions included on the census and surveys—one to determine race and the other to determine Hispanic origin.

When Hispanics answer the census and surveys, most identify themselves as white. In the 2006 American Community Survey, 52 percent of the nation's Hispanics checked the "white" box on the race question.[2] Only 3 percent checked the "black," "Asian," "American Indian" and "Native Hawaiian" boxes, and 4 percent checked the box indicating they were two or more races. Those figures add up to just 59 percent, however. Where are the remaining Hispanics? It turns out, Hispanics are as torn about their race as everyone else. Not finding the term "Hispanic" listed as an option on the race question, 41 percent of Hispanics checked the box "some other race" instead. Of the 19 million people across the nation who checked "some other race," fully 96 percent were Hispanic.

Factoid source: Bureau of the Census, 2006 American Community Survey, http://www.census.gov/acs/www/ (accessed October 1, 2007).

NUMBER OF AMERICANS WHO IDENTIFY THEIR ANCESTRY AS GERMAN: 51 MILLION

It's not fair. How come Hispanics get the ethnic question on government surveys all to themselves? Who decided to lavish attention on just one group while forcing Germans, Swedes, and Poles to make do with goofy bumper stickers and corny festivals? Who made this decision? The Office of Management and Budget made it. Is it fair? No, it is politics.

Every few years, OMB bureaucrats sit down and hash out the government's official rules on race and ethnicity. After much discussion and public input (read: lobbying) they settle on the definition and name of each racial group and decide which groups will have their names listed on the census and surveys. You can imagine the fisticuffs in the conference room. The last set of OMB decisions was drawn up in 1997, establishing the rules for the 2000 census and surveys to follow.[3] Those rules created the 63 different racial groups that characterize us today. If you wonder whether racial categories are arbitrary, a review of the rules will confirm that the lines are drawn by politics, not biology. The OMB rules defined the six racial groups (including "other") now recognized by the federal government. They determined that Hispanics alone would be singled out in a separate ethnicity question. They established that all other ethnic groups could lay claim to their roots only on a separate fill-in-the-blank ancestry question.

Fast forward from survey design to survey results: Responses to the ancestry question reveal Germans—not Hispanics—to be the largest ethnic group in the United States, with 51 million Americans identifying their ancestry as German.[4] In second place are the Irish with 36 million, followed by the English with 28 million. In fourth place, a feisty 20 million are so fed up with the politics of it all that they identify their ancestry as, simply, American.

Factoid source: Bureau of the Census, 2006 American Community Survey, http://www.census.gov/acs/www/ (accessed October 1, 2007).

MEDIAN AGE OF MULTIRACIAL AMERICANS: 21

Until the 2000 census, we did not know how many Americans were multiracial because the government demanded we choose one race over another when answering a census or survey. The rules changed in 2000, and demographers waited expectantly to see how the change would reconfigure racial identity. Much to everyone's relief (or disappointment), racial identity barely budged. Only 2 percent of the population said it was multiracial, a drop in the bucket—or the melting pot—of America.

In the years since the 2000 census, there has been no surge in the number proclaiming a multiracial identity. Not only that, but the demographic profile of the multiracial population raises doubts about the long-term stability of the category. The median age of the multiracial is just 21 years old—in other words, nearly half are children.[5] This compares with a much older median age of 36 for the total population. There is a reason for this skew in the age profile of the multiracial. When the Census Bureau fields a survey, respondents report their race to the interviewer—unless they are under age 18. For children, parents report the race. Apparently, many mixed race couples are unwilling to lock their child into a single racial identity. But many children, upon reaching adulthood, will choose one race over another. The multiracial population shrinks as teenagers turn into young adults and make their own decisions about racial identity.[6]

For now, at least, the multiracial category is transitory. It is often discarded as young adults are pressured to pick sides by a society hung up about race. But respected figures such as Tiger Woods and Barack Obama may break our obsession with rigid racial categories. If the rich and famous are embracing their multiracial identity, how long can it be before a hundred million Americans are scouring their family trees for evidence of diversity?

Factoid source: Bureau of the Census, National Population Estimates, http://www.census.gov/popest/national/asrh/NC-EST2007-sa.html (accessed June 11, 2008).

INTERRACIAL COUPLES AS A PERCENTAGE OF TOTAL MARRIED COUPLES: 4

So how many interracial couples are there anyway? You will wish you never asked. If you think racial categories are confusing, just try applying them to two people simultaneously. That is what you need to do if you want to count interracial couples.

Historically, interracial marriage has been all about *Guess Who's Coming for Dinner*. Marriages between blacks and whites were once illegal in many states and are still uncommon. The number of such marriages has more than doubled since 1980, however, rising from 167,000 to 403,000 today.[7] But these marriages account for less than 1 percent of the nation's 59 million married couples.

Expand the definition of mixed marriages to include Asians, American Indians, and other races, and the number of interracial couples grows to 2.3 million—or 4 percent of all couples. The most common interracial couple is a white husband and an Asian wife (530,000).[8] Take another step in expanding the definition of mixed marriage to include Hispanics, and the number grows to 4.3 million—or 7 percent of married couples. The most common mix is a non-Hispanic white husband and a Hispanic wife (989,000).

Another way to look at interracial marriage is to examine which race and Hispanic origin groups are most likely to intermarry. Among all black spouses, for example, 11 percent are in a mixed marriage.[9] Among all Asian spouses, the figure is a larger 24 percent, and it rises to 27 percent among Hispanics. In contrast, only 8 percent of non-Hispanic white spouses have married outside their group. Why are non-Hispanic whites so much less likely to marry someone different? Probability has a lot to do with it. Because non-Hispanic whites outnumber everyone else, chances are they will meet and fall in love with someone very much like themselves.

Factoid source: Bureau of the Census, America's Families and Living Arrangements: 2006, Detailed Tables, http://www.census.gov/population/www/socdemo/hh-fam/cps2006.html (accessed June 4, 2007).

PERCENTAGE OF CEOS WHO ARE
NON-HISPANIC WHITE: 87

Why make such a fuss over racial and ethnic identity? Actually, there is a good reason for wanting to be uniquely identified in the socioeconomic statistics collected by the census and surveys. How else can you determine whether you are being treated fairly? That's why the federal government separated Native Hawaiians from Asians in the latest revisions of its racial standards, concluding: "The Native Hawaiians presented compelling arguments that the standards must facilitate the production of data to describe their social and economic situation and to monitor discrimination."[10]

Proving discrimination can be difficult, however, because bias is not the only factor creating differences among groups. Other factors include education, marital status, and age. The average non-Hispanic white person is much older than the average Hispanic or black person, for example. These age differences are not subtle. Blacks and Hispanics account for 33 percent of the nation's young adults, but for only 15 percent of its retirees.[11] Because careers and earnings peak in middle age, the older age of non-Hispanic whites makes it more likely they will be higher on the socioeconomic scale than blacks or Hispanics. Age differences partly explain why 87 percent of CEOs are non-Hispanic white and, conversely, why 53 percent of construction workers are black or Hispanic.[12] They partly explain why the home-ownership rate is 76 percent for non-Hispanic whites and less than 50 percent for blacks and Hispanics.[13] They partly explain why the net worth of non-Hispanic whites is greater than the net worth of blacks and Hispanics.[14]

Age partly explains these differences, but it does not completely explain them. Discrimination also explains why blacks and Hispanics lag behind non-Hispanic whites. Without the government's rules on collecting data by race and Hispanic origin, we would not even know these differences existed, let alone try to explain them.

Factoid Source: Bureau of Labor Statistics, Labor Force Statistics from the Current Population Survey, Table 11, http://www.bls.gov/cps/home.htm (accessed June 11, 2008).

BLACK SHARE OF THE AMERICAN POPULATION: 14

Only 14 percent you say? If this surprises you, then join the crowd. Most Americans wildly overestimate the size of the black population. When asked to guess how many Americans are black, the public puts the number at a much higher 30 percent, according to a poll of racial attitudes.[15]

It is painfully obvious Americans are not demographers. They get most of their information about the population not from a census or surveys, but from a much less reliable source: the news. Although many Americans claim they do not trust either the press or television, the media's influence can be insidious.[16] We tend to believe what we see and read. This might explain why most of the public greatly overestimates the size of the black population. It would also explain why most Americans think blacks are the majority of the nation's poor.[17] Wrong again. Blacks account for 25 percent of the poverty population.[18] *Non-Hispanic whites* are a much larger 44 percent share.

These gaffes would be little more than a mildly interesting footnote in a social science journal if it were not for their serious consequences. According to political scientist Martin Gilens, Americans think blacks are the majority of the poor because that is what they see in the media. Unlike the public, Gilens is not guided by gut instinct when he says this. He actually analyzed news stories on TV and in news magazines over the years and found the media depicting the wrong people when reporting on poverty. The media portray blacks rather than whites in most of their stories about the poor, showing blacks an average of 57 percent of the time—more than double the black share of the poverty population.[19] No wonder the public thinks most of the poor are black.

These media distortions have consequences, says Gilens. Most of those who believe the poor are primarily black say the poor themselves are to blame for their predicament.[20] Those who believe the poor are primarily white are more likely to lay the blame for poverty on bad luck rather than bad character.

Factoid source: Bureau of the Census, National Population Estimates, http://www.census.gov/popest/national/index.html (accessed June 11, 2008).

PERCENTAGE OF BLACK PARENTS WHO ARE SATISFIED WITH THE PUBLIC ELEMENTARY SCHOOL IN THEIR AREA: 71

It must be tedious to be told, continuously, how you don't measure up. When this happen in a family, we call the family dysfunctional. The never-good-enough child is a scapegoat for the family's problems. When it happens in the larger society, we call it normal. Our scapegoat is the black population.

The nation's 41 million blacks suffer a daily diet of media reports detailing their lesser status. It is a toxic drip of ghettos and gangs, poverty and prisons. True, blacks and whites are not yet socioeconomic equals, but enough already. Just as the media focuses disproportionately on blacks when reporting on poverty, it focuses disproportionately on black shortcomings when reporting on blacks in general. Yet media stories and the hearsay they generate is all that millions of Americans know about blacks. Nearly half the public admits their opinions about blacks come not from direct experience, but from the media, things they have heard, and a "general sense" of things.[21]

Let's set the record straight: *the black population is decidedly middle class.* The evidence is overwhelming. According to data collected by the government and rarely reported in the news, most blacks are not poor. Among black married couples, 22 percent have incomes of $100,00 or more. The 82 percent majority of blacks are high school graduates, and most go to college. Blacks are more likely to be managers and professionals than ser-vice workers. Among black householders aged 45 or older, most are home-owners. Three out of four blacks say there is no crime in their neighborhood.

Perhaps most important is this statistic: 82 percent of blacks are satisfied with their lives, according to a Gallup poll.[22] The same poll finds one area of dissatisfaction, however. Sixty-eight percent of blacks are not satisfied with the way blacks are treated by our society. Maybe they object to being the scapegoat.

Factoid source: Bureau of the Census, American Housing Survey National Tables: 2005, http://www.census .gov/hhes/www/housing/ahs/ahs05/ahs05.html (accessed July 22, 2007).

PERCENTAGE OF WHITES WHO FEEL
VERY WARMLY TOWARD BLACKS: 20

How do blacks and whites really feel about each other? Considering everything, you might think black feelings toward whites would be less than charitable. But in fact, blacks regard whites more highly than whites regard blacks. When asked how warmly they feel toward whites, the 68 percent majority of blacks report positive feelings, with 37 percent saying their feelings are very warm.[23] When a similar question is asked of whites, a smaller 58 percent have positive feelings toward blacks, and only 20 percent feel very warm.

Given our history, how can so many blacks feel so good about whites? And whites—what is it with them anyway? The answers lie not in psychology but in probability. It is all in the numbers.

With 41 million blacks and nearly 200 million whites in the United States, blacks are outnumbered five to one. Consequently, blacks are more likely to know whites than whites are likely to know blacks. Sixty-one percent of blacks live in an integrated neighborhood, for example, compared with 44 percent of whites.[24] Most blacks work alongside whites, while many whites have no contact with blacks at all. Among whites living in states such as Idaho, Maine, Montana, and Vermont, the chances are less than 1 in 100 that the person next to them will be black. For blacks living even in the states with the most blacks, however, more than 60 percent of the people around them will be white. Because most blacks know whites personally, they are less likely to fall back on stereotypes when forming an opinion about them.

Not so for whites. When whites are asked how they formed their opinion about blacks, only 55 percent say their feelings are based on personal contact.[25] For the rest—or nearly half the white population—their feelings toward blacks are based on what they have heard, seen, or read—in other words, what is in the media. If that makes you shudder, then you get the point.

Factoid source: Survey Documentation and Analysis, Computer-Assisted Survey Methods Program, University of California, Berkeley, General Social Surveys, 1972–2006 Cumulative Data Files, GSS Variable FEELBLKS, http://sda .berkeley.edu/cgi-bin32/hsda?harcsda+gss06 (accessed October 2, 2007).

PERCENTAGE OF HISPANICS WITH
A HIGH SCHOOL DIPLOMA: 60

Nostalgic for the way things used to be? If you are one of the nation's 46 million Hispanics, probably not. Hispanics are reliving the lifestyle of our past, a lifestyle most Americans left behind a generation ago. In many ways, the demographics of the Hispanic population are an anachronism, a socioeconomic profile that has not been seen among the middle class of the United States for thirty or forty years. Warm and fuzzy it is not.

Let's start with money. Hispanic incomes are straight out of the 1950s, literally. The median income of the average Hispanic man is just $23,452—an income surpassed by the average American man all the way back in 1959, after adjusting for inflation.[26] The $46,561 median income of Hispanic couples today is about the same as the median income of the average American couple nearly three decades ago—in 1969, after adjusting for inflation.

There's a reason Hispanics don't make much money. They are poorly educated. At a time when most Americans have at least some college experience, only 60 percent of Hispanics have even graduated from high school—a level of education so low that the average American exceeded it more than thirty years ago.[27] Immigrants from Mexico and other Latin American countries, where schooling is often cut short, explain these educational shortcomings.

Hispanics make little money despite hard work. The labor force participation rate of Hispanic men harkens back, in fact, to 1964—the last time 81 percent of men aged 16 or older were in the labor force.[28] You have to go back even further to match the family life of Hispanics. Half of Hispanic households include children under age 18. The average household has not been that child friendly since 1963.[29]

It is hard to party like it's 1963 when you have twenty-first-century bills to pay. That is why Hispanics are America's new lower class.

Factoid source: Bureau of the Census, 2007 Current Population Survey Annual Social and Economic Supplement, http://pubdb3.census.gov/macro/032007/perinc/toc.htm (accessed October 2, 2007).

PERCENTAGE OF CALIFORNIA RESIDENTS
WHO SPEAK SPANISH AT HOME: 28

Call it a *fait accompli* or, more appropriately, *hecho consumado*. Like it or not, the United States is becoming a bilingual nation. And Spanish is what puts the "bi" in the "lingual." Of the more than 50 million people in the United States who speak a language other than English at home, most speak Spanish. In California, more than one in four residents speaks Spanish at home.

We are being dragged—some of us kicking and screaming—into the modern, multilingual world. It's about time. Europe is way ahead of us on this, with 53 percent of Europeans speaking more than one language, according to a Eurobarometer survey.[30]

Some people think the growing use of Spanish is a cause for concern. To stem the Spanish tide, they are writing laws to make English the official language. Their worries are unfounded, however. No one believes more strongly in the importance of learning English than Spanish-speaking immigrants. Among Hispanics born outside the United States, fully 91 percent say immigrants need to speak English to succeed, according to a Pew Hispanic Center/Kaiser Family Foundation poll.[31] Three out of four children of Hispanic immigrants speak English predominately (45 percent) or English and Spanish equally (32 percent).

Separated from most of the world by two oceans, Americans have not had much experience rubbing shoulders with other languages and cultures. Now our turn has come, and we should be polite about it. The younger generations are getting the message. Thirty-eight percent of young adults are already bilingual, according to a National Geographic–Roper Public Affairs poll.[32] Others are working on it. The percentage of high school students taking Spanish more than doubled to 30 percent over the past two decades.[33] For the growing share of students who speak Spanish at home, that is probably an easy A.

Factoid source: Bureau of the Census, 2006 American Community Survey, http://www.census.gov/acs/www/ (accessed October 2, 2007).

HISPANIC SHARE OF BIRTHS: 24

Stay-at-home moms. Large families. Traditionalists are rejoicing at the renewal of these trends in the United States. But something else is at work. The youthful Hispanic population—46 million strong and half younger than age 28—is muscling its way into government statistics and moving the numbers around. In fact, any trend involving children, young adults, or young families can no longer be fully understood until the Hispanic influence is measured. Let's look at the influence of Hispanics on two of the media's favorite trends.

Trend One: More stay-at-home moms. The *New York Times* got this one wrong by suggesting the small decline in women's labor force participation over the past few years has been due to women's changing priorities.[34] In fact, the lower participation rates of Hispanic women explain much of the decline. Among women aged 25 to 34, labor force participation drifted down from a high of 76.4 percent in the 1990s to 74.5 percent today. But remove Hispanics from the equation, and the labor force participation of women in the age group would rise to 76.8 percent—an all-time high.[35]

Trend Two: Larger families. *Life* magazine goofed on this one by announcing the expansion of the American family when in fact the Hispanic population is doing the expanding. Between 2000 and 2006, the number of third-order or higher births increased by 84,000. With much fanfare *Life* illustrated its cover story, "Why Americans Are Having More Kids," with a non-Hispanic white couple, the Fergusons, and their three children.[36] *Life* should have put the Garcias on the cover instead, because Hispanics account for the entire increase in the nation's third-order or higher births. Between 2000 and 2006, the number of Hispanics having a third or higher birth *increased* by 89,000; the number of non-Hispanic whites having a third or higher birth *decreased* by 7,000.[37]

Hispanics are turning back the clock to the 1950s. They, perhaps more than any other racial or ethnic group in the United States, personify traditional family values.

Factoid source: National Center for Health Statistics, *Births: Preliminary Data for 2006,* National Vital Statistics Report, Vol. 56, No. 7, December 5, 2007, p. 6.

HISPANIC CONTRIBUTION TO
US POPULATION GROWTH: 50 PERCENT

Whenever things go sour, it is a good idea to find someone to blame, a scapegoat to divert attention from the real source of our problems. The best scapegoats are the downtrodden because they have the hardest time fighting back. Until recently, blacks filled the role, but most blacks have climbed into the middle class and are no longer available for the position. So, those looking for someone to blame have been forced to find another target.

Enter the Hispanic population. The nation's Hispanics are an ideal scapegoat for these economically challenged times. Supposedly, the quarry is immigrants and illegals in particular. But the real target is Hispanics, since they became the nation's largest minority group in 2000, surpassing blacks. Today, the nation's 46 million Hispanics account for 15 percent of the US population—enough to attract unwanted attention. Adding fuel to the fire, Hispanics are the engine of our population growth. Between 2000 and 2007, the US population grew by 20 million, and Hispanics accounted for half the increase.[38]

These are fighting words for the over-the-hill gang, who see getting ahead as a zero-sum game. They think Hispanics threaten their well-being, and they aren't going to take it anymore. Things are getting ugly. The Southern Poverty Law Center counted 144 extremist groups actively harassing immigrants in 2007, primarily in the border states of Arizona, California, and Texas.[39] And who is fanning these flames? One guess. Politicians know an opportunity when they see one. All fifty states introduced legislation in 2007 targeted at immigrants.[40] But these efforts will not stem the growth of the Hispanic population because most of it is occurring in the maternity wards, not at the border crossings. Each year the United States population expands by another 3 million, including 500,000 Hispanic immigrants and 1 million Hispanic newborns.

Factoid source: Bureau of the Census, National Population Estimates, http://www.census.gov/popest/national/asrh/NC-EST2007-compchg.html (accessed May 1, 2008).

PART IV

YOUR STUFF

Chapter 16
SPENDING

RANK OF GASOLINE AMONG ITEMS ON WHICH HOUSEHOLDS SPEND THE MOST: 6

The Great American Shopping List. You can learn a lot about life in the United States by taking a look at the list—the inventory of every product and service purchased by American households ranked by how much we spend on each item. The list is long, with more than 350 different products and services. The federal government collects the information by surveying thousands of households each month, asking them how much they spend on everything from cookies and crackers to recreational vehicles. The government uses the data to create the all-important Consumer Price Index.

You might expect to be dazzled by what is at the top of America's shopping list, given our reputation as free spenders. But disappointment is the more likely response. Big screen TVs do not appear among the top ten, twenty, or even thirty items. In fact, spending on televisions ranks a lowly 77 on the list.[1] The number one item is not glamorous at all—Social Security tax is the single biggest expense for the average American household. Most of the other items among the top ten on the list are equally mundane—federal income tax, property tax, car payments, groceries, mortgage interest, gasoline, health insurance, and electricity. Are we having fun yet? Only one item on the top-ten list even remotely sounds like fun—eating out. The fact is, American households devote almost all of their hard-earned dollars to painfully utilitarian items. This is the kind of list your mother would write, with dental services in 38th place and candy at 108, retirement savings at 24 and video games at 190, donations to religious organizations at 14 and dating services at 360.

The Great American Shopping List shows our free-spending reputation to be undeserved. Most Americans are just trying to pay the bills.

Factoid source: Author's calculations based on unpublished tables from the Bureau of Labor Statistics 2006 Consumer Expenditure Survey.

PERCENTAGE OF THE AVERAGE
HOUSEHOLD BUDGET DEVOTED TO FOOD: 13

Food, clothing, and shelter are the basic necessities of life. Throughout history, supplying ourselves with the basics has consumed most of our time and money. In 1901, the average American family devoted 80 percent of its income to those three items.[2] No longer. Families today spend a smaller 50 percent of their budget on food, clothing, and shelter, and our spending on transportation now exceeds our spending on food. If we were to coin a phrase to describe our new priorities, it would be "shelter, transportation, and food." For some reason, it doesn't have quite the same ring to it, but it more accurately reflects modern lifestyles.

If you think food is expensive today, you don't know how lucky you are. In 1901, the average household spent 43 cents of every dollar earned on food for the family. Today we spend only 13 cents of every dollar on food. If we were to spend as much on food today as we did back then, groceries and restaurant meals would cost the average household $21,000 a year instead of just $6,000.[3]

Clothing, too, was once a budget buster, accounting for 14 percent of household expenditures in 1901. Today, the figure is just 4 percent as mass production and low-cost imports have sent clothing prices into a downward spiral. Our standard of living has improved so much, in fact, that we now spend more on entertainment than we do on clothes.

Shelter is another story. With the homeownership rate and housing prices far higher than they once were, shelter consumes a larger share of the household budget. In 1901, the average household devoted 23 percent of its spending to housing. Today, the figure is a much larger 34 percent, making housing our number-one spending priority. The number-two priority, transportation, consumes a substantial 18 percent of our budget today. In 1901, when the automobile was nothing more than a rich man's hobby, the government did not even single out transportation as a separate spending category.

Factoid source: Bureau of Labor Statistics, 2006 Consumer Expenditure Survey, Standard Tables, http://www.bls.gov/cex/home.htm (accessed December 2, 2007).

PERCENTAGE OF THE FOOD DOLLAR
SPENT EATING OUT: 44

The government tracks our spending on food with the kind of detail that would make a grocer swoon. Apples, oranges, butter, margarine, cookies, crackers—the Consumer Expenditure Survey records how much we spend on more than one hundred grocery items. The survey also measures how much we spend at the grocery store's biggest rival—the restaurant. It's an epic battle, and right now restaurants appear to be winning.

Remember when eating out was fun? Those were the days before fast food, when families strictly limited their restaurant excursions because eating out was expensive, time consuming, and something to be savored. In 1960, the average household devoted only 21 percent of its food budget to what the Bureau of Labor Statistics calls food away from home.[4] Then along came McDonalds, and the rest is history. The nation now has more than 200,000 fast-food restaurants, making eating out convenient and cheap—which is good.[5] But fast-food restaurants transformed eating out into little more than a tool for time management, an experience to be endured rather than enjoyed—which is bad. Evidently we like the convenience more than we hate the experience, since we now devote 44 percent of our food budget to food away from home.

Grocery stores are fighting back, with some success—but only on certain items. Average household spending on the grocery category "miscellaneous prepared food" (translation: the supermarket deli, which is the closest thing a grocery store has to fast food) climbed a whopping 53 percent between 2000 and 2006 after adjusting for inflation.[6] The spending statistics clearly show time-starved shoppers loading their carts with ready-made meals rather than ingredients for cooking. Average household spending on flour fell 47 percent during those years.

Factoid source: Bureau of Labor Statistics, 2006 Consumer Expenditure Survey, Standard Tables, http://www.bls.gov/cex/home.htm (accessed December 2, 2007).

AGE GROUP WITH THE BIGGEST
INCREASE IN SPENDING: 65 AND OLDER

Why has the adjective "free-spending" attached itself like a barnacle to the noun "baby-boom generation"? No matter how hard the social scientists recommend scrubbing the noun clean of the adjective, the pundits and the public let it stick. Face it: we revel in the holier-than-thou feeling we get when we blame boomers (ourselves excepted, of course) for spending too much. And we know it's true because the media said so.

But the media are mistaken. They have attached the free-spending label to the wrong generation. Yes, boomers as a group spend a lot, but not because they lack willpower. They spend a lot because there are a lot of them. Born between 1946 and 1964, they are the single largest generation in American history. With millions of boomers in the peak-spending years of middle age, consumer spending has soared. Since 1984, personal consumption expenditures (defined as all consumer spending) have nearly doubled, after adjusting for inflation.[7] To explain this increase, reporters look around and see McMansions, SUVs, and iced lattes. They assume, wrongly, that boomers are big spenders. In fact, households headed by 35- to 54-year-olds spend just 4 percent more today than households in the same age group spent in 1984, after adjusting for inflation.[8] Boomers held their spending in check despite the soaring cost of housing, health insurance, and college tuition. Their parents are not as disciplined. Householders aged 65 or older are spending 29 percent more than their counterparts did in 1984.

The Greatest Generation is spending freely while boomers frugally husband their resources. Anyone spouting this heresy risks a lightning strike. But some economists go even further: they blame the decline in the nation's savings rate on the increased consumption of older Americans, thanks to guaranteed government benefits.[9] Social Security and Medicare, they say, have freed older Americans from the fear of outliving their wealth, creating a generation of free spenders.

Factoid source: Author's calculations based on Bureau of Labor Statistics, 1984 and 2006 Consumer Expenditure Surveys, http://www.bls.gov/cex/home.htm (accessed December 2, 2007).

NUMBER OF TIMES THE AVERAGE PERSON SHOPS EACH WEEK: 5

Shopping is as American as apple pie. We are supposed to be good at it. We have been urged to shop as a patriotic duty. But are we really a nation of shopaholics, or are we being told we are shopaholics to get us to spend even more?

Everyone has to shop, of course. The average person leaves home to shop five times a week, according to the National Household Travel Survey. But some people shop more than others. The biggest shoppers are neither teenagers nor middle-aged bargain hunters, but older Americans. People ranging in age from 61 to 75 shop more than any other age group, leaving home to go to the store an average of seven times a week.[10]

Other surveys confirm this finding. On an average day, people aged 65 to 74 are more likely than any other age group to go grocery shopping, according to the American Time Use Survey.[11] They are also among those most likely to shop for items other than groceries. Nineteen percent of people aged 65 to 74 go to the grocery store on an average day, and an even larger 25 percent shop at other types of stores. No one goes to the mall more frequently than teenagers and the elderly, according to the International Council of Shopping Centers.[12]

Older Americans have the most free time, which explains why they spend more time shopping. But are they—or anyone else—having the kind of heel-kicking fun implied by the term *shopaholic*? Sadly, no. Studies show shopping to be only mildly amusing at best. According to an examination of how much people enjoy their daily activities, shopping ranks with other chores.[13] Regular shopping has an enjoyment rating of 6.6 on a scale of zero (dislike) to ten (like), alongside cooking, childcare, and commuting to work. Grocery shopping rates an even lower 5.5, below housework. Shopping for necessities is lowest of all at 5.1, below paying bills and ironing.

Factoid source: Author's calculations based on Department of Transportation, 2001 National Household Travel Survey, http://nhts.ornl.gov (accessed August 25, 2007).

AVERAGE ANNUAL SPENDING ON JEWELRY BY HOUSEHOLDS WITH INCOMES OF $150,000 OR MORE: $534

Jewelry, toilet paper, bus tickets—you name it, the federal government's Consumer Expenditure Survey knows how much you and everyone else spends on it—which is why it is a good place to start if you are fantasizing about what life would be like with more money in your bank account. The survey tracks the spending of households by income—all the way up to $150,000 or more, hereafter referred to as "the rich."

The rich spend more than the rest of us on almost everything. Take toilet paper, for example. The average household spends $100 a year on toilet paper. The rich spend $150. Why would the rich spend so much more on this basic necessity? Are they buying the fancy stuff? Do they have more to clean up? Actually, yes. Households with incomes of $150,000 or more are larger than average and include more children because they are likely to be headed by the middle-aged. So they spend more than average on most things. But on some things, they spend much more. Let's take a look at a few of the items on which the rich spend at least five times more than the average household.[14] Surprisingly, diamond rings and gold necklaces do not make the cut. The rich spend only four times more than the average household on jewelry. But many other items do make the quintuple cut. This is what separates the rich from the rest of us:

Nannies. But not day care centers, which are a necessity for working parents.

Private schools. But not college tuition. Now that most children go to college, tuition bills have become more of a middle-class burden.

Wine at restaurants. But not restaurant meals themselves. Eating out is no longer a luxury for most families.

Recreational vehicles. But not camping equipment. The spending numbers suggest that the rich do not like to rough it.

Retirement savings. But not lottery tickets. Luck is not a factor when the rich draw up their retirement plans.

These items, too, separate the rich from the rest: rent, phone cards, Laundromats, and cigarettes. The rich spend less than the average household on all of them.

Factoid source: Unpublished tables from the Bureau of Labor Statistics 2006 Consumer Expenditure Survey.

Chapter 17
HOUSES

PERCENTAGE OF HOUSEHOLDS
OWNING THEIR HOME: 68

They had to walk a mile to get to school, sometimes through a foot of snow. They had no fast-food restaurants, microwaves, televisions, or credit cards. The old folks have a way of turning history into hardship. But, in fact, some things were harder in the past. Consider this and shudder: if you were in the market for a house a century ago, you needed a 50 percent down payment and had to pay off the remainder of the loan in just five years.[1] That is hardship. And it is why a century ago most Americans rented rather than owned their home.

Then things got worse. During the Depression, many homeowners could not keep up with their mortgage payments and lost their homes. The home-ownership rate fell from 48 to 44 percent between 1930 and 1940.[2] The situation was so dire the government created a new agency—the Federal Housing Administration—and a new financing system—the 30-year fixed rate mortgage—to help people out. The rest is history. By 1950, the nation's homeownership rate had climbed to 55 percent.

Today, the homeownership rate stands at a much higher 68 percent. The rate has increased over the past few decades in part because the population is aging, and older people are most likely to own a home. The rate has also grown because financial terms became much more generous—so generous they got some people (and many financial institutions) into trouble all over again. Those generous terms—such as allowing people to buy a house with no down payment at all—turned out to be a bad idea. What do you want to bet these modern-day tales of hardship will be told to the next generation of youth?

Factoid source: Bureau of the Census, Housing Vacancy Survey, Annual Statistics 2007, http://www.census.gov/hhes/www/housing/hvs/annual07/ann07ind.html (accessed June 11, 2008).

PERCENTAGE OF HOMEOWNERS WITH A HOME EQUITY LOAN: 14

Dumb and dumber. The media delights in portraying American consumers as gullible and foolish. One of our financial missteps, the story goes, is that we have been greedy and gobbled up houses we could not afford. Another is that we are frittering away the equity in our homes on plasma TVs and granite countertops. Oh, how we love those stories. The problem is, they aren't true. Few homeowners are stuck with an unmanageable mortgage, and only 14 percent have a home equity loan, according to the American Community Survey.

Yes, horror stories abound, but the number of homeowners caught up in the nightmare is small. Let's look at the big picture. Among the nation's 75 million homeowners, nearly one in three owns their home free and clear—no mortgage at all. Among the 61 percent of homeowners with a mortgage, their median debt amounts to only 55 percent of their home's value, according to the American Housing Survey.[3] This means housing prices could drop a long way before most would be in trouble.

The nation's homeowners have made smart choices in other ways as well. Only 10 percent of those with mortgages gambled with an adjustable rate loan, balloon payments, or other easy-money schemes. Ninety percent of homeowners with mortgages are safely locked into a fixed rate loan with a median interest rate of just 6 percent. Only 3 percent of homeowners owe more than their house is worth. Among the millions who have refinanced over the past few years, 87 percent did so to get a lower interest rate. Only 13 percent refinanced to pocket some cash.

American homeowners appear to be better money managers than the ones employed by the financial institutions pushing the risky schemes. They have more sense even than the former chairman of the Federal Reserve Board, Alan Greenspan, who, as recently as 2004, was extolling the virtues of adjustable rate mortgages and admonishing consumers for not taking advantage of them.[4] Wise money managers that they are, most Americans did not take his advice.

Factoid source: Bureau of the Census, 2006 American Community Survey, http://factfinder.census.gov/home/saff/main.html?_lang=en (accessed June 11, 2008).

AVERAGE PRICE OF A NEW
SINGLE-FAMILY HOME IN 1970: $26,600

Talk about runaway inflation. The average price of a new single family home today is more than eleven times the 1970 price, reaching $305,900 in 2006. Houses used to be cheap—or were they? Some might argue that the $26,600 price of 1970 felt like just as much money to families back then as the $305,900 price feels to families today. Are they right? Whether housing is affordable or a budget buster depends on how much money people make and the kind of house they want to buy. Let's compare the years 1970 and 2006 to get a feel for what happened to housing.

First, the money angle: in 1970, the average price of a new single-family home was three times the median household income, estimated at $8,734 by the Census Bureau. By 2006 the average price of a new home had ballooned to six times the $48,201 median household income.[5] Our incomes have not kept pace with prices. By this calculation, the real price of a new home for the typical household has doubled.

There's more to the story, however. A new house in 1970 had far fewer bells and whistles than the new house of today, making the comparison between then and now more complex. Fortunately, the Census Bureau tracks housing prices while holding housing quality (bedrooms, bathrooms, garages, etc.) constant. It chose 1996 as its standard year and adjusted prices forward and backward to create a set of prices independent of changes in housing quality. The 1970 family would have had to pay $38,000 for the 1996 standard house, or four times its median income. The 2006 family would have had to pay $264,900 for the 1996 standard house, or five times its median income.[6] By holding housing quality constant, the difference in housing prices is greatly reduced but not eliminated. If our home is our castle, then it is costing more than ever to live like a king.

Factoid source: Bureau of the Census, Construction Price Indexes, Constant Quality (Laspeyres) Price Index of New One-Family Houses Sold, http://www.census.gov/const/www/constpriceindex.html (accessed December 2, 2007).

MEDIAN SIZE OF A NEW SINGLE-FAMILY HOME: 2,235 SQUARE FEET

You can see them from an airplane as you come in for a landing. They surround you as you drive through the suburbs of any urban area in the United States: supersized houses. The statistics confirm the eyeball survey. During the past three decades, the median size of a new single-family home in the United States has grown by 43 percent, from 1,560 square feet in 1975 to 2,235 square feet in 2007, according to the Census Bureau.[7] What accounts for this rapid expansion of our living space? Let's look at the facts.

During the first decade of the time period, between 1975 and 1985, the size of a new single-family home increased by a modest 30 square feet. During the next ten years, between 1985 and 1995, the typical new home expanded by a much larger 290 square feet. Between 1995 and 2007, the average new home gained an even greater 355 square feet. What happened during those time periods to inflate the size of homes? The baby-boom generation's entry into the housing market often gets the blame for our McMansion-studded suburbs. Boomers demanded castles, the story goes, and builders responded. But there may be another more surprising explanation: the computer.

Between 1975 and 1985, few households owned a computer. Computer ownership grew from essentially zero in 1975 to a tiny 8 percent in 1985. The median size of a new home barely changed during those years. Between 1985 and 1995, computer ownership climbed to 32 percent of households, and the size of new homes expanded.[8] Between 1995 and 2007, computers became the norm, with three out of four households owning a computer today.[9] The median size of a new home climbed sharply in response.

Blame it on the home office. Computers, monitors, and printers require space, and a growing proportion of homebuyers wanted an additional room—a home office—to house their equipment. Fully 35 percent of the owners of new homes say they have a "room used for business."[10] That room explains why our houses are bigger than ever.

Factoid source: Bureau of the Census, Characteristics of New Housing, Characteristics of New One-Family Houses Sold, http://www.census.gov/const/www/charindex .html#sold (accessed June 11, 2008).

PERCENTAGE OF HOMES WITH AIR CONDITIONING:
1960: 12
2005: 85

Can you say "Global Warming"? The American public may be divided on the causes of global warming, but they are of one mind when it comes to solving the problem—get an air conditioner. The percentage of homes with air conditioning has soared over the past fifty years. Today, fully 62 percent of homes are centrally air-conditioned and another 23 percent are equipped with room units. Of new single-family homes sold in 2007, fully 93 percent had central air conditioning.[11]

The rise of home air conditioning has occurred with the kind of rocket-propelled growth usually reserved for new communications technologies like the telephone, the television, and the Internet. Money is the only thing that can fuel this kind of growth. A quick probe into the history of air conditioning reveals the identity of the moneymen to be none other than developers. In the post–World War II residential building boom, homebuilders substituted central air conditioning for more expensive architectural details, such as overhanging eaves, which once served to cool houses in the summer's heat.[12]

The rise of the South also plays a large role in the air conditioning story. Between 1960 and 2007, the southern states gained 55 million people, accounting for nearly half of the nation's population growth.[13] Air conditioning made the South an appealing place to live, and in turn the region's growth propelled the demand for air conditioning. Other places also benefited from the cooling technology—think Las Vegas, Phoenix, and Palm Springs.

The 70 percent majority of Americans now regard home air conditioning as a necessity, according to a Pew Research Center Survey.[14] This is quite a change in attitude since 1973, when only 26 percent of the public believed air conditioning was necessary.[15] Air conditioning is more important today, the public says, than the cell phone, the television, or the computer.

Factoid source: Bureau of the Census, "Tracking the American Dream—Fifty Years of Housing Changes," *Statistical Brief,* April 1994, p. 2; and American Housing Survey National Tables: 2005, http://www.census.gov/hhes/www/housing/ahs/ahs05/ahs05.html (accessed May 11, 2007).

PERCENTAGE OF AMERICANS
WHO LIVE IN A GATED COMMUNITY: 6

The average American inhabits the vast middle of the bell curve of housing. Most of us consider ourselves lucky to be there, too, except when television exposes us to houses of the rich and famous, showing us how much better it could be—like Xanadu 2.0, the 50,000 square-foot lakeshore mansion owned by Bill Gates. That's when we stare enviously at the top of the curve, wishing our house was one of the 2 percent with waterfront property or one of the 6 percent securely ensconced in the rarified atmosphere of a gated community, with access restricted to residents only.

The middle of the bell curve is a comfortable, three-bedroom house in the suburbs. Sixty-four percent of the nation's households live in a single-family detached home—the pinnacle of the American Dream. The statistical medians show the house was built in 1973 and sits on one-third of an acre, according to the Census Bureau's American Housing Survey.[16] The government does not say how many houses have white picket fences.

Naturally, when you're in the middle of the bell curve, you see more of the same when you look out the window. More of the same describes the view from the living room window of the typical American home. Eighty-one percent of us report single-family detached houses within 300 feet of our home. In a testament to America's wide-open spaces, the average person is more likely to see woods and fields than apartment buildings or highways when looking out the window. Thirty-eight percent see open space, park, woods, farm, or ranchland. A smaller 27 percent look out upon apartment buildings, and only 13 percent see four-lane highways.

Except for twinges of envy every now and then, most Americans are satisfied with their house. On a scale of one to ten, 71 percent rate their house an eight or higher. It may be no Xanadu, but it is home.

Factoid source: Bureau of the Census, American Housing Survey National Tables: 2005, http://www.census .gov/hhes/www/housing/ahs/ahs05/ahs05.html (accessed May 12, 2007).

VACATION HOMES AS A PERCENTAGE OF THE NATION'S HOUSING STOCK: 3

On any given day, 18 million housing units sit vacant. That's a lot of empty space—enough to house the populations of the nation's three largest metropolitan areas (New York, Los Angeles, and Chicago) with room to spare. Many of the vacant units are begging for someone to call them home: 6 million are for sale or rent and have no takers. Another 6 million are being held off the market, most likely because the owner is waiting for a better price. Four million vacant housing units are seasonal—occupied only a few weeks or months of the year.[17] These are the nation's vacation homes.

Ah, vacation! Ah, vacation homebuyers! For years the real estate market has been eagerly anticipating a crush of second-home buyers as the population ages. The excitement is well founded, since the percentage of households owning a vacation home rises with age to a peak of 6 percent in the 55-to-64 age group—the age group now expanding with the large baby-boom generation.[18] But no crush of buyers has appeared so far, despite the efforts of real estate pundits to massage the numbers by adding investment properties and timeshares to the mix. Rather than surging as anticipated, the number of vacation homes is growing at about the same pace as the housing stock. Seasonal homes have accounted for 3 percent of the nation's housing units for the past fifty years.[19]

It may be that middle-aged Americans are too squeezed by college costs and retirement savings to even think about taking on a second mortgage payment. But if they did, where would they be most likely to find such a retreat? Not at the Hamptons or South Beach. The three states in which vacation homes account for the largest percentage of housing units are Maine (16 percent), Vermont (15 percent), and New Hampshire (10 percent).[20]

Factoid source: Bureau of the Census, Historical Census of Housing Tables—Vacation Homes, http://www.census.gov/hhes/www/housing/census/historic/vacation.html (accessed May 29, 2007).

Chapter 18
CARS

NUMBER OF REGISTERED VEHICLES
ON THE HIGHWAYS: 251 MILLION

Americans love automobiles. That much we know. But why do we have so many automobiles, why do we spend so much money on them, and why do we use them to the exclusion of all other modes of transportation? Is our car-crazed culture something uniquely American, or is there another explanation for this obsession?

There is another explanation: cars are the primary mode of transportation in the United States because we live in one of the largest countries in the world. We rank third in square miles—behind only Russia and Canada. Both of those countries include large tracts of uninhabitable land. Given our size and temperate climate, it could be argued that no other country on earth has as many places to go within its borders. No wonder we depend on personal rather than public transportation to get from point A to point B.

But we have a problem. The number of vehicles is expanding much faster than highway miles. Since 1960, the number of miles of paved road in the United States has more than doubled, increasing by 114 percent.[1] This falls far short of the increase in registered vehicles, the number growing by 237 percent and rising to 251 million. The number of vehicles, in fact, first exceeded the number of licensed drivers more than two decades ago.[2] No wonder getting from point A to point B is harder than ever. It's called congestion. The Federal Highway Administration studies congestion and devises ingenious ways to measure it. One measure is called "travel reliability."[3] It works this way: As traffic becomes more congested, your best guess about how long it will take you to get to point B becomes increasingly unreliable because you might end up in a traffic jam. The only way to guarantee your on-time arrival is to leave earlier and spend more time in the car. They call this the "buffer index." And it is growing.

Factoid source: Bureau of Transportation Statistics, Table 1-11, http://www.bts.gov/publications/national _transportation_statistics/html/table_01_11.html (accessed June 11, 2008).

AMOUNT OF TIME AMERICANS SPEND DRIVING ON AN AVERAGE DAY: 63 MINUTES

If you wonder where the time goes, here is your answer. The automobile steals your time, and it is becoming increasingly bold about doing so. Americans spend more than one hour a day behind the wheel. A calculator will show you how it all adds up: 383 hours a year of driving, or 16 full days of high anxiety. No wonder we feel stressed out.

It is a rare day when we do not drive somewhere. Government researchers study our comings and goings, and here is their finding: on an average day, 88 percent of Americans leave their home to go somewhere else, according to the National Household Travel Survey.[4] The average person leaves home not just once, but four times a day. The average trip is 10 miles and 20 minutes long. Nearly nine out of ten trips are by automobile.

The demographics determine who is most likely to be on the road. The percentage of people who leave home on an average day peaks in middle age then falls with advancing age to just 52 percent of people aged 85 or older. Women are as likely as men to leave the house, although men travel greater distances. Men drive an average of 41 miles a day, women a shorter 25 miles. One reason for the greater number of miles logged by men is their commute. Not only are men more likely to work, but they drive longer distances to get to work. The average working man commutes 14 miles, his female counterpart only 10. For some activities, however, women are more often behind the wheel. During a year's time, women travel 914 miles driving other people (mostly their children) around. Men log a smaller 751 miles a year as chauffeurs.

Factoid source: Department of Transportation, 2001 National Household Travel Survey, Online Analysis Tool, http://nhts.ornl.gov/index.shtml (accessed November 20, 2005).

RANK OF CAR PAYMENTS AMONG ITEMS ON WHICH THE AVERAGE HOUSEHOLD SPENDS THE MOST: 3

Geography alone does not explain our car-driven culture. China and Brazil are almost as large as the United States, but they have far fewer cars per capita. We opt for cars over trains or buses or bicycles because most of us—citizens of the wealthiest nation in the world—can afford to buy and maintain them. The cost is steep, however. Car payments rank third among items on which the average household spends the most, behind only Social Security taxes and mortgage interest. We spend more on car payments than we do on groceries, health insurance, or federal income taxes. Gasoline ranks sixth on the list, not to mention vehicle insurance and repairs. Yet, despite the stiff cost, almost no one decides to forego owning a vehicle. Only 9 percent of households do not own an automobile. Fifty-eight percent own at least two.[5]

Here's another American eccentricity: chances are, the two or three cars you own are not parked where they should be—in the garage. Most of us have a garage, and many of us have enough garage space to park three or more cars. But only 15 percent of us park any car in the garage, according to the National Association of Homebuilders.[6] We don't park our cars in the garage because our garage is full of other things—garages have become self-storage units for all of our stuff. Why do we have so much stuff? Back to the geography lesson: Americans have 3.7 million square miles to fill, stretching from sea to shining sea. We are only doing what comes naturally. For thousands of years, *Homo sapiens* have been busy filling empty space. Human nature, it seems, abhors a vacuum.

Factoid source: Author's calculations based on unpublished tables from the Bureau of Labor Statistics 2006 Consumer Expenditure Survey.

AVERAGE AMOUNT SPENT
ON A NEW CAR: $25,000

Over the past half-century, family incomes in the United States have nearly doubled, after adjusting for inflation. This growing affluence has allowed us to do some foolish things, like spend too much money on cars. The average household lavishes $8,000 a year on automobiles—a figure that includes car payments, gasoline, new tires, oil changes, repairs, insurance, and so on.[7] For every $100 we spend, we devote $17 to automobiles. This is more than we spend on food, clothing, entertainment, health care, taxes, or any other item except the ultimate money pit—our house. It sounds crazy, and it is.

Unlike a house, vehicles do not appreciate in value. (OK, sometimes houses don't either.) Once we drive the new car off the lot, its value plummets and continues its downward slide until we cry uncle. Then we trade in the junker for a new car and the torture begins all over again, with our money disappearing like tread on a tire. The process is especially painful for those who owe more than their car is worth when they trade it in. Car dealers call this being "upside down," which makes it sound like a lot more fun than it is. Fortunately, most households manage to stay right side up, but just barely.

It's a paradox. Automobiles are one of our biggest expenses, yet they are also an important household asset—second only to checking accounts in the proportion of households owning them, according to the Survey of Consumer Finances.[8] The automobile's value begins to fall a soon as we put pedal to the metal, yet our driveways are full of these bulky assets. Just how much are they worth? For the average household, the median value of (all) their automobiles is just $14,200, well below what we pay for just one of them.

Factoid source: Author's calculations based on unpublished tables from the Bureau of Labor Statistics 2006 Consumer Expenditure Survey.

PERCENTAGE OF US HOUSEHOLDS WITH PUBLIC TRANSPORTATION IN THEIR AREA: 54

There is nothing cocky about why Americans spurn public transportation in favor of personal vehicles. The fact that barely half of US households have access to public transportation, and just a handful use it, has more to do with our relatively low population density than an unwillingness to rub shoulders with the masses. With only 84 people per square mile, the United States is much less densely populated than most European countries. Population density explains Europe's stellar public transportation systems. France has 289 people in each of its square miles, Germany 609, and the United Kingdom 650—nearly eight times our density.[9] Imagine multiplying every American, every car, and every mile of pavement by a factor of eight and you begin to understand why public transportation is more important in the United Kingdom than in the United States.

Our car-loving culture is the creation of a low-density geography. It is fed by our (usually) bustling economy, which allows us to spend lavishly on personal transportation. Change the mix a bit—crowd more of us together and make owning a vehicle prohibitively expensive—and public transportation would become the preferred mode of getting from here to there. This is not just empty speculation. For proof, look no further than densely populated New York City, where parking spaces can cost more than an entire house costs in many parts of the country. New York has the highest rate of public transit commuting in the United States.[10] In 2006, the 54 percent majority of workers in New York City used public transportation to get to work. Only 24 percent drove to work alone. Most households in New York City do not even own a car.

Factoid source: Bureau of the Census, 2005 American Housing Survey, http://www.census.gov/hhes/www/housing/ahs/ahs05/ahs05.html (accessed November 29, 2007).

PERCENTAGE OF LONG-DISTANCE TRIPS TRAVELED BY AUTOMOBILE: 90

Even when traveling long distances, Americans overwhelmingly choose to travel by car. Airplanes are the second choice, but they account for only 7 percent of long-distance trips (defined as trips of 50 or more miles). The bus and the train combined account for only 3 percent of long-distance travel, barely registering on the scale.

The immense size of the United States makes air travel the most efficient way to get from one place to another when the measure is in thousands rather than hundreds of miles. The average airplane trip carries the traveler a median of 2,068 miles, according to the National Household Travel Survey.[11] The average long-distance car trip is just 194 miles.

The United States is one of only a handful of countries in the world where a traveler can journey for one, two, or even three thousand miles in one direction and still remain within the borders of a single nation. Travel a thousand miles from New York and you will be in Kansas—just halfway across the country. But travel a thousand miles from London and you could be in Poland, Italy, or Spain. Travel 2,500 miles from New York and you arrive in Los Angeles. But travel 2,500 miles from Paris and you could find yourself in Iraq. The distance between London and Paris is only 211 miles, about the same as the distance between New York and Washington, DC. The miles that transport travelers into a different culture in Europe take them only to a different area code in the United States.

Our sprawling geography makes us uniquely American—big, bold, and (OK, we admit it) sometimes boorish. But take a European (or a Latin American or an Asian) and plant him in our vast geography and he will turn into one of us—a big, bold, and boorish American. Our 3.7 million square miles of mountains, prairies, and coastline have worked this alchemy on newcomers for hundreds of years.

Factoid source: Bureau of Transportation Statistics, "National Household Travel Survey Long-Distance Travel Quick Facts," http://www.bts.gov/programs/national _household_travel_survey/long_distance.html (accessed November 27, 2006).

PERCENTAGE OF HOUSEHOLDS
WITH ONE OR MORE BICYCLES: 44

Our car craze has had some unintended consequences: sprawl and spread. The two are inextricably linked because, as roadways grow in number and size, the opportunities for bicycling and walking shrink and waistlines expand. With traffic increasingly congested, bicycling has become perilous on all but designated bike paths, which are scarce in most communities. Few children ride their bike to school anymore, and many adults are afraid to venture onto crowded streets with their bicycles. The percentage of people aged 7 or older who rode a bicycle more than once in the past year fell from 24 to 14 percent in the past decade, according to the National Sporting Goods Association.[12] Most households no longer even own a bicycle.

Walking, like bicycling, is becoming an endangered activity as networks of highways surround neighborhoods, forcing residents into cars to get to stores and jobs. The results can be measured at our waistline. A study by the National Center for Smart Growth at the University of Maryland examined the effect of the car culture on obesity. The researchers compared the weight of nearly 11,000 people living in different types of neighborhoods in Atlanta.[13] Those living in the most residential suburbs, where cars are king, weighed significantly more than those living in mixed-use (or walking) communities.

After decades of indulging in cars, we are beginning to worry about where our gluttony is taking us. Our newfound concern is unlikely to change our behavior, however, because—in the end—geography rules. Americans will expand into the space around them until they are prevented from doing so either by crowds or costs. But don't hold your breath waiting for the day we adopt the European model of getting from here to there via mass transportation. It won't happen until our population approaches the 2 billion mark, when we will be as densely populated as Germany.

Factoid source: US Department of Transportation, 2001 National Household Travel Survey, Online Analysis Tool, http://nhts.ornl.gov/index.shtml (accessed November 20, 2005).

Chapter 19
TECHNOLOGY

PERCENTAGE GOING ONLINE
YOUNG: 92
OLD: 37

Sex, drugs, and rock 'n' roll once divided young from old. Today, the Internet is the great divider. The difference in Internet use between young adults (those under age 30) and the oldest adults (those aged 65 or older) is a gaping 55 percentage points, according to the Pew Internet & American Life Project. Rapid technological change, coupled with enormous differences in technology adoption by age, means young adults and their grandparents are no longer on the same wavelength, literally.

The chasm is even deeper than the online numbers suggest because most of the oldest adults depend on agonizingly slow dial-up connections. Only 19 percent of people aged 65 or older have broadband Internet access. In contrast, most 18- to 29-year-olds have a high-speed connection to the Internet, according to Pew.[1] Because of their dial-up connection, older Americans cannot access the increasingly important visual applications of the Web such as Google Earth and YouTube. Cell phones are another gulf between the generations, with only about one-third of Americans aged 65 or older owning a cell phone versus near universal ownership among the young and middle-aged.[2]

What we have is a failure to communicate. The younger generations find what they need to know online. The oldest generation gets its information from newspapers and television. The younger generations are available 24/7 by cell phone. The oldest generation depends on landline phones and is out of touch if not at home. The younger generations are frustrated because they cannot text their parents and grandparents. The oldest generation wonders why the kids never write.

To track these differences, Pew created a typology of technology users that says it all. At the one extreme are technological Omnivores who have almost everything. At the other extreme is a group labeled Off the Network, who have almost nothing.[3] The median age of the Omnivores is 28. The median age of those Off the Network is 64. Like the communications gap between immigrants and their American-born offspring, old and young no longer speak the same language.

Factoid source: Pew Internet & American Life Project, Demographics of Internet Users, http://www.pewinternet.org/trends/User_Demo_2.15.08.htm (accessed March 18, 2008).

MEDIAN AGE OF THE AUDIENCE FOR NETWORK EVENING NEWS: 61

If you love the way things have always been, then this will break your heart: average household spending on newspapers and magazines has fallen by 60 percent, after adjusting for inflation, since the pre-Internet days of 1991.[4] A number like that means things are going to change—big time. Yet, like a cartoon character who has run off a cliff, we're still pedaling madly in the air and ignoring the fact that the ground beneath us has disappeared. We are about to plummet into a world where daily newspapers, network news, glossy magazines, landline telephones, the written letter, and even the phone book will no longer play a central role in our lives.

For the traditional media, the demographics are deadly. Only 35 percent of Americans now read a daily newspaper, down from 69 percent in the early 1970s, according to the General Social Survey.[5] Even worse, while readership remains high among the elderly (66 percent), it has plummeted in the young adult age group. Among people under age 30, the percentage reading a daily newspaper fell from 48 to 16 percent during the past three decades. Ditto for the network evening news. Its audience has collapsed from 52 million viewers in 1980 to just 23 million today, according to Nielsen Media Research.[6] The fatal blow is this: half the remaining viewers are aged 61 or older. As younger adults replace "off the network" generations, the bleeding is only going to get worse.

A Harris poll shows what is in store in the not-too-distant future.[7] Today, the largest share of Americans gets its news and information from television. But when asked where they think they will get their news and information five years from now, the largest share says the Internet. Things are about to get very unpleasant for those who love the way things have always been.

Factoid source: Project for Excellence in Journalism, "The State of the News Media 2008," http://www.stateofthenewsmedia.org/2008 (accessed June 11, 2008).

NUMBER OF TELEVISION CHANNELS RECEIVED BY THE AVERAGE HOUSEHOLD: 119

Cell phone? Check. Internet service? Check. More than one hundred television channels? Check. The list goes on, and we have it all: iPod, HDTV, Tivo, texting, digital camera, DVDs, YouTube—a veritable treasure trove of high-tech toys that could barely be imagined just a decade or two ago. In 1985, the average home received only nineteen channels on its television set, according to Nielsen Media Research.[8] You might think the one hundred-plus channels now streaming into our home, captured by Tivo, and displayed on a fifty-inch plasma screen with surround sound would have us jumping up and down with joy. Instead, we still say there's nothing on TV.

At least, that's what social scientists have discovered when they ask Americans whether they find life exciting, routine, or dull. Despite the marvels at our fingertips, the percentage of people who find life exciting has barely increased over the past three decades. In 1973—before an apple was an Apple—just 46 percent of Americans said life was exciting, according to the General Social Survey.[9] Thirty years later, the proportion is 50 percent. Yes, it is a bit higher than it once was, but the gain is ho-hum considering the revolution in technology. What are we waiting for—holograms, warp speed, and time travel?

Even more curious is this: young adults are no more likely to find life exciting than their counterparts thirty years ago. Among 18- to 29-year-olds, the same 52 percent think life is exciting—as if nothing has happened in the meantime. In contrast, the middle-aged are on fire. The percentage of 50- to 64-year-olds who find life exciting has surged, rising from just 40 percent in the early 1970s to 52 percent today. Maybe that's because the middle-aged are uniquely positioned to appreciate the miracle of technology. They are young enough to enjoy the high-tech cornucopia but old enough to remember the interminable wait for Saturday morning cartoons.

Factoid source: Nielsen Media Research, "Average U.S. Home Now Receives a Record 118.6 TV Channels," June 6, 2008, http://www.nielsenmedia.com (accessed June 11, 2008).

PERCENTAGE OF WAKING HOURS PEOPLE AGED 65 OR OLDER SPEND WATCHING TELEVISION: 25

The first parents to lecture their children about watching too much television are now themselves glued to the tube. People aged 65 or older devote nearly four hours a day to television—one-quarter of their waking hours and more than any other age group. Don't let them fool you, either. The television is not just turned on for company while they busy themselves with other tasks. Older Americans spend 3.76 hours a day watching television as a "primary activity," according to the American Time Use Survey. The survey defines "primary activity" as the main activity being done at a given time. This means people aged 65 or older spend one-quarter of their waking hours *watching* television, not eating, reading, or vacuuming while the TV happens to be on.

The elderly may be the most addicted to television, but they are not alone in their obsession. Americans of all ages spend a lot of time watching TV. If you rank all the activities we do in a day by the amount of time we devote to them, television is third in time use—behind only sleeping and working. On average, Americans enjoy nearly five hours of leisure each day, spending more than half of it in front of their television set. Nobody sits there longer than the elderly, which explains why the television audience is so much older than the population as a whole. And it is getting older. As video games, iPods, Facebook, and text messaging lure younger generations away from the tube, the television audience is aging. The median age of prime time viewers for the top five broadcast networks hit a paunchy 48 in the 2006–07 television season, according to *TV Guide*, more than ten years older than the median age of the population as a whole.[10]

What does a television advertiser have to do to reach the nation's younger generations? Maybe they should start texting.

Factoid source: Calculations by the author based on unpublished tables from the Bureau of Labor Statistics 2005 American Time Use Survey.

PERCENTAGE WHO HAVE BEEN ANNOYED BY THE CELL PHONE USE OF OTHERS IN PUBLIC: 82

Before cell phones, who knew *Homo sapiens* wanted to talk so much? Our prehistoric ancestors, maybe, since they were the last to live within shouting distance of everyone they knew. The African savannahs might have been humming with conversation as ancient humans discussed the latest hunt and gathering. But as our species migrated to distant lands without a way to talk to those left behind, we were forced to repress our need to stay in touch. Out of this melancholy, perhaps art was born. We told stories, wrote poems, and drew pictures to mourn the loss.

It has been thousands of years since we could strike up a conversation at will with any friend or family member. Only in the past ten years, as cell phones proliferated, have we rediscovered our addiction to continuous communication with those we care about. The cell phone, in fact, has revealed talk to be one of our most powerful urges—powerful enough to transform household spending patterns. If you make a list of every item the average household buys in a year and sort the list by how much we spend on each item, no other product or service has moved up in the ranks more than cell phone service. In 1997, few households spent on cell phone service, which ranked a lowly 112th in the list—lower than spending on postage.[11] Today, cell phone service is in 22nd place—above important categories such as alcoholic beverages and prescription drugs.[12]

Interestingly, while 82 percent of the public has gotten annoyed with someone else's public cell phone use, only 8 percent of cell phone users think they have annoyed others with their calls.[13] They were too busy talking to notice.

Factoid source: Lee Rainie and Scott Keeter, *How Americans Use Their Cell Phones*, Pew Internet & American Life Project, April 3, 2006, p. 1.

PERCENTAGE OF YOUNG ADULTS WHO ARE CELL-PHONE-ONLY USERS: 31

Houston, we have a problem. Most of what we know about ourselves as Americans comes from surveys. Telephone surveys. Using landline phones. Uh-oh.

With cell phones proliferating, survey researchers began to wonder whether something was wrong. The National Center for Health Statistics decided to take a look. In a word, wow. Among 18- to 24-year-olds, nearly 31 percent cannot be reached on a landline phone because they are cell-phone-only users. Among 25- to 29-year-olds, the figure is an even larger 35 percent. These stunning statistics have survey researchers tearing their hair out, in their understated way. The researchers conclude, "The potential for bias due to undercoverage remains a real and growing threat to surveys conducted only on landline telephones."[14] It is a quiet scream.

The abandonment of landline phones has occurred with alarming speed. The percentage of 25- to 29-year-olds with only cell phones tripled in just three years. Their telephone preferences stand in sharp contrast to middle-aged and older Americans. In the 30-to-44 age group, a smaller 16 percent use cell phones only; among 45- to 64-year-olds, just 8 percent; among people aged 65 or older, a tiny 2 percent. It may be just a matter of time, however, before most age groups are cell-phone-only users. The government's household spending statistics reveal the growing dominance of the cell over the landline phone. Householders up to the age of 55 now devote more dollars to cell phone service than they do to landline service.[15]

Survey researchers are facing the facts. They know cell phones must be included in their survey samples. But that means the price of learning about life in the United States will go up. Analysts at the Pew Research Center estimate that cell phone interviews cost twice as much as their landline equivalents.

Factoid source: Stephen J. Blumberg and Julian V. Luke, *Wireless Substitution: Early Release of Estimates from the National Health Interview Survey, July–December 2007*, May 13, 2008, National Center for Health Statistics, p. 7.

MEDIAN LENGTH OF A CELL PHONE CALL: 2 MINUTES

Public Schools: 1, Parents: 0. That was the score in May 2007, when the New York State Supreme Court upheld the New York City Department of Education's ban on the possession of cell phones in the city's public schools. That's *possession*, not use. New York City's public school students are not permitted to bring cell phones to school, period. Only someone born in the electronic dark ages could have formulated such a draconian policy. Coincidentally, New York City Public School Chancellor Joel Klein was born in 1946, the year of the first-ever mobile telephone call.

Times have changed, but not in the New York City public schools. Parents in New York are rightly having a fit, unable to communicate with their children before, during, or after school. They are so upset they took the school district to court, arguing that the ban interfered with the constitutional right of parents and children to make family decisions. They lost.

New York City's educational bureaucracy needs a lesson in twenty-first-century family dynamics and the central role played by the cell phone. Among families with school-aged children, more than 70 percent of mothers and fathers work.[17] The cell phone allows working parents to be there for their kids, a stand-in for the stay-at-home mom. Family communications drive the cell phone market. The median length of a cell phone call is two minutes—just enough time to make sure everything is OK, adjust schedules, make plans. Knowing this, most schools have crafted reasonable cell phone rules, allowing students to carry a phone but forbidding them from using it during the school day. When the phone rings, says a dean of students at a more enlightened school district in Wilmington, Delaware, more often than not the caller is a parent.[18]

Factoid source: Federal Communications Commission, *Trends in Telephone Service* (Washington, DC: FCC, February 2007), pp. 11–18.

NUMBER OF FIRST-CLASS LETTERS MAILED IN THE UNITED STATES: 40 BILLION

Pity the poor letter. For centuries it has been our friend, our confidant, the only means of staying in touch with friends and family far away. Then came the Internet. Once we went online, there was no going back. Now the writing paper lies unused, along with envelopes and postage stamps, in a desk drawer rarely opened. Between 1994 and 2007, the annual number of first-class letters mailed in the United States fell from 55 to 40 billion, a 27 percent decline.

The postal service is concerned. Letters have long been its main source of revenue, and the revenue stream is drying up: in 2007, letters generated only 26 percent of postal service revenue, down from 39 percent in 1994.[19] What remains of revenue from first-class mail is increasingly dependent on the shrinking number of people who are off the net, who prefer stationery to keyboards and checkbooks to online banking. A look at the demographics of those standing in line at the post office reveals the customers of postage stamps to be decidedly old. Americans aged 55 or older are responsible for a disproportionate share of spending on postage today, according to the Consumer Expenditure Survey. During an average week, no one is more likely to buy postage than householders aged 55 or older.[20]

In 2005, for the first time, first-class mail fell from its number-one position in the volume of mail processed by the nation's post offices. Nevertheless, the postal service reported total mail volume reaching a record high that year. Mail volume set another record in 2006 and remained close to the record in 2007—despite the continuing decline in first-class volume. That can mean only one thing: the postal service is delivering more junk mail than ever.

Factoid source: United States Postal Service, Revenue, Pieces, and Weights Reports, http://www.usps.com/financials/rpw/ (accessed June 11, 2008).

NUMBER OF PAY PHONES
IN THE UNITED STATES: 1 MILLION

Would someone hand Jim Rockford a cell phone? The intrepid private eye, star of the 1970s television series *The Rockford Files* (now in syndication heaven on a television set near you), had the misfortune of working BCP— that's Before Cell Phones—forcing him to depend on pay phones to make his crucial calls to clients and police while on the run. The same technological woes beset Thomas Magnum of *Magnum, P.I.*, as well as *Miami Vice* detective Sonny Crockett, and every other cop and detective working the streets in the BCP era.

Fox Mulder and Dana Scully of *The X-Files* were more fortunate. They were on the job ACP—or After Cell Phones. When the series started in the early 1990s, few US households had a cell phone, giving the show a decidedly high-tech edginess.

Unlike Rockford, most of us are not stuck in the BCP era. We were born there, but emigrated to ACP as cell phone technology became cheap and ubiquitous. More than three out of four adults in the United States live in households with at least one cell phone, according to a study by the National Center for Health Statistics.[21]

It is a good thing that Jim Rockford has retired, because if he refused to use a cell phone (and, given his age, he just might), he would have a difficult time finding a pay phone today. The number of pay phones in the United States fell from 2 million in 1997 to 1 million in 2006, according to the FCC.[22] This makes life harder for the one in five Americans who have only landline phones or no phone at all. For those in need of a pay phone, several Internet sites are devoted to them in an obsessive sort of way.[23] The Pay Phone Directory lists 3,500 pay phones remaining in California—including 31 in Jim Rockford's old stomping ground, Malibu.

Factoid source: Federal Communications Commission, *Trends in Telephone Service* (Washington, DC: FCC, February 2007), pp. 7–11.

Chapter 20
PLAY

AVERAGE HOURS OF LEISURE PER DAY: 5

So you think you're working harder than ever? Pack up the tiny violins and cancel the pity party. Most academic studies show we have more leisure time today than in the past, or at least no less. It all depends on how you define "leisure." Does it include school? Caring for pets? Playing with kids? The statistics can be manipulated any which way—but the conclusion is the same: You are not working harder than your parents did.

Making the case that leisure time has increased is a study by the Federal Reserve Bank of Boston. The researchers examine changes in time use by men and women aged 21 to 65 over the past forty years.[1] Yes, women are more likely to have a job, but they are doing less housework. Yes, men are vacuuming more, but they are spending less time on the job. All told, the researchers conclude that men and women today have nearly seven more hours of leisure per week than their counterparts did in 1965.

Making the case that leisure time has been stable is a study by the National Bureau of Economic Research. Yes, we work fewer hours than we once did, but we are spending most of those work-free hours in school. Sitting in a classroom, taking a test, and writing a paper is not leisure time, say the researchers.[2] After accounting for schoolwork, they conclude that we have about the same amount of leisure time today as our counterparts did not just a generation ago, but a century ago.

Despite all this evidence to the contrary, Americans still believe they are overworked. The 59 percent majority says the average worker has to work harder today to earn a decent living than he did twenty or thirty years ago, according to the Pew Research Center.[3] Maybe it all depends on how you define "decent."

Factoid source: Bureau of Labor Statistics, 2006 American Time Use Survey, http://www.bls.gov/news.release/atus.toc.htm (accessed July 18, 2007).

ON A SCALE OF 1 TO 10, ACTIVITY AMERICANS RANK AS THE MOST ENJOYABLE: SEX

That's what you call a no-brainer. It is easy to name the activity Americans think is most enjoyable. But which activity ranks second, third, or fifth? Is doing the laundry more fun than paying bills? How does sleep compare with cooking? You might think no one would bother to ask simple questions like these, probing how much we like or dislike each of our daily activities, but you would be wrong. Social scientists have surveyed, recorded, and analyzed every minute of our 24-hour day as they try to describe the human condition.

Misery it is not. When survey researchers asked a representative sample of Americans to rate their daily activities by how much they enjoy doing them on a scale of 1 (least enjoyable) to 10 (most enjoyable), the average rating for all activities is a decidedly cheery 7.[4] In other words, most of us do not mind getting out of bed in the morning. But we do like being in bed more than anything else. Sex ranks as the single most enjoyable activity, with a rating of 9.3. Close behind is playing sports (9.2). Only two other activities rate above a 9.0—fishing, and participating in art or music. The least enjoyable activity is taking the car to a repair shop (4.6). Also below 5.0 on the scale are going to the doctor, doing the laundry, and cleaning the house. No surprises there.

But there are surprises elsewhere. Cooking ranks a below-average 6.6 on the scale, less enjoyable than going to work or attending meetings. People enjoy playing with children (8.8) much more than physically caring for children (6.4). They like to eat out (8.2), but they like to sleep even more (8.5). In fact, Americans enjoy sleeping more than they enjoy watching television (7.8)—maybe because the television puts them to sleep.

Factoid source: John P. Robinson and Geoffrey Godbey, *Time for Life: The Surprising Ways Americans Use Their Time* (University Park: Pennsylvania State University Press, 1997), p. 340.

PERCENTAGE WHO HAVE READ A BOOK
FOR PLEASURE IN THE PAST YEAR: 57

Maybe Oprah's book club explains it, or Harry Potter's magical spell, or the lure of the skinny latte. Whatever the reason, books appear to be surviving the Internet revolution—not unscathed, mind you, but for the most part intact. Yes, spending on books has fallen painfully. Between the pre-Internet year of 1991 and the decidedly post-Internet year of 2006, average household spending on books was down 28 percent, after adjusting for inflation.[5] This decline, while substantial, is so much less than the Tower-of-Terror-like plummet experienced by newspapers and magazines (down 60 percent) that book spending seems stable in comparison. As yet, there is no substitute for the efficiency and convenience of a printed book. Despite much fanfare each time a new "electronic book" is introduced, e-book sales have been slow at best.

The Internet has left scars, however. Americans are reading less than they once did—but not a lot less. According to a National Endowment for the Arts survey of reading, the percentage of Americans who had read a book for pleasure in the past year fell only slightly between 1992 and 2002, from 61 to 57 percent.[6] Even more important than the overall numbers are the healthy demographics of book readers. People of all ages—even young adults—are still drawn to books. Among 18- to 24-year-olds, a substantial 52 percent had read a book for pleasure in the past year. This was down from 59 percent in 1992, but the decline was surprisingly small considering the revolution in communications that occurred during the decade.

Who knows, maybe the old-fashioned activity of reading print on paper will survive the Internet. Reading still ranks among the top items on America's daily to-do list. In fact, if you take all the activities we do in a day and rank them by how much time we devote to each one, reading is an impressive number ten—well above computer use, in nineteenth place.[7]

Factoid source: National Endowment for the Arts, *To Read or Not to Read: A Question of National Consequence*, Research Report 47, November 2007, p. 7.

PERCENTAGE OF MEN WHO HUNT: 12

Where have all the manly men gone? ABC's *Monday Night Football* desperately wanted to know back in 2005 when its ratings skidded to an all-time low after thirty-five years of broadcasting. It gave up on football. Now others are wondering where men have gone. Fewer men are tramping through the fields with their hunting rifles, according to the latest survey from the US Fish and Wildlife Service. Nor are there as many men plying the waters, fishing pole in hand.

Even more dramatically, men appear to be taking up activities that would have made their father's lips curl in disgust. Case in point: bird-watching. Men these days are more likely to watch birds than shoot them. According to estimates from the National Survey of Fishing, Hunting, and Wildlife-Associated Recreation, the nation's bird-watchers outnumber hunters and fishermen combined.[8] Between 1996 and 2006, the number of anglers fell by 15 percent, to 30 million. The number of hunters fell by 10 percent, to 13 million. But bird-watching is a different story. The number *watching* wildlife increased by 13 percent during those years. Forty-eight million Americans have made a hobby of watching birds, nearly half of them men.

It seems obvious that our fathers, husbands, and sons are turning into what California governor and former body builder Arnold Schwarzenegger famously called "girly men." That would explain a few other things—like the fact that husbands have doubled the amount of time they spend caring for children and doing housework over the past few decades.[9] Or that only one in four men still thinks a woman's place is in the home.[10] Or that three out of four men believe it is more important for a man to spend time with his family than to be successful in his career.[11] Where have you gone, Joe DiMaggio?

Factoid source: Author's calculations based on National Sporting Goods Association, Sports Participation, http://www.nsga.org/public/pages/index.cfm?pageid=864 (accessed September 4, 2007).

ANNUAL NUMBER OF VACATION DAYS
FOR THE AVERAGE AMERICAN WORKER: 13

Something is wrong with this picture. Americans live in the third-largest country in the world, yet we have almost no time to travel the fifty states. The average worker gets only 13 days a year of vacation to explore the country's 3.7 million square miles. In contrast, the French are allotted 37 vacation days to see their much smaller 211,000 square miles. Maybe it is time for a new quality of life statistic, the Oh Say Can You See Indicator, calculated by dividing vacation days by square miles times one million. The higher the number the better. In France, the indicator is a lofty 175.4. In the United States, it is a measly 3.5. You can bet the French are much more familiar with their geography than we are with ours.

If you combine the stinginess of employers in doling out vacation days with the increasingly busy schedules of two-earner families, it is no wonder many Americans have seen little of the United States outside of airports and amusement parks. It also explains another sorry statistic. Although the US population is groaning past the 300 million mark, the number of visitors to the national parks has declined. The figure peaked at 287 million in 1999. By 2007 it had fallen to 276 million.[12] According to an Orbitz survey, 27 percent of Americans have not traveled at all in the past year.[13] Expedia finds only 14 percent of workers planning to take a full two weeks off at one time—the minimum required to see much of the United States.[14] The American road trip may be going the way of train travel—fondly remembered but rarely undertaken. Parks in the vast middle of the United States, such as Badlands National Park in South Dakota, are experiencing some of the greatest declines. Since hitting a peak of 1.5 million visitors in 1991, the number venturing into the Badlands has fallen by 42 percent. And it's not because of the name.

Factoid source: Infoplease.com, Average Number of Vacation Days Around the World Per Year, http://www .infoplease.com/ipa/A0922052.html (accessed July 21, 2007).

PERCENTAGE OF CHILDREN BICYCLING MORE THAN ONCE IN THE PAST YEAR: 40

Baseball, basketball, bicycling, ice hockey, skiing, soccer, softball, tennis, and volleyball: children are abandoning an alphabet soup of activities. The bicycle was once the way kids got around. No longer. Only 40 percent of children aged 7 to 11 have bicycled more than once in the past year, according to the National Sporting Goods Association, down from 57 percent ten years earlier.[15] The organization's annual surveys are finding steep declines in children's participation in a wide variety of sports.

Other studies show fewer children venturing outside at all. A survey by Hofstra University professor Rhonda Clements documents a seemingly precipitous decline in children's outdoor play.[16] She asked mothers with children aged 3 to 12 how often their child plays outdoors and how often the mother herself played outdoors as a child. While 70 percent of the mothers reported playing outside daily as a child, only 31 percent say their children play outside every day.

American children are auditioning for the role of couch potato for a number of reasons. The mothers surveyed by Clements faulted television and video games, but electronic media are not entirely to blame. Granted, kids have more to do indoors than ever before, and staying in touch with friends from a distance is easy with cell phones and instant messaging. But another and perhaps more likely reason children stay indoors is that the outdoors is lonely. Only about one-third of American households even include children under age 18, down from nearly half in 1950. Many children are in after-school care and not at home to play in the neighborhood. To meet up with their friends, kids must travel from one far-flung suburb to another, which means scheduling a play date and finding someone to drive—not an easy task now that both mom and dad go to work. According to a government survey of parents with children aged 9 to 13, transportation problems and a lack of time are two of the biggest obstacles to their children's participation in organized and free-time physical activities.[17]

Factoid source: National Sporting Goods Association, Research and Statistics, http://www.nsga.org (accessed August 12, 2007).

PERCENTAGE OF ADULTS EXERCISING VIGOROUSLY FOR AT LEAST TEN MINUTES DURING THE PAST WEEK: 39

Don't move. That appears to be our command as we sit mesmerized in front of our big-screen TV, drive to the mall and battle for the closest parking space, and eschew two-story houses because we do not want to climb stairs. It seems like we will do whatever we can to avoid exercise. Even the word "exercise" sounds ugly. We might talk the talk, but we don't walk the walk—literally. Perhaps the biggest clue to our true feelings about exercise is how much we have to force ourselves to do it. No one has to tell us to watch television, eat ice cream, or have sex. But we have to force ourselves—at the urging of the media, our doctor, and our spouse—to exercise. That's how much we hate it.

In the good old days, people exercised the natural way—while hunting for food. Mounting a treadmill and running a couple of miles while listening to "Stairway to Heaven" was entirely unnecessary. We are the most sedentary bunch of humans ever to lounge about the planet, which explains, in part, why most of us are overweight. In the past week, only 39 percent of Americans aged 18 or older engaged in even ten minutes of vigorous physical activity, according to the National Health Interview Survey.[18]

Other data confirm this finding. The National Sporting Goods Association finds our participation falling since the mid-1990s in many of our once favorite sports. Fewer people are riding bikes, swimming, playing tennis, or skiing.[19] A larger percentage of people are working out with equipment, but only 20 percent have done so more than once in the past year. Many of those who paid dearly for exercise equipment are probably using it as a clothes hanger. Exercise walking is the single most popular "sport" (note the air quotes), but only 33 percent participate.

How do we get ourselves moving again? How do we get off the couch, out of the car, up the stairs, and onto the treadmill? Don't hold your breath waiting for an answer.

Factoid source: National Center for Health Statistics, *Summary Health Statistics for U.S. Adults: National Health Interview Survey, 2006,* Vital and Health Statistics, Series 10, No. 235, Table 28.

PART V

YOUR BODY

Chapter 21
HEALTH

PERCENTAGE OF ADULTS WHOSE HEALTH IS EXCELLENT OR VERY GOOD: 54

We are living longer, but are we living better? The answer may be no. The percentage of adults who rate their health as excellent or very good has fallen by 4.5 percentage points since 1995. Although life expectancy in the United States is at a record high, the percentage reporting their health as very good or excellent is declining. These contradictory trends are an unexpected finding, and they call into question the basic paradigm of modern medicine—that improvements in diagnosis and treatment will result not just in a longer life, but in a better life too.

According to the federal government's Behavioral Risk Factor Surveillance System, the percentage of adults aged 18 or older who report being in excellent or very good health fell from 58.7 to 54.2 percent between 1995 and 2007.[1] The aging of the population explains some of the drop, but an examination of the trends by age reveals the greatest decline occurring among people aged 25 to 54 rather than the elderly.

A study by researchers at the University of Pennsylvania corroborates these findings. In an analysis of data from the Health and Retirement Study (HRS), the researchers examined the health of three cohorts of Americans as they approached retirement age. They conclude that today's 51- to 56-year-olds—baby boomers—are worse off than their parents were at the same age: "Boomers indicate they have relatively more difficulty with a range of everyday physical tasks, but they also report having more pain, more chronic conditions, more drinking and psychiatric problems, than their HRS earlier counterparts," they report.[2]

What accounts for this decline in health? The authors of the study offer several suggestions, such as the growing problem of obesity. Another possibility is that today's middle-aged complain more about health problems than previous generations. Or as the researchers phrase it: "younger cohorts are less accepting of physiological changes."[3] Interestingly, the middle-aged also report a worsening of their mental health.

Factoid source: Centers for Disease Control and Prevention, Behavioral Risk Factor Surveillance System, Prevalence Data, http://apps.nccd.cdc.gov/brfss/index.asp (accessed June 12, 2008).

DAYS OF POOR MENTAL HEALTH
IN THE PAST MONTH: 3.4

Feeling blue, depressed, stressed out? You are not alone. The average American is under the weather—mentally—more than three days a month. This is up from 2.9 days a little more than a decade ago in the early 1990s. The additional half-day of poor mental health may not seem like much of an increase, but it has raised alarms among researchers in the healthcare field. They want to know what's wrong. Why are Americans feeling stressed out and depressed more frequently than in the past?

Young adults experience the most mental health problems. People aged 18 to 24 are mentally under the weather an average of 4.3 days a month.[4] Their woes stem from the struggle to establish an identity. Typically, mental problems decline with age as things settle down. But this pattern has changed. The latest data show a spike in mental problems among the middle-aged. The number of poor mental health days has climbed steeply among 45- to 54-year-olds since the early 1990s, from 2.9 to 3.7. Now the 45-to-54 age group is second only to young adults in feeling depressed and stressed out.

What do the middle-aged have to complain about? Actually, the list is a long one. Here are a few of the entries. 1) Job insecurity: the percentage of men aged 45 to 49 who have worked for their employer for ten or more years fell from 51 to 43 percent during the past decade.[5] 2) Income insecurity: the median income of men aged 45 to 54 is lower today than it was in 2000, after adjusting for inflation.[6] 3) Housing insecurity: the homeownership rate of 45- to 54-year-olds actually fell between 2000 and 2006, the only age group to lose ground during the housing boom.[7] The middle-aged are in distress. They stand at the edge of a cliff with tech-savvy younger adults crowding them from behind and no safety net below to catch them if they fall.

Factoid source: Centers for Disease Control and Prevention, Health Related Quality of Life, Prevalence Data, http://apps.nccd.cdc.gov/HRQOL/ (accessed December 4, 2007).

PERCENTAGE OF AMERICANS UNDER AGE 65 WITHOUT HEALTH INSURANCE: 18

Considering everything, the percentage of Americans without health insurance is surprisingly low. In our employer-based system, finding a job with health insurance can be difficult. Paying for health insurance can be prohibitive. Given these problems, it is nothing short of miraculous that only 18 percent of the population under age 65 does not have insurance. (Nearly everyone aged 65 or older is covered by the federal government's Medicare program.)

Health insurance has become a massive game of musical chairs. Among Americans under age 65, only 32 percent have employer-provided health insurance from their own job, according to the Current Population Survey.[8] Another 31 percent have snagged a seat only through the employer-provided benefits of spouses, partners, or parents. The government's health insurance program for the poor, Medicaid, covers an additional 13 percent. Only 7 percent of people under age 65 can afford to buy their own individual health insurance policies.

Our economy and family life are contorted by the effort to grab a seat in the health insurance game. The insurance conundrum has lowered our rate of self-employment below that of most other developed countries.[9] It forces parents with young children into full-time jobs because part-time work is rarely covered by insurance. Married couples must decide which spouse will provide the health insurance, which puts many in the perilous position of being a divorce away from losing coverage. No wonder the 56 percent majority of the public worries about losing health insurance because of a job loss.[10]

Despite all these concerns, the federal government has yet to address the health insurance problem in any meaningful way. It is no mystery where the "What, me worry?" attitude comes from. Congress is covered by the federal government's premier health insurance plan. And anyone ever elected to the House or Senate, after only five years of service, continues to receive this coverage—even if thrown out of office—until eligible at age 65 for Medicare.[11]

Factoid source: Bureau of the Census, 2007 Current Population Survey Annual Social and Economic Supplement, Health Insurance Coverage: 2006, http://pubdb3 .census.gov/macro/032007/health/toc.htm (accessed September 21, 2007).

AVERAGE ANNUAL OUT-OF-POCKET SPENDING BY HOUSEHOLDS ON PRESCRIPTION DRUGS: $393

Americans are popping more pills than ever. Prescription drug use is on the rise as drug companies create a growing array of must-have magic bullets. Nearly half the public—45 percent—took a prescription drug in the past month, up from 38 percent a decade earlier according to government surveys.[12] Prescription drug use is especially common among the elderly, 85 percent of whom took a prescription drug in the past month.

The high cost of prescription drugs can be a shock at the pharmacy counter, leading to calls for the greater use of cheaper generic drugs. This solution may be shortsighted, however, because generics are, by definition, years behind the times. It can take a decade or more before a drug's patent expires and generic equivalents enter the market. Limiting your prescription drug use to generics is like installing Windows 98 on your computer. It might run, but it won't be up to speed.

If you compare the cost of a new drug with the financial benefits that result from its greater effectiveness, the decision on which drug to use is a no-brainer, according to Columbia University economist Frank Lichtenberg. The benefits of new drugs, in fact, are eight times greater than their cost.[13] In a study for the National Bureau of Economic Research, Lichtenberg compared the healthcare expenses of Medicare beneficiaries over a three-year period by health condition and prescription drug use. The beneficiaries using newer drugs spent much less on doctor visits and hospitalizations than those using older drugs. The savings more than made up for the additional expense of the newer drug. This finding was even more important: "People consuming new drugs," says Lichtenberg, "were significantly less likely to die by the end of the survey than people consuming older drugs."[14]

Factoid source: Bureau of Labor Statistics, unpublished tables from the 2006 Consumer Expenditure Survey.

PERCENTAGE WITH A DISABILITY
HIGH SCHOOL GRADUATES: 19
COLLEGE GRADUATES: 8

Can you walk a quarter mile? Are you in a wheelchair? Can you hear normal conversation? Are you able to climb, stand, sit, stoop, reach, grasp, lift, push, pull? Can you manage your bills? Go grocery shopping? Are you missing a limb, an eye? Do you use crutches? Can you work? Do you have trouble getting along with others? These are just some of the questions used to identify the nation's disabled population. Defining disability, identifying the disabled, and making sense of disability statistics is a heroic but often futile task because there are no generally agreed-upon definitions or counts of the disabled. Disability statistics are a big mess, and unavoidably so. That is what you get when you try to measure how people feel.

Amid the confusion about disability there is one certainty: things are going to change. But no one can agree on the direction of change. Academics in the field are finding evidence to support both an increase and a decrease in disability in the years ahead. On the one hand, data from the Health and Retirement Study show higher rates of disability among people aged 51 to 56 today compared to earlier cohorts.[15] A Rand Corporation Study projects a rise in disability rates because of obesity.[16] But other researchers find disability rates falling among the elderly, a consequence of their growing educational attainment. Nothing improves health like a college degree, with the college educated less than half as likely as high school graduates to be disabled. Education may make a difference because it gives people "the ability to navigate the health care system and implement complex medical regimens," suggest social scientists.[17]

Ultimately, whether disability rates rise or fall depends on how many people decide they are disabled. That threshold is constantly changing as modern medicine creates new pills and more props to turn many disabling conditions into mild inconveniences.

Factoid source: National Center for Health Statistics, *Summary Health Statistics for U.S. Adults: National Health Interview Survey, 2006*, Series 10, No. 235, 2007, Table 18.

PERCENTAGE OF SURGERIES
PERFORMED ON OUTPATIENTS: 63

A couple of decades ago, the average patient remained in the hospital for more than one week. Those were the days when doctors were in charge and nursing professionals cared for the ailing during their recovery from sickness or surgery. Today, the average length of a hospital stay is less than five days. The length of stay for almost every procedure has fallen over the past few decades. For childbirth, women are in the hospital for only 2.6 days today, down from 3.8 days in 1980. After a heart attack, the number of days patients spend in a hospital has declined from 12.6 to just 5.5.[18] Chances are, if you are scheduled to have surgery, you will not spend even one night in the hospital. The percentage of surgeries performed on outpatients has climbed from just 16 percent in 1980 to fully 63 percent today.[19]

What accounts for this fundamental change in hospital care? Money, of course. Health insurance companies pressure hospitals to discharge patients as soon as possible to cut costs. Treatment protocols have changed too because doctors have discovered patients recover more quickly the sooner they are up and around. No more lying in bed while trained professionals take care of you. Families now bear the burden of patient care.

Does it matter that your wife rather than a nurse is in charge of your postoperative care? The answer, apparently, is *no*. There has been no up-tick in death rates associated with shortened hospital stays. To the contrary, mortality rates are falling and life expectancy is on the rise. A longitudinal study by researchers at Northwestern University's Feinberg School of Medicine finds no evidence of an increase in death rates among Medicare beneficiaries discharged from hospitals for six different conditions as the length of hospital stays fell over the years.[20] The study comes to the reassuring conclusion that financial pressure on hospitals to reduce length of stays has not harmed the health of patients. We have our families to thank for that.

Factoid source: American Hospital Association Annual Survey of Hospitals, reprinted in National Center for Health Statistics, *Health, United States, 2007* (Washington, DC: US Government Printing Office, 2007), p. 352.

PERCENTAGE OF 14-YEAR-OLDS
WITH BRACES: 17

Two physical characteristics distinguish Americans from other people around the world: our excessive weight and our great teeth. Yes, teeth. While British teeth are objects of ridicule on the international stage (much like American bottoms), our teeth are widely admired for being clean, white, and straight. We pay dearly for our Hollywood smiles. Dental insurance is not included in the typical health insurance plan, making a trip to the dentist a financial as well as a physical ordeal. We must dig deep in our pockets to keep up with our teeth.

Dental care ranks third in the household health care budget following only health insurance and prescription drugs. The average household spent $239 out-of-pocket on dental bills in 2006.[21] We spend more going to the dentist than we do going to the movies, which is where we are subjected to all those Hollywood starlets with the great teeth. Maybe that's why we are willing to spend so much on dental care. Most of us see a dentist at least once a year—60 percent of adults and 76 percent of children, evidence of how much importance we place on our teeth.[22]

Money determines who gets to sit in the dentist's chair. Most low-income Americans see a dentist only sporadically, while most high-income Americans go every six months. Among adults with household incomes below $20,000, most have not seen a dentist in more than a year. Among those with incomes of $75,000 or more, most have seen a dentist in the past six months.[23]

Good teeth have long differentiated rich from poor, but the gap may be growing as expensive whitening and straightening become de rigueur in suburbia. Those teens in braces are the mark of money, as much of a status symbol as the Lexus in the driveway.

Factoid source: US Department of Health and Human Services, Agency for Healthcare Research and Quality, Medical Expenditure Panel Survey, Household Component, http://www.meps.ahrq.gov/mepsweb/survey_comp/household.jsp (accessed June 12, 2008).

DECLINE IN THE NUMBER OF NURSING HOME RESIDENTS DURING THE PAST FIVE YEARS: DOWN 136,100

You read it right. Despite the aging of the population, the number of nursing home residents is shrinking, down by more than 100,000 in the past five years. The number of nursing homes is also declining. Where have all the old people gone?

They have found something better to do. Thanks to the heroic efforts of family caretakers and the innovative ideas of businesses, a growing number of the frail elderly are living successfully in their own home or in assisted living facilities. According to the federal government's latest National Nursing Home Survey, the percentage of people aged 65 or older living in a nursing home fell from 4.3 to 3.6 percent between 1999 and 2004.[24] This decline took many by surprise because a rapid expansion of the nursing home population had been predicted due to the aging of the population.

The rise of assisted living facilities—where aging residents live independently in apartments, receiving a variety of housekeeping and healthcare services—explains much of the decline. Unfortunately, there is no official count of the number of people living in assisted living facilities. Rough estimates by the Department of Health and Human Services put the number at about 750,000.[25] The growing popularity of assisted living shows how, with a little help, the frail elderly can remain in their communities, reducing the cost of elder care and improving quality of life. But this can happen only when family and friends are willing to help out. And they are. According to a survey of caregiving, 16 percent of Americans provide unpaid care for someone aged 50 or older.[26] The federal government estimates that 10 million Americans need help with daily tasks such as bathing, dressing, preparing meals, paying bills, and doing housework.[27] Almost all of them get the help they need. Only 11 percent have to pay for it.

Factoid source: National Center for Health Statistics, Trends in Nursing Homes, http://www.cdc.gov/nchs/about/major/nnhsd/Trendsnurse.htm (accessed May 1, 2007).

Chapter 22
WEIGHT

PERCENTAGE OF AMERICANS
WHO ARE OVERWEIGHT: 66

When the United States government reports that Americans have a weight problem, it does not base this finding on anecdotal evidence gathered in a shopping mall. Nor is it based on how many pounds men and women say they weigh. The fact is, when Americans self-report their weight, the numbers come in notoriously shy of the truth because we are in denial about our weight. To counter this problem, the government must spend a lot of money figuring out the facts, literally hitting the road to measure the height and weight of a representative sample of the population.

Here are your tax dollars at work: on any given day, researchers from the National Center for Health Statistics fan out across the country, testing and measuring the public in special mobile examination units—part of the ongoing National Health and Nutrition Examination Survey. Technicians measure the height and weight of a nationally representative sample of Americans to determine their body mass index, or BMI. The BMI is calculated by dividing weight in kilograms by height in meters squared. It sounds complex, but the results are revealing. The BMI calculation determines whether we are underweight, in the healthy weight range, or overweight. According to these measurements, only 32 percent of adults are in the healthy weight range.[1] Fully 66 percent are overweight.

Do Americans recognize the problem they have on their hands—and hips and waistlines? Yes and no. The Pew Research Center has discovered that the public's attitude toward weight is similar to its attitude toward many other important issues. They see the problem—but only on the other guy. Nine out of ten Americans acknowledge that most people are overweight, according to Pew.[2] But only 39 percent say they, themselves, are overweight.

Factoid source: National Center for Health Statistics, *Health, United States, 2007* (Washington, DC: US Government Printing Office, 2007), p. 288.

WEIGHT OF THE AVERAGE AMERICAN WOMAN: 163 POUNDS

The average American woman gained 19 pounds over the past twenty-five years, according to measurements taken by the National Health and Nutrition Examination Survey. The average man gained 17 pounds during those years and now weighs 190. While remarkable, these gains pale in comparison to those revealed by cohort analysis—an examination of the weight gain for a group of people born at the same time. A cohort analysis shows that the weight Americans are gaining is not distributed evenly across the population, but is much greater for some groups than for others. In particular, the baby-boom generation, born between 1946 and 1964, has put on much more weight than its parents.[3]

Take a look at what happened to boomer men. A quarter century ago, the average man aged 20 to 29 (this cohort includes most of the oldest boomers) weighed 168 pounds. Today, the same man (now in his forties) weighs 196 pounds. During those years, he gained a stunning 28 pounds. In contrast, men in his father's birth cohort gained less than half that weight—a smaller 12 pounds.

For boomer women, the picture is even more alarming. A quarter century ago, the average woman aged 20 to 29 weighed 136 pounds. Today, the same woman (now in her forties) weighs 168 pounds. She is 32 pounds heavier than she used to be. This weight gain exceeds that of her male counterparts and is more than double the weight gain experienced by her mother's birth cohort over those years.

Worse, boomers seem to have passed the problem on to their children. Today's 20- to 29-year-olds already weigh 16 to 21 pounds more than boomers weighed as young adults. And they have yet to hit middle age when the spread begins in earnest.

Factoid source: National Center for Health Statistics, *Mean Body Weight, Height, and Body Mass Index, United States 1960–2002,* Advance Data No. 347, October 27, 2004, p. 8.

PERCENTAGE OF WOMEN
WHO ARE TRYING TO LOSE WEIGHT: 32

The average woman will not tell you how much she really weighs. You can accuse her of lying, indulging in wishful thinking—or maybe embracing the popular principal of truthiness. It doesn't matter. She knows what she wants to weigh, and the facts be damned. Women carve several pounds from reality when reporting their weight, according to a Gallup survey.[4] Women say they weigh 156 pounds, but the government's measurements show reality to be a larger 163. Even after falsifying the record, however, their proportions remain far from ideal. Women say their ideal weight is 138 pounds, according to Gallup.

Men are not immune from the pressure to stretch the truth to make themselves feel better, if not look better. A Pew Research Center survey finds men adding inches to their height. Men say they are 5 feet, 11 inches tall, on average, according to Pew.[5] But government measurements show the average American man, in fact, to be just 5 feet, 9 inches in height.

With the average woman actually weighing a full 25 pounds more than her ideal weight, you would think most would be trying to shed pounds. Sales of diet books, diet supplements, low-fat foods, gym memberships, and exercise equipment seem to suggest that Americans are taking charge. Well, maybe not so much. Yes, many are throwing money at the problem, but few have committed themselves to changing the numbers when they step on the scale. According to the Gallup survey, the 68 percent majority of women would like to lose weight but only 32 percent are actively trying to lose pounds. The rest have chosen the easy way out by moving the goalpost. Since Gallup first asked the question in 1990, the average woman's ideal weight has increased by nine pounds.

Factoid source: Gallup Poll, "Personal Weight Situation," http://www.gallup.com/poll/7264/Personal-Weight -Situation.aspx (accessed June 12, 2008).

AVERAGE HEIGHT OF AMERICAN MEN: 5' 9"

Ask the man on the street to list the reasons why Americans weigh more than they did twenty-five years ago and one reason he might suggest is that they are taller. It is a common misconception. After all, since life expectancy has been climbing one would assume height (and therefore weight) should be increasing too.

Nice try, but no cigar. Yes, life expectancy has been rising steadily over the past century, but we have not been getting taller along with those extra years. Since 1900, life expectancy at birth grew from 47 years to the record high of 78 years today. At the same time, the height of (native-born) American men climbed from 170 centimeters in 1900 to 177 centimeters in 1950. Then our height stalled, according to Richard Steckel, professor of economics at Ohio State University and one of the leading experts on trends in height.[6]

American men were the tallest in the world for more than two centuries. But when we stopped getting taller, we lost our number-one position. Men in the United States are now significantly shorter than men in Belgium, the Czech Republic, Denmark, Germany, the Netherlands, Norway, and Sweden, according to an analysis by John Komlos and Benjamin E. Lauderdale in *Social Science Quarterly*.[7] They find significant height differences between Americans and Europeans even after limiting their analysis to native-born whites and blacks, excluding Hispanics and Asians. The Dutch are now the tallest men in the world, they report, surpassing American men by two inches.

What stopped our growth? Steckel's historical research shows a population's height is directly related to socioeconomic conditions such as nutrition and health care. Komlos and Lauderdale suggest fast food and limited access to health care in the United States as possible factors. More recently, the height of Americans has begun to increase again, but relative to our European counterparts we are still—literally—coming up short.

Factoid source: National Center for Health Statistics, *Mean Body Weight, Height, and Body Mass Index, United States 1960–2002,* Advance Data No. 347, October 27, 2004, p. 10.

PERCENTAGE OF DOCTOR VISITS IN WHICH PATIENTS ARE ADVISED TO LOSE WEIGHT: 5

We are in denial about our weight, and we have run out of excuses to explain away the gains. But don't think the medical establishment will help us control the problem. Few patients are lectured about their weight at the doctor's office. Among the nearly 1 million visits Americans made to a physician in 2005, only 15 percent included patient counseling on diet and nutrition, a smaller 11 percent received information about exercise, and a tiny 5 percent heard advice about losing weight.[8]

It is not that doctors are hesitant about giving advice. For proof, just ask smokers, 61 percent of whom have been told by a doctor in the past year to quit smoking.[9] Doctors are more than willing to give advice about smoking because fewer than 6 percent of them smoke, according to a survey by Mathematica Policy Research.[10] When it comes to smoking, doctors are good role models.

Doctors are not good role models for the overweight, however. They, like most Americans, tip the scales, making their advice about the importance of weight loss more than a bit suspect. A survey of physicians and their attitudes toward obesity published in the journal *Obesity Research* found the average body mass index of doctors to be just over the line at 25.5, placing most of them in the overweight category.[11] One in eight is obese, with a body mass index of 30.0 or higher. The fact that many doctors are as fat as their patients doesn't keep them from thinking unkind thoughts about the person on the exam table, however. The majority of the surveyed doctors think the obese are unattractive and weak willed. "Primary care physicians view obesity as largely a behavioral problem and share our broader society's negative stereotypes about the personal attributes of obese persons," the authors conclude.[12] Physician, heal thyself.

Factoid source: National Center for Health Statistics, *National Ambulatory Medical Care Survey: 2005 Summary*, Advance Data No. 387, 2007, p. 30.

NUMBER OF CALORIES CONSUMED PER DAY
BY THE AVERAGE AMERICAN WOMAN: 1,884

Why have Americans gained so much weight over the past twenty-five years? Only two factors can explain the increase. We are either eating more or exercising less. An analysis by the National Bureau of Economic Research finds overeating to be the bigger part of the problem, accounting for more than 75 percent of our weight gain.[13] Just how much more are we eating? A survey by the federal government shows the average woman consuming 1,884 calories a day, up from the 1,525 calories consumed by the average woman twenty-five years ago.[14] Do the math and that's an additional 359 calories a day—the equivalent of a cheeseburger. The average man has boosted his daily caloric intake by 238 calories over the past twenty-five years—or the equivalent of a small order of French fries.

Some researchers think restaurant meals themselves are behind America's weight gain. Another study by the National Bureau of Economic Research shows that the more restaurants per capita, the greater a population's weight gain over the past quarter century. In "The Super Size of America: An Economic Estimation of Body Mass Index and Obesity in Adults," the researchers found that 54 percent of the increase in Americans' body mass index between 1976 and 2000 can be explained by the increase in restaurants per capita.[15] "The existence of numerous restaurants per capita facilitates caloric intake," the NBER researchers conclude.

The authors do not know why weight gain is linked to restaurant density, but here is a theory: As fast food became part of the daily diet, and as the number of fast-food restaurants grew, Americans ate out more often and ate more whenever they ate out. The increasingly fierce competition among restaurants for customers created an arms race of sorts, boosting portion size to get people in the door. Bigger portions mean more calories and growing waistlines.

Factoid source: National Center for Health Statistics, *Health, United States, 2007* (Washington, DC: US Government Printing Office, 2007), p. 285.

PERCENTAGE OF TEENAGERS WHO EAT FAST FOOD ON AN AVERAGE DAY: 48

Fast food is as American as apple pie. In fact, fast-food restaurants even sell apple pie, or something approximating it. Burgers, fries, and sodas have become American staples because working mothers no longer have time to cook family meals. That explains why the busiest people—parents with children—are the best customers of fast-food restaurants.[16] And it explains why the people most likely to eat in fast-food restaurants—parents with children—are the ones gaining the most weight.

For every dollar that married couples with children spend in restaurants, they hand over nearly half of it—44 cents—at the fast-food counter. Single parents devote an even larger 53 percent of their restaurant dollars to fast food.[17] Now you know why nearly half of teenagers eat fast food on an average day, according to the California Health Interview Survey. Among black teenagers—whose mothers are most likely to work—the 58 percent majority eat fast food every day.[18] Don't forget the soda. Two-thirds of teenagers drink a (non-diet) soda every day. According to a study in the journal *Pediatrics*, teenagers who eat fast food on a given day consume 379 more calories than those who do not.[19]

When the Pew Research Center asked the public to explain why so many Americans are overweight, the largest share—75 percent—said it was a lack of exercise.[20] But they are wrong, according to an analysis by the National Bureau of Economic Research.[21] Overeating is the far more important factor, accounting for three-quarters of our weight gain over the past few decades. Two all-beef patties with all the works is the modern-day siren song. The only mystery is how one-third of the population has managed to maintain a healthy weight.

Factoid source: Theresa A. Hastert et al., "More California Teens Consume Soda and Fast Food Each Day Than Five Servings of Fruits and Vegetables," *UCLA Health Policy Research Brief*, September 2005, p. 1.

Chapter 23
DEATH

LIFE EXPECTANCY AT BIRTH
1900: 47 YEARS
2006: 78 YEARS

You can always spot the demographer at a cocktail party. He is the guest in the corner earnestly discussing life and death. One of the finest arrows in his quiver of conversation starters is life expectancy—how many years you can expect to live.

Here is the boring part: Life expectancy is a statistical measure of the average length of life based on age-specific mortality rates in a given year. Life expectancy at birth has grown by more than thirty years since 1900 because medical science has conquered many infectious diseases. Our ancestors did not drop dead at the age of 47. Some of them lived well into old age. But so many people died in infancy and childhood that the average length of life was pulled down to 47.

Here is the interesting part: Life expectancy is growing at every age—which means you are likely to live longer than you might have a few decades ago. Life expectancy at age 65, for example, has grown from 12 years in 1900 to 19 years today.[1] This seven-year gain is one reason Congress increased the age at which older Americans could claim full Social Security benefits, boosting the age of eligibility from 65 to 67 for people born in 1960 or later.

But, you protest, this means the frail elderly will be hobbling into the office. Not so, says the cocktail party demographer. His colleagues have gone beyond straightforward life expectancy calculations to determine how many hale and hearty years people have left—or, what demographers call "healthy" life expectancy. At age 65, Americans can expect about half their remaining years to be free of disability.[2] In other words, they have about ten good years left—and since fewer can afford to retire, many people will be spending those years in the office.

Factoid source: National Center for Health Statistics, *Health United States, 2007* (Washington, DC: US Government Printing Office, 2007): p. 175; and *Deaths: Preliminary Data for 2006*, http://www.cdc.gov/nchs/deaths.htm (accessed June 12, 2008).

LEADING CAUSE OF DEATH IN THE
UNITED STATES: HEART DISEASE

You don't have to be a doctor to figure out what's going to kill you. Just take a look at the leading causes of death, a list published each year by the federal government. More than 2 million Americans die each year, and heart disease is at the top of the list.

The cause-of-death list looked very different in 1900, when the number-one-killer was the category "pneumonia and influenza."[3] Second was tuberculosis, and in third place diarrhea. Back then, heart disease ranked only fourth as a cause of death.

But heart disease was on the move. It became the leading cause of death in 1910 and has been number-one ever since, except for the years 1918, 1919, and 1920 when the Spanish flu pushed influenza to the top. Year after year, the heart disease death rate climbed as it consolidated its power. The rate peaked in 1963 at 375.5 deaths per 100,000 population. Then, to the surprise of all, the scourge began to recede. The death rate fell slowly at first, then with increasing speed. Today, the death rate from heart disease (210.2 deaths per 100,000 population) is 44 percent below the 1963 peak. Research shows lifestyle change to be the most important reason for the decline— Americans are less likely to smoke, have lowered their cholesterol, and are controlling their blood pressure.

Don't get too excited, however. Even if we could eliminate heart disease entirely, our life expectancy would rise by only a few years. That is because we are pushing life expectancy to the biological limit of the human life span. According to James F. Fries of Stanford University School of Medicine, the life span—which he defines as "the average longevity in a society without disease or accident"—is somewhere between 85 and 100 years.[4] Others disagree, arguing there may be no maximum. Chances are, something on the list will get us before we ever know who's right.

Factoid source: National Center for Health Statistics, *Deaths: Preliminary Data for 2006*, National Vital Statistics Reports, Vol. 56, No. 16, June 11, 2008, p. 5.

NUMBER OF AMERICAN WOMEN DYING FROM PREGNANCY OR CHILDBIRTH IN 2006: 787

Until recently, childbirth was a leading cause of death among women in the United States. Today, it is close to the bottom of a very long list of causes, not far above death row executions. If childbirth were as risky today as it was less than a century ago, then more than 25,000 women, rather than 787, would have died giving birth in 2006.[5] By virtually eliminating the risks of childbirth, medical science has boosted women's life expectancy. But this is not why women live longer than men.

The most recent calculations by the federal government show life expectancy at birth to be five years greater for females (80.7 years) than for males (75.4 years).[6] The size of the gap has fluctuated over the years, but the gap itself existed long before death from childbirth fell to the bottom of the cause-of-death list. Documentation of the longer life expectancy of females extends back hundreds of years, and the female advantage occurs in almost every country in the world.

In 1900, females born in the United States could expect to live about three years longer than males.[7] The life expectancy gap grew over the decades as the risks of dying in childbirth were reduced. Between 1970 and 1990, the gap was at least seven years. Since then, the gap has been reduced along with mortality rates from heart disease.

But the gap has not gone away—nor will it, according to researchers who have studied the matter. Daniel L. Kruger and Randolph M. Nesse, writing in *Evolutionary Psychology*, say the difference is rooted in evolutionary biology. Males—particularly young adults—compete with one another through risk-taking behavior to attract females. Those risks shorten men's lives. "Being male is now the single largest demographic risk factor for early mortality in developed countries," the researchers conclude.[8]

Factoid source: National Center for Health Statistics, *Deaths: Preliminary Data for 2006*, National Vital Statistics Reports, Vol. 56, No. 16, June 11, 2008, p. 19.

INCREASE IN LIFE EXPECTANCY FOR EACH ADDITIONAL YEAR OF EDUCATION: 7 MONTHS

Something is going on, but no one can explain it. Mortality rates are falling for the US population as a whole, but they remain stubbornly high among the least educated. After controlling for age, those without a high school diploma are three times more likely to die in a given year than those with at least some college experience.[9]

So what else is new? Even the man on the street would wager, correctly, that high school dropouts are not as healthy as the college crowd. They can see with their own eyes what the research shows: The less educated fare poorly on almost every measure of health, including self-reported health status, disability, obesity, and chronic conditions such as arthritis, heart conditions, and asthma. That's what you get when you behave badly, says the man on the street. The less educated are more likely to smoke, drink, use illegal drugs, and forego seat belts. It all seems so obvious, except for one thing: bad behavior does not explain the gap. Even after controlling for risky behavior, differences in health by education persist. They persist even when controlling for income, health insurance status, age, race, and gender. There seems to be some mystery factor—call it the X factor—linking education to better health and higher life expectancy.

Maybe this does require further study. When social scientists David M. Cutler and Adriana Lleras-Muney pursued the X factor with a one-two punch of data analysis and a massive literature review, they came up with no definitive answer but an intriguing possibility—the educated think differently. "Education might matter for health not just because of the specific knowledge one obtains in school," they suggest, "but rather because education improves general skills, including critical thinking skills and decision-making abilities."[10] Their conclusion: more research is necessary.

Factoid source: David M. Cutler and Adriana Lleras-Muney, *Education and Health: Evaluating Theories and Evidence*, National Bureau of Economic Research, NBER Working Paper 12352, June 2006, p. 21.

LIFETIME ODDS OF DYING IN AN ACCIDENT: 1 IN 34

No wonder they made a movie called *Snakes on a Plane*. Snakes rank number one on the list of things that scare people the most, with 36 percent of Americans saying they are very afraid of them, according to a Harris Poll.[11] Yet the lifetime odds of dying by snake bite are minuscule—just one in 628,000. Dogs are also on the fright list, although only 2 percent of the public is very afraid of them. Yet death by dog bite is four times more likely than death by snake.[12]

Every year in the United States, more than 100,000 people die an accidental death, which makes accidents the fifth most important cause of death, following the diseases of old age—heart disease, cancer, stroke, and chronic respiratory disease. Whether you die by snake or dog bite, it will be duly noted in the official mortality tables—the government's meticulous recording of every death. In the accident category, the government tracks more than 500 different causes.[13] Take the most common cause of accidental death, the car crash, for example. When the government says car, it means car—not pickup truck, SUV, motorcycle, bus, streetcar, tractor, or all-terrain vehicle, each of which gets its own listing. On top of that, the government parses car crashes into collisions with pickup trucks, buses, trains, and so on—more than sixty deadly combinations. The list rivals a Stephen King novel for horror.

According to the government's mortality tables, 27 people died by dog bite in the United States in 2004—cause of death classification W54. Only six people died by snake bite (cause of death classification X20). Fortunately, no one died that year from cause of death W59—getting crushed by a snake.

Factoid source: National Safety Council, "The Odds of Dying From . . ." http://www.nsc.org/research/odds.aspx (accessed June 12, 2008).

AFTERWORD

My editor warned me not to end this book on a down note. The last sentence—the one about getting crushed by a snake—comes pretty close to being a bummer. Yuck. So, to lighten the mood, I am adding these few paragraphs to reassure you that your future is most probably snake free. In fact, you have bigger problems than snakes—the biggest being your status as a high-flying American in a world being leveled by the Internet.

Does this mean you are doomed? Far from it. Does it mean your life will change? Yes, and it already has. If you don't feel it, your children most certainly will as household incomes lag behind the rising cost of a middle-class lifestyle. Does this mean your life and the lives of your children will be less than you hoped? Not necessarily. Individual Americans will prosper despite and because of the changing status of our place in the world. Prosperity will just have to be redefined. That's the work we have to do.

By now, you have probably heard enough. So I'm stepping down from the soapbox and leaving you, at long last, in silence. But for those who can't get enough (you know who you are), and for those who, in the days ahead, hunger for the real story, the news behind the numbers, take refuge in my blog, DemoMemo.blogspot.com. There, I will be telling all who wander by their life story from a demographer's perspective.

NOTES

CHAPTER. 1 FAMILY

1. Bureau of the Census, *Historical Statistics of the United States: Colonial Times to 1970, Part 1* (Washington, DC: US Government Printing Office, 1975), pp. 53, 56.

2. Frank Newport et al., "Americans and Their Pets," Gallup Poll, December 21, 2006, http://www.gallup.com/poll/25969/Americans-Their-Pets.aspx (accessed November 25, 2007).

3. American Veterinary Medical Association, *U.S. Pet Ownership and Demographics Sourcebook, 2002*, as reported in Bureau of the Census, *Statistical Abstract of the United States: 2007* (Washington, DC: US Government Printing Office, 2007), p. 765.

4. Bureau of Labor Statistics, unpublished tables from the 2005 American Time Use Survey.

5. Author's calculations based on Bureau of Labor Statistics, unpublished tables from the 2000 and 2006 Consumer Expenditure Surveys.

6. Stephanie Coontz, *The Way We Never Were* (New York: Basic Books, 1992), p. 25.

7. Bureau of the Census, *Historical Statistics*, p. 50.

8. Bureau of the Census, Families and Living Arrangements, Historical Time Series—Families, http://www.census.gov/population/www/socdemo/hh-fam.html (accessed September 16, 2007).

9. Bureau of the Census, *Examining American Household Composition: 1990 and 2000*, Census 2000 Special Report CENSR-24 (Washington, DC: US Government Printing Office, 2005), p. 22.

10. Survey Documentation and Analysis, Computer-Assisted Survey Methods Program, University of California, Berkeley, General Social Surveys, 1972–2006 Cumulative Data Files, GSS Variable KIDJOY, http://sda.berkeley.edu/cgi-bin32/hsda?harcsda+gss06 (accessed September 25, 2007).

11. National Center for Health Statistics, *Fertility, Family Planning, and Reproductive Health of U.S. Women: Data from the 2002 National Survey of Family Growth*, Vital and Health Statistics, Series 23, No. 25, 2005, p. 7.

12. National Center for Health Statistics, *Fertility, Contraception, and Fatherhood: Data on Men and Women from Cycle 6 of the 2002 National Survey of Family Growth*, Vital and Health Statistics, Series 23, No. 26, 2006, pp. 120–21.

13. Ibid., pp. 110–11.

14. Daniel Gilbert, *Stumbling on Happiness* (New York: Vintage Books, 2007), p. 242.

15. Ibid., p. 243–44.

16. Bureau of the Census, "Median and Average Sales Prices of New One-Family Homes Sold in United States," http://www.census.gov/const/www/charindex.html#sold; Historical Income Data, http://www.census.gov/hhes/www/income/histinc/p38ar.html; and 2007 Current Population Survey Annual Social and Economic Supplement, http://pubdb3.census.gov/macro/032007/perinc/new05_000.htm (accessed November 25, 2007).

17. Survey Documentation and Analysis, Computer-Assisted Survey Methods Program, University of California, Berkeley, General Social Surveys, 1972–2006 Cumulative Data Files, GSS Variables FECHLD and FEPRESCH, http://sda.berkeley.edu/cgibin32/hsda?harcsda+gss06 (accessed September 25, 2007).

18. National Center for Education Statistics, National Household Education Survey, Initial Results from the 2005 NHES Early Childhood Program Participation Survey, http://nces.ed.gov/pubs2006/earlychild/tables.asp (accessed February 18, 2007).

19. Survey Documentation and Analysis, Computer-Assisted Survey Methods Program, University of California, Berkeley, General Social Surveys, 1972–2006 Cumulative Data Files, GSS Variable MAWRKGRW, http://sda.berkeley.edu/cgi-bin32/hsda?harcsda+gss06 (accessed September 16, 2007).

20. National Center for Education Statistics, National Household Education Survey, Initial Results from the 2005 NHES Early Childhood Program Participation Survey, http://nces.ed.gov/pubs2006/earlychild/tables.asp (accessed February 18, 2007).

21. Ibid.

22. Bureau of the Census, "A Child's Day: 2004 (Selected Indicators of Child Well-being), Survey Income and Program Participation," detailed tables, http://www.census.gov/population/www/socdemo/2004_detailedtables.html (accessed October 31, 2007).

23. J. Duke, "Physical Activity Levels among Children Aged 9 to 13—United States, 2002," *Mortality and Morbidity Weekly Report* 52 (August 22, 2003): 785–88.

24. Bureau of the Census, "A Child's Day: 2004."

25. Bureau of the Census, "School Enrollment, October 2005," detailed tables, http://www.census.gov/population/www/socdemo/school/cps2005.html (accessed February 19, 2007).

26. Bureau of the Census, "A Child's Day: 2004."

27. Survey Documentation and Analysis, Computer-Assisted Survey Methods Program, University of California, Berkeley, General Social Surveys, 1972–2006 Cumulative Data Files, GSS Variable SPANKING, http://sda.berkeley.edu/cgi-bin32/hsda?harcsda+gss06 (accessed September 16, 2007).

28. Duane F. Alwin, "Historical Changes in Parental Orientations to Children," *GSS Social Change Report* 28 (Chicago: National Opinion Research Center, 1987), p. 30.

29. Survey Documentation and Analysis, Computer-assisted Survey Methods Program, University of California, Berkeley, General Social Surveys, 1972–2004 Cumulative Data Files, GSS Variables HELLPOTH, WORKHARD, THNKSELF, http://sda.berkeley.edu/cgi-bin32/hsda?harcsda+gss06 (accessed September 16, 2007).

30. Centers for Disease Control and Prevention, "KidsWalk: Then and Now—Barriers and Solutions," http://www.cdc.gov/nccdphp/dnpa/kidswalk/then_and _now.htm (accessed August 13, 2007).

31. S. Martin and S. Carlson, "Barriers to Children Walking to or from School—United States, 2004," *Mortality and Morbidity Weekly Report* 54 (September 30, 2005): 949–52.

32. Pew Research Center, *Families Drawn Together by Communications Revolution*, February 21, 2006, p. 8.

33. National Poverty Center, "Family Support during the Transition to Adulthood," *Policy Brief* 3 (August 2004): 2.

34. Pew Research Center, *Families Drawn Together*, p. 2.

35. Ibid. p. 13.

36. Bureau of the Census, "America's Families and Living Arrangements: 2006," http://www.census.gov/population/www/socdemo/hh-fam/cps2006.html (accessed November 25, 2007).

37. Survey Documentation and Analysis, Computer-Assisted Survey Methods

Program, University of California, Berkeley, General Social Surveys, 1972–2006 Cumulative Data Files, GSS Variables SIBMOST, SIBVISIT, and SIBCALL, http:// sda.berkeley.edu/cgi-bin32/hsda?harcsda+gss06 (accessed September 16, 2007).

38. Pew Research Center, *Families Drawn Together*, p. 9.

39. Miller McPherson, Lynn Smith-Lovin, and Matthew E. Brashears, "Social Isolation in America: Changes in Core Discussion Networks over Two Decades," *American Sociological Review* 71 (June 2006): 353–75.

40. Jeffrey Boase et al., *The Strength of Internet Ties*, Pew Internet & American Life Project, January 25, 2006, p. 5.

41. Ibid., p. 3.

CHAPTER 2. MEN AND WOMEN

1. Bureau of the Census, "2007 Current Population Survey Annual Social and Economic Supplement," http://pubdb3.census.gov/macro/032007/perinc/toc.htm (accessed September 25, 2007).

2. National Center for Health Statistics, *Fertility, Contraception, and Fatherhood: Data on Men and Women from Cycle 6 of the 2002 National Survey of Family Growth*, Vital and Health Statistics, Series 23, No. 26, 2006, pp. 64, 93–94.

3. Bureau of the Census, "Characteristics of New Housing, Characteristics of New One-Family Houses Sold," http://www.census.gov/const/www/charindex .html#sold (accessed June 5, 2007).

4. Bureau of Labor Statistics, "Consumer Expenditure Survey, 1984 and 2006 Standard Tables," http://www.bls.gov/cex/csxstnd.htm (accessed November 25, 2007).

5. National Center for Education Statistics, "Digest of Education Statistics 2006," http://nces.ed.gov/programs/digest/ (accessed July 30, 2007).

6. Chinhui Juhn and Kevin M. Murphy, *Wage Inequality and Family Labor Supply*, National Bureau of Economic Research, NBER Working Paper 5459, February 1996.

7. Finis Welch, "Growth in Women's Relative Wages and Inequality among Men: One Phenomenon or Two?" *American Economic Review* 90 (May 2000): 444–49.

8. Bureau of Labor Statistics, "Labor Force Characteristics from the Current Population Survey," http://www.bls.gov/cps/home.htm (accessed August 18, 2007).

9. Survey Documentation and Analysis, Computer-Assisted Survey Methods Program, University of California, Berkeley, General Social Surveys, 1972–2006 Cumulative Data Files, GSS Variables FEFAM and FEPRESCH, http://sda.berkeley .edu/cgibin32/hsda?harcsda+gss06 (accessed September 25, 2007).

10. Suzanne M. Bianchi, John P. Robinson, and Melissa A. Milkie, *Changing Rhythms of American Family Life* (New York: Russell Sage Foundation, 2006), p. 64.

11. Ibid., p. 93.

12. Frank Avenilla, Emily Rosenthal, and Pete Tice, "Fathers of U.S. Children Born in 2001: Findings from the Early Childhood Longitudinal Study, July 2006," http://nces.ed.gov/pubsearch/pubsinfo.asp?pubid=2006002 (accessed August 23, 2007).

13. Bianchi et al., *Changing Rhythms*, p. 64.

14. Ibid., p. 93.

15. Author's calculations based on Bureau of Labor Statistics, unpublished data from the 2005 American Time Use Survey.

16. Survey Documentation and Analysis, Computer-Assisted Survey Methods Program, University of California, Berkeley, General Social Surveys, 1972–2006 Cumulative Data Files, GSS Variable HHWKFAIR, http://sda.berkeley.edu/cgi-bin32/hsda?harcsda+gss06 (accessed September 25, 2007).

17. Bianchi et al., *Changing Rhythms*, p. 55.

18. Bureau of the Census, *Custodial Mothers and Fathers and Their Child Support: 2003*, Current Population Reports, P60–230, July 2006, p. 3.

19. National Center for Health Statistics, *Fertility, Contraception, and Fatherhood*, p. 94.

20. Ibid., p. 106.

21. Ibid., p. 107.

22. Pew Research Center, *Families Drawn Together by Communications Revolution*, February 21, 2006, p. 8.

23. Pew Research Center, *Motherhood Today—Tougher Challenges, Less Success*, May 2, 2007, p. 4.

CHAPTER 3. SEX

1. Bureau of the Census, "Families and Living Arrangements, Historical Time Series," http://www.census.gov/population/www/socdemo/hh-fam.html#history (accessed June 15, 2007).

2. National Center for Health Statistics, *Teenagers in the United States: Sexual Activity, Contraceptive Use, and Childbearing, 2002*, Vital and Health Statistics, Series 23, No. 24, 2004, p. 18.

3. National Center for Health Statistics, *Fertility, Family Planning, and Reproductive Health of U.S. Women: Data from the 2002 National Survey of Family Growth*, Vital and Health Statistics, Series 23, No. 25, 2005, p. 79.

4. National Center for Health Statistics, *Teenagers in the United States*, p. 23.

5. Ibid., pp. 36–37.

6. Ibid., pp. 27–28.

7. Survey Documentation and Analysis, Computer-Assisted Survey Methods Program, University of California, Berkeley, General Social Surveys, 1972–2006 Cumulative Data Files, GSS Variable PREMARSX, http://sda.berkeley.edu/cgi -bin32/hsda?harcsda+gss06 (accessed October 4, 2007).

8. National Center for Health Statistics, *Fertility, Family Planning, and Reproductive Health of U.S. Women*, p. 99.

9. National Center for Health Statistics, *Use of Contraception and Use of Family Planning Services in the United States: 1982–2002*, Advance Data, No. 350, 2004, p. 17.

10. National Center for Health Statistics, *Teenagers in the United States*, p. 29.

11. National Center for Health Statistics, *Fertility, Contraception, and Fatherhood: Data on Men and Women from Cycle 6 of the 2002 National Survey of Family Growth*, Vital and Health Statistics, Series 23, No. 26, 2006, p. 78.

12. Ibid., p. 84.

13. "Family Planning Takes a New Perspective," *Drug Store News*, November 6, 2006, pp. 32, 34.

14. Survey Documentation and Analysis, Computer-Assisted Survey Methods Program, University of California, Berkeley, General Social Surveys, 1972–2006 Cumulative Data Files, GSS Variables ABANY, ABRAPE, and ABHEALTH, http:// sda.berkeley.edu/cgi-bin32/hsda?harcsda+gss06 (accessed October 4, 2007).

15. Guttmacher Institute, "Emergency Contraception (EC) Played Key Role in Abortion Rate Declines," December 17, 2002, http://www.guttmacher.org/media/ nr/2002/12/17/nr_340602.html (accessed June 19, 2007).

16. Pew Research Center for the People & the Press, *Pragmatic Americans Liberal* and *Conservative on Social Issues*, August 3, 2006, p. 3.

17. National Center for Health Statistics, *Sexual Behavior and Selected Health Measures: Men and Women 15–44 Years of Age, United States, 2002*, Advance Data, Vital and Health Statistics, No. 362, September 15, 2005, pp. 32–33.

18. Ibid., p. 26.

19. Lydia Saad, "Tolerance for Gay Rights at High-Water Mark," Gallup Poll, May 29, 2007, http://www.gallup.com/poll/27694/Tolerance-Gay-Rights-High-Water-Mark.aspx (accessed November 25, 2007).

20. Pew Research Center for the People & the Press, *Pragmatic Americans*, pp. 8, 10, 12.

21. Harris Interactive, "Seven Out of Ten Heterosexuals Today Know Someone Gay," October 10, 2006, http://www.harrisinteractive.com/news/allnewsbydate.asp ?NewsID=1099 (accessed November 25, 2007).

CHAPTER 4. MARRIAGE AND DIVORCE

1. National Center for Health Statistics, *Fertility, Family Planning, and Reproductive Health of U.S. Women: Data from the 2002 National Survey of Family Growth*, Vital and Health Statistics, Series 23, No. 25, 2005, pp. 86, 88.

2. David Popenoe, "Marriage and Family: What Does the Scandinavian Experience Tell Us?" The State of Our Unions 2005, National Marriage Project, Rutgers University, July 2005, http://marriage.rutgers.edu/Publications/SOOU/TEXT SOOU2005.htm (accessed March 22, 2007).

3. Bureau of the Census, "Families and Living Arrangements, Historical Time Series," http://www.census.gov/population/www/socdemo/hh-fam.html (accessed September 24, 2007).

4. Bureau of the Census, *Historical Statistics of the United States, Colonial Times to 1970*, Part 1 (Washington, DC: US Government Printing Office, 1975), p. 20.

5. National Center for Health Statistics, *Fertility, Family Planning, and Reproductive Health of U.S. Women*, p. 89.

6. Bureau of the Census, "Number, Timing, and Duration of Marriages and Divorces: 2004," detailed tables, http://www.census.gov/population/www/socdemo/marr-div/2004detailed_tables.html (accessed September 24, 2007).

7. National Center for Health Statistics, *Fertility, Contraception, and Fatherhood: Data on Men and Women from Cycle 6 of the 2002 National Survey of Family Growth*, Vital and Health Statistics, Series 23, No. 26, 2006, p. 69.

8. Norval D. Glenn, "The Recent Trend in Marital Success in the United States," *Journal of Marriage and the Family* 53 (May 1991): pp. 261–70.

9. Bureau of the Census, "Families and Living Arrangements," http://www.census.gov/population/www/socdemo/hh-fam.html (accessed September 24, 2007).

10. Bureau of the Census, "Number, Timing, and Duration of Marriages and Divorces: 2004."

11. Survey Documentation and Analysis, Computer-Assisted Survey Methods Program, University of California, Berkeley, General Social Surveys, 1972–2006 Cumulative Data Files, GSS Variable DIVLAW, http://sda.berkeley.edu/D3/GSS06/Docyr/gs06.htm (accessed September 24, 2007).

12. Norval D. Glenn, *With This Ring . . . A National Survey on Marriage in America* (Gaithersburg, MD: National Fatherhood Initiative, 2005), p. 29.

13. National Center for Health Statistics, *Fertility, Contraception, and Fatherhood*, pp. 72–73.

14. Glenn, *With This Ring*, p. 32.

15. Ibid., p. 29.

16. Ibid., p. 32.

17. Bureau of the Census, "Number, Timing, and Duration of Marriages and Divorces: 2004."

18. Glenn, *With This Ring*, p. 32.

19. National Marriage Project, *The State of Our Unions, 2006* (Piscataway, NJ: Rutgers University, 2006), p. 23.

20. Bureau of the Census, "Number, Timing, and Duration of Marriages and Divorces: 2004."

21. Bureau of the Census, "Families and Living Arrangements: 2006," http://www.census.gov/population/www/socdemo/hh-fam.html (accessed September 24, 2007).

22. Bureau of the Census, "Number, Timing, and Duration of Marriages and Divorces: 2004."

23. Andrew Kochera, Audrey Straight, and Thomas Guterbock, "Beyond 50.05 A Report to the Nation on Livable Communities: Creating Environments for Successful Aging," *AARP Research Report*, May 2005, p. 48.

CHAPTER 5. BABIES

1. National Center for Health Statistics, *Nonmarital Childbearing in the United States, 1940–99*, National Vital Statistics Report, Vol. 48, No. 16, October 18, 2000, p. 17.

2. Ibid., p. 31.

3. National Center for Health Statistics, *Births: Preliminary Data for 2006*, National Vital Statistics Report, Vol. 56, No. 17, December 5, 2007, p. 6.

4. National Center for Health Statistics, *Fertility, Family Planning, and Reproductive Health of U.S. Women: Data from the 2002 National Survey of Family Growth*, Vital and Health Statistics, Series 23, No. 25, 2005, p. 52.

5. Carol B. Stack, *All Our Kin* (New York: Harper & Row, 1974), p. 52.

6. Gallup Poll, "Moral Issues," http://www.gallup.com/poll/1681/Moral-Issues.aspx (accessed November 26, 2007).

7. Heather Mason Kiefer, "Are Out-of-Wedlock Births Morally Acceptable?" Gallup Poll, June 15, 2003, http://www.gallup.com/poll/8839/OutofWedlock-Births-Morally-Acceptable.aspx (accessed November 26, 2007).

8. National Center for Health Statistics, *Fertility, Contraception, and Fatherhood: Data on Men and Women from Cycle 6 of the 2002 National Survey of Family Growth*, Vital and Health Statistics, Series 23, No. 26, 2006, pp. 122–23.

9. National Center for Education Statistics, *Digest of Education Statistics 2007*, table 40, http://nces.ed.gov/programs/digest/d07/tables_2.asp (accessed June 12, 2008).

10. Bureau of Labor Statistics, "Labor Force Statistics from the Current Population Survey," table 11: Employed persons by detailed occupation, sex, race, and Hispanic or Latino ethnicity, ftp://ftp.bls.gov/pub/special.requests/lf/aat11.txt (accessed June 12, 2008).

11. Sarah Cohn, "Board Diversity Increases Slowly," Institutional Shareholder Services, June 30, 2006, http://blog.issproxy.com/2006/06/000110print.html (accessed March 16, 2007).

12. Congressional Research Service, *Membership of the 109th Congress: A Profile*, November 29, 2006, http://www.senate.gov/reference/resources/pdf/RS22007.pdf (accessed March 16, 2007).

13. Sanford Levinson, "Our Broken Constitution," *Los Angeles Times*, October 16, 2006, p. B13.

14. National Center for Health Statistics, *Estimated Pregnancy Rates by Outcome for the United States, 1990–2004* National Vital Statistics Reports, Volume 56, No. 15, April 14, 2008, p. 12.

15. National Center for Health Statistics, *Fertility, Family Planning, and Reproductive Health of U.S. Women*, p. 60.

16. Ibid., p. 56.

17. Ibid., p. 93.

18. Survey Documentation and Analysis, Computer-Assisted Survey Methods Program, University of California, Berkeley, General Social Surveys, 1972–2006 Cumulative Data Files, Variable CHLDIDEL, http://sda.berkeley.edu/cgi-bin32/hsda?harcsda+gss06 (accessed September 14, 2007).

19. National Center for Health Statistics, *Births: Preliminary Data for 2006*, p. 6.

20. Bureau of the Census, "Fertility of American Women," http://www.census.gov/population/www/socdemo/fertility.html (accessed March 19, 2007).

21. CIA World Factbook, https://www.cia.gov/cia/publications/factbook/index.html (accessed September 11, 2007).

22. National Center for Health Statistics, *Fertility, Family Planning, and Reproductive Health of U.S. Women*, p. 122.

23. Ibid., p. 123.

24. Bureau of the Census, *Adopted Children and Stepchildren: 2000*, Census 2000 Special Reports, October 2003, pp. 2, 12.

CHAPTER 6. SCHOOL

1. Bureau of the Census, "Educational Attainment," historical tables, http://www.census.gov/population/www/socdemo/educ-attn.html (accessed June 10, 2008).

2. Ibid.

3. Ibid.

4. Bureau of Labor Statistics, "Labor Force Statistics from the Current Population Survey," http://www.bls.gov/cps/home.htm (accessed June 13, 2007).

5. Bureau of the Census, "Current Population Surveys, School Enrollment—Historical Tables," http://www.census.gov/population/www/socdemo/school.html (accessed June 10, 2008).

6. National Center for Education Statistics, "Adult Education Survey of the 2005 National Household Education Surveys Program," http://nces.ed.gov/pubs 2006/adulted/01.asp (accessed June 11, 2007).

7. Xianglei Chen and Kathryn Chandler, *Efforts by Public K-8 Schools to Involve Parents in Children's Education: Do School and Parent Reports Agree?* National Center for Education Statistics Statistical Analysis Report, September 2001, p. iii.

8. Bureau of the Census, "A Child's Day: 2004 (Selected Indicators of Child Well-Being), Survey Income and Program Participation," detailed tables, http://www.census.gov/population/www/socdemo/2004_detailedtables.html (accessed October 31, 2007).

9. Chen and Chandler, *Efforts by Public K-8 Schools*, p. 32.

10. Lowell C. Rose and Alec M. Gallup, *The 39th Annual Phi Delta Kappa/Gallup Poll of the Public's Attitudes Toward the Public Schools*, September 2007, p. 39.

11. Tom W. Smith, "Why Our Neck of the Woods Is Better Than the Forest," *Public Perspective* (June/July 1998): 50.

12. Ibid., p. 52.

13. Bureau of the Census, "American Housing Survey National Tables: 2005," http://www.census.gov/hhes/www/housing/ahs/ahs05/ahs05.html (accessed June 12, 2007).

14. National Center for Education Statistics, "The Condition of Education," http://nces.ed.gov/programs/coe/2007/section1/indicator04.asp (accessed June 12, 2007).

15. Rose and Gallup, *39th Annual Phi Delta Kappa/Gallup Poll*, p. 37.

16. Lowell C. Rose and Alec M. Gallup, *The 35th Annual Phi Delta Kappa/Gallup Poll of the Public's Attitudes Toward the Public Schools*, September 2003, p. 50.

17. D. Princiotta and S. Bielick, *Homeschooling in the United States: 2003*, National Center for Education Statistics 2006–042 (Washington, DC: US Department of Education, 2005), pp. 5–6.

18. Ibid., p. 13.

19. National Center for Education Statistics, "Digest of Education Statistics:

2007," http://nces.ed.gov/programs/digest/d07/tables_2.asp (accessed June 10, 2008).

20. Author's calculations based on Bureau of Labor Statistics 2006 Consumer Expenditure Survey Standard Tables, http://www.bls.gov/cex/home.htm (accessed December 3, 2007).

21. Bureau of the Census, "2007 Current Population Survey Annual Social and Economic Supplement," http://www.census.gov/hhes/www/income/dinctabs.html (accessed September 15, 2007).

22. Bureau of the Census, "A Child's Day: 2004."

23. Alexander W. Astin et al., *The American Freshman: Thirty-five Year Trends* (Los Angeles: Cooperative Institutional Research Program, Higher Education Research Institute, University of California, Los Angeles, December 2002), p. 56.

24. National Center for Education Statistics, "Digest of Education Statistics: 2007."

25. Ibid.

26. John H. Pryor et al., *The American Freshman: National Norms for Fall 2007* (Los Angeles: Cooperative Institutional Research Program, Higher Education Research Institute, University of California, Los Angeles, December 2007), p. 32.

27. National Center for Education Statistics, "Digest of Education Statistics 2007."

28. Bureau of the Census, "2007 Current Population Survey Annual Social and Economic Supplement."

29. Claudia Goldin, Lawrence F. Katz, and Ilyana Kuziemko, *The Homecoming of American College Women: The Reversal of the College Gender Gap*, National Bureau of Economic Research, NBER Working Paper No. 12139, March 2006, p. 3.

30. National Center for Education Statistics, "Digest of Education Statistics 2007."

31. Author's calculations based on $19,300 in undergraduate debt in 1999, adjusted for inflation to 2007 dollars, data from National Center for Education Statistics, "The Condition of Education," http://nces.ed.gov/programs/coe/2004/section5/indicator38.asp#info (accessed April 7, 2007).

32. Bureau of the Census, "Historical Income Table-Families," http://www.census.gov/hhes/www/income/histinc/f09ar.html; and National Center for Education Statistics, "Digest of Education Statistics: 2007."

33. Sandy Baum and Marie O'Malley, *College on Credit: How Borrowers Perceive Their Education Debt, Results of the 2002 National Student Loan Survey*, Final Report, Nellie Mae Corporation, February 6, 2003, p. 12.

34. Ibid., p. v.

35. AllianceBernstein Investments, "Fast Facts: American Families and Their

College Savings Efforts, 2006," http://www.alliancebernstein.com/CSC/StoryPage .aspx?cid=40397 (accessed April 8, 2007).

36. Ibid.

37. Vanguard Group, "Vanguard/Upromise Survey Reveals Saving for College Is Top Financial Worry among Parents," January 5, 2006, http://onlinepressroom .net/vanguard/ (accessed April 8, 2007).

38. John Hancock, "John Hancock Research Shows Financial Gifts for College Education Popular and Necessary," November 1, 2006, http://www.johnhancock .com/about/news/news_nov0106.jsp (accessed April 8, 2007).

39. MetLife Mature Market Institute, "The MetLife Grandparents Poll," June 2006, http://www.metlife.com/WPSAssets/81911529701150382761V1FGrandparent Poll.pdf (accessed April 8, 2007).

40. Pryor et al., *The American Freshman*, p. 22.

41. David M. Cutler and Adriana Lleras-Muney, *Education and Health: Evaluating Theories and Evidence*, National Bureau of Economic Research, NBER Working Paper 12352, June 2006, p. 21.

42. Author's calculations based on 2007 Current Population Survey Annual Social and Economic Supplement, http://pubdb3.census.gov/macro/032007/perinc/ toc.htm; and http://www.census.gov/hhes/www/income/histinc/incpertoc.html (accessed September 16, 2007).

43. Mark Gongloff, "Education May Not Be the Answer," CNN/Money.com, February 23, 2004, http://money.cnn.com/2004/02/19/news/economy/education/ index.htm (accessed June 11, 2007).

44. NBC News/*Wall Street Journal* Survey, March 2–5, 2007, Study #6071, http://online.wsj.com/public/resources/documents/wsj070705_March2007-poll.pdf (accessed June 11, 2007).

CHAPTER 7. WORK

1. Bureau of the Census, "American Housing Survey National Tables: 2005," http://www.census.gov/hhes/www/housing/ahs/ahs05/ahs05.html (accessed May 2, 2007).

2. Bureau of the Census, *Journey to Work: 2000*, Census 2000 Brief, March 2004, p. 5.

3. Bureau of the Census, "2006 American Community Survey," http://www .census.gov/acs/www/ (accessed October 10, 2007).

4. Peter Gordon, Bumsoo Lee, and Harry W. Richardson, *Travel Trends in U.S. Cities: Explaining the 2000 Census Commuting Results* (Los Angeles: Lusk Center for Real Estate, University of Southern California, April 2004), p. 4.

5. Pew Research Center, *Public Says American Work Life Is Worsening, but Most Workers Remain Satisfied with Their Jobs*, August 30, 2006, p. 14.

6. Ibid., p. 1.

7. Bureau of Labor Statistics, *Employee Tenure in 2006*, USDL 06–1563, September 8, 2006, Table 2.

8. Ann Huff Stevens, *The More Things Change, the More They Stay the Same: Trends in Long-Term Employment in the United States, 1969–2002*, National Bureau of Economic Research, NBER Working Paper 11878, December 2005, p. 2.

9. Bureau of Labor Statistics, "Labor Force Statistics from the Current Population Survey," http://www.bls.gov/cps/home.htm (accessed June 10, 2008).

10. Bureau of Labor Statistics, *Handbook of Labor Statistics* (Washington, DC: US Government Printing Office, 1989), pp. 26, 242.

11. Pew Research Center for the People & the Press, *Trends in Political Values and Core Attitudes: 1987–2007*, March 22, 2007, p. 35.

12. Bureau of Labor Statistics, "Labor Force Statistics from the Current Population Survey," custom tables, http://data.bls.gov/PDQ/outside.jsp?survey=ln (accessed June 10, 2008).

13. Bureau of the Census, "America's Families and Living Arrangements: 2006," http://www.census.gov/population/www/socdemo/hh-fam/cps2006.html (accessed May 4, 2007).

14. Bureau of the Census, "School Enrollment—Social and Economic Characteristics of Students: October 2006," http://www.census.gov/population/www/socdemo/school/cps2006.html (accessed June 10, 2008).

15. Bureau of the Census, "Disability Data from the Current Population Survey," http://www.census.gov/hhes/www/disability/disabcps.html (accessed May 4, 2007).

16. Social Security Online, "Annual Statistical Supplement, 2006," table 5.D4, http://www.ssa.gov/policy/docs/statcomps/supplement/2006/ (accessed October 10 2007).

17. Bureau of Labor Statistics, "Labor Force Statistics from the Current Population Survey," custom tables.

18. Bureau of the Census, "A Child's Day: 2004 (Selected Indicators of Child Well-Being), Survey Income and Program Participation," detailed tables, http://www.census.gov/population/www/socdemo/2004_detailedtables.html (accessed October 31, 2007).

19. Congressional Budget Office, "What Is Happening to Youth Employment Rates?" November 2004, http://www.cbo.gov/showdoc.cfm?index=6017 &sequence=0 (accessed May 3, 2007).

20. Daniel Aaronson, Kyung-Hong Park, and Daniel Sullivan, "Explaining the Decline in Teen Labor Force Participation," Chicago Fed Letter 234, Federal

Reserve Bank of Chicago, January 2007, http://www.chicagofed.org/publications/fedletter/cfljanuary2007_234.pdf (accessed May 3, 2007).

21. Pew Research Center, *Public Says American Work Life Is Worsening, but Most Workers Remain Satisfied with Their Jobs*, August 30, 2006, p. 2.

22. *Frontline*, "Can You Afford to Retire?" http://www.pbs.org/wgbh/pages/frontline/retirement/etc/script.html (accessed May 7, 2007).

23. GAO, *Employer-Sponsored Health and Retirement Benefits—Efforts to Control Employer Costs and the Implications for Workers*, GAO-07-355, March 2007, p. 18.

24. Employee Benefit Research Institute, *Employment-Based Health Benefits: Access and Coverage, 1988–2005*, EBRI Issue Brief 303, March 2007, pp. 6, 9.

25. David G. Blanchflower, "Self-Employment: More May Not Be Better," paper presented at the Conference on Self-Employment organized by the Economic Council of Sweden, March 2004, p. 22.

26. Paul Fronstin, *Sources of Health Insurance and Characteristics of the Uninsured: Analysis of the March 2006 Current Population Survey*, Employee Benefit Research Institute, EBRI Issue Brief 298, October 2006, p. 11.

27. Bureau of the Census, "2006 American Community Survey," http://www.census.gov/acs/www/ (accessed October 11, 2007).

28. Bureau of Labor Statistics, *Work at Home in 2004*, USDL 05–1768, September 22, 2005, p. 1 and tables 1, 7.

29. Bureau of Labor Statistics, "Employed Persons by Detailed Occupation, Sex, and Age, Annual Average 2007," unpublished table from the "2007 Current Population Survey."

30. Corporation for National and Community Service, Office of Research and Policy Development, *Volunteering in America: 2007 State Trends and Rankings in Civic Life*, Washington, DC, 2007, p. 4.

31. Bureau of Labor Statistics, *Volunteering in the United States, 2007*, January 23, 2008, p. 2.

32. R. A. Stebbins and M. Graham, eds., *Volunteering as Leisure/Leisure as Volunteering* (Oxfordshire, UK: CABI Publishing, 2004).

CHAPTER 8. MONEY

1. Bureau of the Census, "Current Population Survey, Historical Income Tables—People," http://www.census.gov/hhes/www/income/histinc/incpertoc.html (accessed September 20, 2007).

2. Jodie T. Allen and Michael Dimock, *A Nation of "Haves" and "Have-Nots"?* Pew Research Center, September 13, 2007, p. 1.

3. Bureau of the Census, "Current Population Surveys, Historical Income Data," http://www.census.gov/hhes/www/income/histinc/inchhtoc.html (accessed September 28, 2007).

4. Survey Documentation and Analysis, Computer-Assisted Survey Methods Program, University of California, Berkeley, General Social Surveys, 1972–2006 Cumulative Data Files, GSS Variable HAPPY, http://sda.berkeley.edu/cgi-bin32/hsda?harcsda+gss06 (accessed September 28, 2007).

5. Daniel Kahneman et al., *Would You Be Happier If You Were Richer? A Focusing Illusion*, Princeton University Center for Economic Policy Studies, CEPS Working Paper 125, May 2006, p. 6.

6. Erzo F. P. Luttmer, *Neighbors as Negatives: Relative Earnings and Well-Being*, National Bureau of Economic Research, NBER Working Paper 10667, August 2004, p. 25.

7. Brian K. Bucks, Arthur B. Kennickell, and Kevin B. Moore, "Recent Changes in U.S. Family Finances: Evidence from the 2001 and 2004 Survey of Consumer Finances," *Federal Reserve Bulletin* 92 (February 2006): A8.

8. Bureau of the Census, "Historical Income Data, Current Population Survey tables," http://www.census.gov/hhes/www/income/histinc/inchhtoc.html (accessed September 28, 2007).

9. Bureau of Labor Statistics, "Labor Force Statistics from the Current Population Survey," http://www.bls.gov/cps/home.htm (accessed May 28, 2008).

10. Andrew Chamberlain and Gerald Prante, "Generational Equity: Which Age Groups Pay More Tax, and Which Receive More Government Spending?" *Tax Foundation Special Report* 156 (Washington, DC: Tax Foundation, June 2007), p. 12.

11. Ibid., p. 15.

12. Ibid.

13. C. Y. Cyrus Chu and Ronald D. Lee, "The Co-evolution of Intergenerational Transfers and Longevity: An Optimal Life History Approach," *Theoretical Population Biology* 69 (2006): 193–201.

14. Bureau of the Census, "2007 Current Population Survey Annual Social and Economic Supplement," http://pubdb3.census.gov/macro/032007/faminc/toc.htm (accessed November 28, 2007).

15. Alexander W. Astin et al., *The American Freshman: Thirty-five Year Trends* (Los Angeles: Cooperative Institutional Research Program, Higher Education Research Institute, University of California–Los Angeles, December 2002), p. 106.

16. John H. Pryor et al., *The American Freshman: National Norms for Fall 2005* (Los Angeles: Cooperative Institutional Research Program, Higher Education Research Institute, University of California, Los Angeles, December 2005), pp. 56, 76.

17. Bureau of the Census, "2007 Current Population Survey Annual Social and Economic Supplement," http://pubdb3.census.gov/macro/032007/faminc/toc.htm (accessed November 28, 2007).

18. Bureau of the Census, "Current Population Surveys, Historical Income Tables—Families," http://www.census.gov/hhes/www/income/histinc/incfamdet .html (accessed July 31, 2007).

19. Arlene Dohm and Lynn Shniper, "Occupational Employment Projections to 2016," *Monthly Labor Review* (November 2007): 86–125.

20. New Strategist Publications, *American Incomes: Demographics of Who Has Money*, 6th ed. (Ithaca, NY: New Strategist, 2007), pp. 275–90.

21. Pew Research Center, *Luxury or Necessity? Things We Can't Live Without: The List Has Grown in the Past Decade*, December 14, 2006, p. 4.

22. US Department of Labor, "History of Federal Minimum Wage Rates Under the Fair Labor Standards Act, 1938–2007," http://www.dol.gov/esa/minwage/ chart.htm (accessed July 29, 2007).

23. Bureau of Labor Statistics, "Characteristics of Minimum Wage Workers: 2007," http://www.bls.gov/cps/minwage2007.htm (accessed April 1, 2008).

24. Allen and Dimock, *A Nation of "Haves" and "Have-Nots"?* p. 1.

25. Gallup Poll, "Taxes and Tax Cuts," http://www.gallup.com/poll/1714/ Taxes.aspx (accessed June 10, 2008).

26. Luttmer, *Neighbors as Negatives*, p. 25.

27. Matthew Miller, "The Forbes 400," September 20, 2007, http://www .forbes.com/2007/09/19/richest-americans-forbes-lists-richlist07-cx_mm_0920rich _land.html (accessed November 28, 2007).

28. City-Data.com, Allen, South Dakota, http://www.city-data.com/city/Allen-South-Dakota.html (accessed August 10, 2007).

29. Bucks et al., "Recent Changes," p. A8.

30. Bureau of the Census, "1985 and 2005 American Housing Surveys for the United States," http://www.census.gov/hhes/www/housing/ahs/nationaldata.html (accessed July 23, 2007).

31. Paul Taylor, Cary Funk, and April Clark, *We Try Hard. We Fall Short. Americans Assess Their Saving Habits*, Pew Research Center, January 24, 2007, p. 8.

32. Ibid., p. 15.

33. Ibid., pp. 8, 14.

34. Bucks et al., "Recent Changes," p. A26.

35. Ibid., p. A32.

36. Ibid., p. A29.

37. Paul Taylor, Cary Funk, and April Clark, *What Americans Pay For—And How*, Pew Research Center, February 7, 2007, p. 6.

38. Ibid., p. 17.

39. Bucks et al., "Recent Changes," p. A35.

40. Robert B. Avery and Michael S. Rendall, "Inheritance and Wealth," Cornell University Philanthropy Roundtable, November 11, 1993.

41. Jagadeesh Gokhale and Laurence J. Kotlikoff, "The Baby Boomers' Mega-Inheritance—Myth or Reality?" Federal Reserve Bank of Cleveland, *Economic Commentary*, October 1, 2000, http://www.clevelandfed.org/Research/Commentary/2000/1001.pdf (accessed July 26, 2007).

42. John Gist and Carlos Figueiredo, *In Their Dreams: What Will Boomers Inherit?* AARP Public Policy Institute, June 2006, pp. 3, 6.

43. Gordon M. Fisher, "The Development and History of the Poverty Thresholds," *Social Security Bulletin* 55 (1992), http://www.ssa.gov/history/fisheron poverty.html (accessed June 8, 2007).

44. Robert Rector, "Not So Poor: The Luxury of American Poverty," *National Review* 51 (1999): 28–29.

45. Bureau of the Census, "Extended Measures of Well-Being: Living Conditions in the United States, 2003," detailed tables, http://www.census.gov/population/www/socdemo/p70–110.html (accessed July 11, 2007).

46. Pew Research Center, *Luxury or Necessity?* p. 1.

47. Bureau of the Census, *Dynamics of Economic Well-Being: Participation in Government Programs, 2001 through 2003—Who Gets Assistance?* Current Population Reports, P70–108, October 2006, pp. 18, 20–22.

48. Alberto Alesina, Edward Glaeser, and Bruce Sacerdote, *Why Doesn't the U.S. Have a European-Style Welfare System?* National Bureau of Economic Research, NBER Working Paper 8524, October 2001, p. 65.

49. Ibid., p. 39.

50. Ibid., p. 33.

CHAPTER 9. RETIREMENT

1. B. Douglas Bernheim, Jonathan Skinner, and Steven Weinberg, *What Accounts for the Variation in Retirement Wealth among U.S. Households?* National Bureau of Economic Research, NBER Working Paper 6227, October 1997, p. 4.

2. Employee Benefit Research Institute, Retirement Confidence Survey, http://www.ebri.org/surveys/rcs/ (accessed April 16, 2008).

3. John Karl Scholz, Ananth Seshadri, and Surachai Khitatrakun, "Are Americans Saving 'Optimally' for Retirement?" *Journal of Political Economy* 114 (2006): 607–43.

4. Laurence J. Kotlikoff, "Is Conventional Financial Planning Good for Your

Financial Health?" February 2006, http://www.esplanner.com/Download/Financial%20Health%2002–16–2006.pdf (accessed June 26, 2007).

5. Employee Benefit Research Institute, Benefit FAQs, http://ebri.org/publications/benfaq/index.cfm?fa=retfaq14 (accessed June 27, 2007).

6. Averages calculated by the author for the three cohorts analyzed in James H. Moore Jr., "Projected Pension Income: Equality or Disparity for the Baby-Boom Cohort?" *Monthly Labor Review* (March 2006): 64.

7. Craig Copeland, "Retirement Plan Participation and Retirees' Perception of Their Standard of Living," Employee Benefit Research Institute, *Issue Brief* 289 (January 2006): 6.

8. Bureau of Labor Statistics, *National Compensation Survey: Employee Benefits in Private Industry in the United States, March 2007*, August 2007, p. 9.

9. Jack Vanderhei and Sarah Holden, "401(k) Plan Asset Allocation, Account Balances, and Loan Activity in 2006," Employee Benefit Research Institute, *Issue Brief* 308 (August 2007): 11.

10. Bureau of the Census, "2007 Current Population Survey Annual Social and Economic Supplement," http://pubdb3.census.gov/macro/032007/perinc/toc.htm (accessed October 6, 2007).

11. Ken McDonnell, "Income of the Elderly Population Age 65 and Over, 2005," Employee Benefit Research Institute, *Notes* (May 2007): 3.

12. Employee Benefit Research Institute, Retirement Confidence Survey, http://www.ebri.org/surveys/rcs/ (accessed April 16, 2008).

13. Brian K. Bucks, Arthur B. Kennickell and Kevin B. Moore, "Recent Changes in U.S. Family Finances: Evidence from the 2001 and 2004 Survey of Consumer Finances," *Federal Reserve Bulletin* 92 (February 2006): A-13, A-14.

14. Author's calculations based on median Social Security income of $11,501 in 2006, a twenty-year retirement, 5 percent rate of return, and a 3 percent rate of inflation.

15. Laurence J. Kotlikoff, Ben Marx, and Pietro Rizza, *Americans' Dependency on Social Security*, National Bureau of Economic Research, NBER Working Paper 12696, November 2006, p. 4.

16. Social Security and Medicare Board of Trustees, "The 2008 Annual Report of the Board of Trustees of the Federal Old-Age and Survivors Insurance and Federal Disability Insurance Trust Funds," http://www.socialsecurity.gov/OACT/TR/TR08/ (accessed March 25, 2008).

17. Congressional Budget Office, "Updated Long-Term Projections for Social Security," June 2006, http://www.cbo.gov/ftpdocs/72xx/doc7289/06–14-LongTerm Projections.pdf (accessed June 28, 2007).

18. Centers for Medicare and Medicaid Services, "Data Compendium 2006," http://www.cms.hhs.gov/DataCompendium/ (accessed September 3, 2007).

19. Bureau of the Census, "National Population Estimates," http://www.census.gov/popest/national/asrh/NC-EST2007-sa.html (accessed June 11, 2008).

20. Bureau of the Census, "America's Families and Living Arrangements: 2006," detailed tables, http://www.census.gov/population/www/socdemo/hh-fam/cps2006.html (accessed September 3, 2007).

21. Employee Benefit Research Institute, Retirement Confidence Survey, http://www.ebri.org/surveys/rcs/ (accessed April 16, 2008).

22. Amy Finkelstein, *The Aggregate Effects of Health Insurance: Evidence from the Introduction of Medicare*, National Bureau of Economic Research, NBER Working Paper 11619, April 2006, p. 30.

23. Bureau of the Census, "Current Population Survey Annual Social and Economic Supplements," http://www.census.gov/hhes/www/poverty/histpov/perindex.html (accessed July 2, 2007).

24. Center for Financing, Access and Cost Trends, Agency for Healthcare Research and Quality, "Medical Expenditure Panel Survey, 2005," http://www.meps.ahrq.gov/mepsweb/survey_comp/household.jsp (accessed June 11, 2008).

25. *ABC News*/Kaiser Family Foundation/*USA Today*, *Health Care In America 2006 Survey*, Publication 7573, October, 2006, p. 10.

CHAPTER 10. TROUBLES

1. National Sleep Foundation, 2003, 2005, and 2007 *Sleep in America* surveys (Washington, DC: National Sleep Foundation, 2003, 2005, and 2007), p. 7.

2. Bureau of Labor Statistics, unpublished tables from the 2006 American Time Use Survey.

3. Tom W. Smith, *Troubles in America: A Study of Negative Life Events across Time and Sub-Groups*, GSS Topical Report 40 (Chicago: National Opinion Research Center, 2005), p. 20.

4. Ibid., p. 11.

5. Ibid., p. 18.

6. Ibid., p. 11.

7. Survey Documentation and Analysis, Computer-Assisted Survey Methods Program, University of California, Berkeley, General Social Surveys, 1972–2006 Cumulative Data Files, GSS Topical Module: Troubles, http://sda.berkeley.edu/cgi-bin32/hsda?harcsda+gss06 (accessed October 9, 2007).

8. Lydia Saad, "Perceptions of Crime Problem Remain Curiously Negative," Gallup Poll, October 22, 2007, http://www.gallup.com/poll/102262/Perceptions-Crime-Problem-Remain-Curiously-Negative.aspx (accessed November 30, 2007).

9. Lowell C. Rose and Alec M. Gallup, *The 39th Annual Phi Delta Kappa/*

Gallup Poll of the Public's Attitudes Toward the Public Schools, September 2007, pp. 39–40.

10. Jeffrey M. Jones, "Low Trust in Federal Government Rivals Watergate Era Levels," Gallup Poll, September 26, 2007, http://www.gallup.com/poll/28795/Low-Trust-Federal-Government-Rivals-Watergate-Era-Levels.aspx (accessed November 30, 2007).

11. Survey Documentation and Analysis, Computer-Assisted Survey Methods Program, University of California, Berkeley, General Social Surveys, 1972–2006 Cumulative Data Files, GSS Variable TRUST, http://sda.berkeley.edu/cgi-bin32/hsda?harcsda+gss06 (accessed September 29, 2007).

12. Joseph Carroll, "Americans' Crime Worries," Gallup Poll, October 19, 2006, http://www.gallup.com/poll/25081/Americans-Crime-Worries.aspx (accessed November 30, 2007).

13. National Center for Health Statistics, "Classification of Death and Injury Resulting from Terrorism," http://www.cdc.gov/nchs/about/otheract/icd9/terrorism_code.htm (accessed April 13, 2007).

14. National Center for Health Statistics, "Appendix I: Classification for Mortality," http://www.cdc.gov/nchs/about/otheract/icd9/appendix1.htm (accessed April 13, 2007).

15. National Center for Health Statistics, "Mortality Tables," http://www.cdc.gov/nchs/data/dvs/mortfinal2002_workipt4.pdf (accessed October 9, 2007).

16. National Center for Health Statistics, *Deaths: Preliminary Data for 2006*, National Vital Statistics Report, Vol. 56, No. 16, June 11, 2008, p. 5.

17. Bureau of Justice Statistics, "Criminal Victimization, 2006," *Bureau of Justice Statistics Bulletin* (December 2007): 3.

18. Survey Documentation and Analysis, Computer-Assisted Survey Methods Program, University of California, Berkeley, General Social Surveys, 1972–2006 Cumulative Data Files, GSS Variables SEMIGUNS, GUNSALES, and GUNS911, http://sda.berkeley.edu/cgi-bin32/hsda?harcsda+gss06 (accessed September 29, 2007).

19. Howard Schuman and Stanley Presser, "Attitude Measurement and the Gun Control Paradox," *Public Opinion Quarterly* 41 (Winter 1977–78): 427–38.

20. Clive Beauchamp, "In the Wake of Columbine: Who Is Winning the Great American Gun War?" Paper presented at the Australasian Political Studies Association 2000 Conference, October 4–6, 2000.

21. Sanford Levinson, "Our Broken Constitution," *Los Angeles Times*, October 16, 2006, p. B13.

22. Survey Documentation and Analysis, Computer-Assisted Survey Methods Program, University of California, Berkeley, General Social Surveys, 1972–2006 Cumulative Data Files, GSS Variable OWNGUN, http://sda.berkeley.edu/cgi-bin32/hsda?harcsda+gss06 (accessed September 29, 2007).

23. Roy Walmsley, *World Prison Population List*, 7th ed., International Centre for Prison Studies, King's College London School of Law, undated, pp.1–3.

24. Bureau of Justice Statistics, "Prisoners in 2006," *Bureau of Justice Statistics Bulletin*, (December 2007): 3.

25. Pew Charitable Trusts, "Public Safety and Performance Statistics and Facts," http://www.pewpublicsafety.org/statistics/index.aspx (accessed April 17, 2007).

26. Bureau of the Census, 2006 American Community Survey, http://factfinder.census.gov/home/saff/main.html?_lang=en (accessed April 14, 2008).

27. Pew Charitable Trusts, *Public Safety, Public Spending: Forecasting America's Prison Population 2007–2011* (Washington, DC: Pew Charitable Trusts, 2007), p. 21.

28. Survey Documentation and Analysis, Computer-Assisted Survey Methods Program, University of California, Berkeley, General Social Surveys, 1972–2006 Cumulative Data Files, GSS Variable CAPPUN, http://sda.berkeley.edu/cgi-bin32/hsda?harcsda+gss06 (accessed September 29, 2007).

29. Amnesty International, "Death Penalty—Abolitionist and Retentionist Countries," http://www.amnesty.org/en/death-penalty/abolitionist-and-retentionist-countries (accessed June 11, 2008).

30. Bureau of Justice Statistics, "Key Crime and Justice Facts at a Glance," http://www.ojp.gov/bjs/glance.htm#cptrends (accessed October 9, 2007).

31. Death Penalty Information Center, "Number of Executions by State and Region Since 1976," http://www.deathpenaltyinfo.org/article.php?scid=8&did=186 (accessed June 11, 2008).

32. Death Penalty Information Center, "Innocence: List of the Freed from Death Row," http://www.deathpenaltyinfo.org/article.php?scid=6&did=110 (accessed October 9, 2007).

33. SAMHSA, Office of Applied Studies, "Results from the 2006 National Survey on Drug Use and Health," table 1–12B, http://www.oas.samhsa.gov/nsduh/2k6nsduh/tabs/Sect1peTabs11to18.pdfm (accessed November 30, 2007).

34. Survey Documentation and Analysis, Computer-Assisted Survey Methods Program, University of California, Berkeley, General Social Surveys, 1972–2006 Cumulative Data Files, GSS Variable GRASS, http://sda.berkeley.edu/cgi-bin32/hsda?harcsda+gss06 (accessed September 29, 2007).

35. Centers for Disease Control and Prevention, "Healthy Youth! National Trends in Risk Behaviors, Youth Risk Behavior Surveillance System," http://www.cdc.gov/HealthyYouth/yrbs/index.htm (accessed June 11, 2008).

36. SAMHSA, Office of Applied Studies, "National Survey on Drug Use and Health, 2006," appendix G: Selected Prevalence Tables, tables G2 and G6, http://www.oas.samhsa.gov/nsduh/2k6nsduh/AppG.htm#TabG-2 (accessed October 9, 2007).

37. SAMHSA, Office of Applied Studies, "National Survey on Drug Use and

Health, 2006," appendix B: Statistical Methods and Measurement, table B-6, http://www.oas.samhsa.gov/nsduh/2k6nsduh/AppB.htm# (accessed October 9, 2007).

38. National Center for Health Statistics, *Health, United States, 2007* (Washington, DC: US Government Printing Office, 2007), p. 266.

39. National Center for Health Statistics, *Summary Health Statistics for U.S. Adults: National Health Interview Survey, 2006*, Provisional Report, Vital and Health Statistics, Series 10, No. 235, 2007, Table 24.

40. Institute for Social Research, University of Michigan, "Monitoring the Future Survey, 2007," table 10, http://monitoringthefuture.org/data/07data.html (accessed June 11, 2008).

41. USDA, Economic Research Services, "Data Sets, Food Availability: Spreadsheets," http://www.ers.usda.gov/Data/FoodConsumption/FoodAvailSpreadsheets.htm#beverage (accessed October 9, 2007).

42. National Institute on Alcohol Abuse and Alcoholism, "Self-Reported Amounts and Patterns of Alcohol Consumption," http://www.niaaa.nih.gov/Resources/DatabaseResources/QuickFacts/AlcoholConsumption/dkpat25.htm (accessed October 9, 2007).

43. Kim Bloomfield et al., "International Comparisons of Alcohol Consumption," National Institute on Alcohol Abuse and Alcoholism, December 2003, http://pubs.niaaa.nih.gov/publications/arh27–1/95–109.htm (accessed October 9, 2007).

CHAPTER 11. GEOGRAPHY

1. National Geographic and Roper Public Affairs, National Geographic–Roper Public Affairs 2006 Geographic Literacy Study, May 2006, http://www.nationalgeographic.com/roper2006/findings.html (accessed April 19, 2007).

2. Bureau of the Census, "American Community Survey, 2006 Ranking Tables," http://factfinder.census.gov/servlet/GRTSelectServlet?ds_name=ACS_2006_EST_G00_&_lang=en&_ts=208202084886 (accessed September 19, 2007).

3. Conference Board of Canada, "The Potential Impact of a Western Hemisphere Travel Initiative Passport Requirement on Canada's Tourism Industry: A Report," July 29, 2005, http://www.corporate.canada.travel/en/ca/research_statistics/industryResearch/economic_political/economic_political.html (accessed April 19, 2007).

4. National Geographic and Roper Public Affairs, National Geographic–Roper Public Affairs 2006 Geographic Literacy Study.

5. National Geographic and Roper Public Affairs, National Geographic–Roper 2002 Global Geographic Literacy Survey, November 2002, http://www.nationalgeographic.com/geosurvey2002/ (accessed April 19, 2007).

6. Mastercard, "New Zealand Is Dream Destination for U.S. Travelers: MasterCard Advisors Survey Report," June 22, 2006, http://www.mastercard.com/nz/press_office/060622.html (accessed April 19, 2007).

7. Bureau of the Census, "Selected Historical Decennial Census Population and Housing Counts," http://www.census.gov/population/www/censusdata/hiscendata.html (accessed April 19, 2007).

8. Bureau of the Census, "Geographic Mobility: 2005 to 2006," detailed tables, http://www.census.gov/population/www/socdemo/migrate/cps2006.html (accessed October 16, 2007).

9. Bureau of the Census, "Geographical Mobility/Migration, Historical Data," http://www.census.gov/population/www/socdemo/migrate.html (accessed October 16, 2007).

10. Bureau of the Census, "2005 American Community Survey Gulf Coast Area Data Profiles, New Orleans–Metairie–Kenner, LA Metropolitan Statistical Area," http://www.census.gov/acs/www/Products/Profiles/gulf_coast/tables/tab1_katrinaK0100US2203v.htm (accessed September 19, 2007).

11. Greater New Orleans Community Data Center, "How Many New Orleanians Are Still Displaced? Where Are They?" http://www.gnocdc.org/ (accessed September 19, 2007).

12. Bureau of the Census, "The 2007 Statistical Abstract, Statistical Abstract State Rankings," http://www.census.gov/compendia/statab/rankings.html (accessed September 2, 2007).

13. Bureau of the Census, "National and State Population Estimates," http://www.census.gov/popest/states/NST-comp-chg.html (accessed September 2, 2007).

14. Bureau of the Census, "American Community Survey, 2006 Ranking Tables," http://factfinder.census.gov/servlet/GRTSelectServlet?ds_name=ACS_2006_EST_G00_&_lang=en&_ts=208202084886 (accessed September 19, 2007).

15. Ibid.

16. Self-Storage Association, "Self-Storage Industry Fact Sheet," http://www.selfstorage.org/pdf/FactSheet.pdf (accessed June 11, 2008).

CHAPTER 12. IMMIGRANTS

1. Pew Research Center for the People & the Press and Pew Hispanic Center, *America's Immigration Quandary*, March 30, 2006, p. 30.

2. Bureau of the Census, "Foreign-Born Population of the United States, Characteristics of the Population by Generation, Current Population Survey, March 2004," detailed tables (PPL-176), http://www.census.gov/population/www/socdemo/foreign/ppl-176.html (accessed April 5, 2007).

3. United Nations Population Division, "World Migrant Stock: The 2005 Revision," http://esa.un.org/migration/index.asp?panel=1 (accessed June 24, 2007).

4. Bureau of the Census, "National and State Population Estimates," http://www.census.gov/popest/states/NST-comp-chg.html (accessed June 11, 2008).

5. Department of Homeland Security, "2007 Yearbook of Immigration Statistics," http://www.dhs.gov/ximgtn/statistics/publications/LPR07.shtm (accessed June 11, 2008).

6. Bureau of the Census, "Nativity of the Population and Place of Birth of the Native Population: 1850 to 1990," http://www.census.gov/population/www/documentation/twps0029/tab01.html (accessed April 5, 2007).

7. Bureau of the Census, "2006 American Community Survey," http://factfinder.census.gov/servlet/DatasetMainPageServlet?_program=ACS&_submenuId=&_lang=en&_ts= (accessed September 13, 2007).

8. Rasmussen Reports, "85% Support English as Official Language of U.S.," June 9, 2006, http://www.rasmussenreports.com/public_content/politics/85_support_english_as_official_language_of_u_s (accessed September 22, 2007).

9. U.S. English, Inc., "States with Official English Laws," http://www.usenglish.org/inc/official/states.asp (accessed September 22, 2007).

10. Lowell C. Rose and Alec M. Gallup, *The 37th Annual Phi Delta Kappa/Gallup Poll of the Public's Attitudes Toward the Public Schools*, September 2005, p. 53.

11. Pew Hispanic Center, "Hispanic Attitudes Toward Learning English," fact sheet, June 7, 2006, from the Pew Hispanic Center/Kaiser Family Foundation 2004 National Survey of Latinos, http://pewhispanic.org/reports/report.php?ReportID=33 (accessed April 6, 2007).

12. Jeffrey S. Passel, "Growing Share of Immigrants Choosing Naturalization," Pew Hispanic Center, March 28, 2007, p. i.

13. US Citizenship and Immigration Services, "Civics (History and Government) Items for the Redesigned Naturalization Test," http://www.uscis.gov/portal/site/uscis (accessed September 28, 2007).

14. Department of Homeland Security, "2007 Yearbook of Immigration Statistics," http://www.dhs.gov/ximgtn/statistics/publications/LPR07.shtm (accessed June 11, 2008).

15. Bureau of the Census, "National and State Population Estimates," http://www.census.gov/popest/states/NST-comp-chg.html (accessed April 8, 2007).

16. Michael Hoefer, Nancy Rytina, and Christopher Campbell, *Estimates of the Unauthorized Immigrant Population Residing in the United States: January 2006*, Office of Immigration Statistics, Department of Homeland Security, August 2007, p. 4.

17. Pew Research Center for the People & the Press and Pew Hispanic Center, *America's Immigration Quandary*, p. 4.

18. Ibid., p. 3.

19. Martin H. Bosworth, "The Earnings Suspense File: Social Security's 'Secret Stash,'" ConsumerAffairs.com, February 22, 2006, http://www.consumer affairs.com/news04/2006/02/ss_secret_stash.html (accessed April 10, 2007).

20. Thomas D. Boswell et al., *Facts about Immigration and Asking "Six Big Questions" for Florida and Miami-Dade County*, Bureau of Economic and Business Research, University of Florida, November 2001, www.bebr.ufl.edu/system/files/ bosmig.pdf (accessed September 23, 2007).

21. Giovanni Peri, *Immigrants' Complementarities and Native Wages: Evidence from California*, National Bureau of Economic Research, NBER Working Paper 12956, March 2007, p. 20.

22. Steven A. Camarota, *The High Cost of Cheap Labor: Illegal Immigration and the Federal Budget*, Center for Immigration Studies, August 2004, p. 6.

23. Pew Research Center for the People & the Press and Pew Hispanic Center, *America's Immigration Quandary*, pp. 17–18.

CHAPTER 13. POLITICS

1. Tom W. Smith and Seokho Kim, "National Pride in Comparative Perspective: 1995/96 and 2003/04," *International Journal of Public Opinion Research* 18 (2006): 127–36.

2. Survey Documentation and Analysis, Computer-Assisted Survey Methods Program, University of California, Berkeley, General Social Surveys, 1972–2006 Cumulative Data Files, GSS Variable AMBETTER, http://sda.berkeley.edu/cgi -bin32/hsda?harcsda+gss06 (accessed September 30, 2007).

3. Bureau of the Census, *Voting and Registration in the Election of November 2004*, Current Population Reports, P20–556, March 2006, p. 4.

4. Bureau of the Census, "2005 Current Population Survey Annual Social and Economic Supplement," http://www.census.gov/hhes/www/income/dinctabs.html (accessed May 16, 2007).

5. Bureau of the Census, "Voting and Registration in the Election of November 2004," detailed tables, http://www.census.gov/population/www/socdemo/ voting/cps2004.html (accessed May 31, 2007).

6. Ibid.

7. Ibid.

8. Bureau of the Census, "Voting and Registration, Historical Time Series Tables," table A-1, http://www.census.gov/population/www/socdemo/voting.html (accessed May 28, 2007).

9. Survey Documentation and Analysis, Computer-Assisted Survey Methods

Program, University of California, Berkeley, General Social Surveys, 1972–2006 Cumulative Data Files, GSS Variable FEPOL, http://sda.berkeley.edu/cgi-bin32/hsda?harcsda+gss06 (accessed September 30, 2007).

10. Survey Documentation and Analysis, Computer-Assisted Survey Methods Program, University of California, Berkeley, General Social Surveys, 1972–2006 Cumulative Data Files, GSS Variable POLVIEWS, http://sda.berkeley.edu/cgi-bin 32/hsda?harcsda+gss06 (accessed September 30, 2007).

11. Survey Documentation and Analysis, Computer-Assisted Survey Methods Program, University of California, Berkeley, General Social Surveys, 1972–2006 Cumulative Data Files, GSS Variable CONPRESS and CONTV, http://sda.berkeley.edu/cgi-bin32/hsda?harcsda+gss06 (accessed September 30, 2007).

CHAPTER 14. RELIGION

1. Survey Documentation and Analysis, Computer-Assisted Survey Methods Program, University of California, Berkeley, General Social Surveys, 1972–2006 Cumulative Data Files, GSS Variable GOD, http://sda.berkeley.edu/cgi-bin32/hsda?harcsda+gss06 (accessed October 4, 2007).

2. European Commission, *Social Values, Science, and Technology*, Special Eurobarometer 225, Wave 63.1, June 2005, appendix table QB2.

3. Pew Global Attitudes Project, *World Publics Welcome Global Trade—But Not Immigration,* October 4, 2007, p. 41.

4. Ibid., p. 43.

5. Survey Documentation and Analysis, Computer-Assisted Survey Methods Program, University of California, Berkeley, General Social Surveys, 1972–2006 Cumulative Data Files, GSS Variable PRAYER, http://sda.berkeley.edu/cgi-bin32/hsda?harcsda+gss06 (accessed October 4, 2007).

6. David W. Moore, "Public Favors Voluntary Prayer for Public Schools," Gallup Poll, August 26, 2005, http://www.gallup.com/poll/18136/Public-Favors-Voluntary-Prayer-Public-Schools.aspx (accessed December 1 2007).

7. Survey Documentation and Analysis, Computer-Assisted Survey Methods Program, University of California, Berkeley, General Social Surveys, 1972–2006 Cumulative Data Files, GSS Variables GODHELP, POSTLIFE, POSTLF1, POSTLF3, POSTLF7, and POSLF10, http://sda.berkeley.edu/cgi-bin32/hsda?harcsda+gss06 (accessed October 4, 2007).

8. Dalia Sussman, "Poll: Elbow Room No Problem in Heaven," *ABC News* Poll, December 20, 2005, http://abcnews.go.com/US/Beliefs/story?id=1422658 (accessed December 1, 2007).

9. Pew Research Center for the People & the Press, "Voters Remain in Neu-

tral as Presidential Campaign Moves into High Gear," February 23, 2007, http://people-press.org/reports/display.php3?ReportID=307 (accessed March 28, 2007).

10. Gallup Poll, "Religion," http://www.gallup.com/poll/1690/Religion.aspx (accessed June 11, 2008).

11. Frank Newport, "Estimating Americans' Worship Behavior, Part II," Gallup Poll, January 10, 2006, http://www.gallup.com/poll/20824/Estimating-Americans-Worship-Behavior-Part.aspx (accessed December 1, 2007).

12. Gallup Poll, "Religion."

13. National Center for Health Statistics, *Fertility, Contraception, and Fatherhood: Data on Men and Women from Cycle 6 of the 2002 National Survey of Family Growth*, Vital and Health Statistics, Series 23, No. 26, 2006, p. 57.

14. National Center for Health Statistics, *Fertility, Family Planning, and Reproductive Health of U.S. Women: Data from the 2002 National Survey of Family Growth*, Vital and Health Statistics, Series 23, No. 25, 2005, p. 80.

15. National Center for Health Statistics, *Fertility, Contraception, and Fatherhood*, p. 123.

16. National Center for Health Statistics, *Fertility, Family Planning, and Reproductive Health of U.S. Women*, p. 52.

17. "Overhaul Church Accounting," *National Catholic Reporter*, March 9, 2007, http://ncronline.org/NCR_Online/archives2/2007a/030907/030907z.htm (accessed March 30, 2007).

18. "Ministry Watch," Best of the Web, Forbes.com, Winter 2005, http://www.forbes.com/bow/b2c/review.jhtml?id=7553 (accessed March 30, 2007).

19. Survey Documentation and Analysis, Computer-Assisted Survey Methods Program, University of California, Berkeley, General Social Surveys, 1972–2006 Cumulative Data Files, GSS Variable EVOLVED, http://sda.berkeley.edu/cgi-bin32/hsda?harcsda+gss06 (accessed October 4, 2007).

20. Ibid.

21. Frank Newport, "Almost Half of Americans Believe Humans Did Not Evolve," Gallup Poll, June 5, 2006, http://www.gallup.com/poll/23200/Almost-Half-Americans-Believe-Humans-Did-Evolve.aspx (accessed December 1, 2007).

22. Pew Research Center for the People & the Press, *Many Americans Uneasy with Mix of Religion and Politics*, August 24, 2006, p. 3.

23. Survey Documentation and Analysis, Computer-Assisted Survey Methods Program, University of California, Berkeley, General Social Surveys, 1972–2006 Cumulative Data Files, GSS Variable SCIFAITH, http://sda.berkeley.edu/cgi-bin32/hsda?harcsda+gss06 (accessed October 4, 2007).

CHAPTER 15. RACE

1. Bureau of the Census, *Overview of Race and Hispanic Origin*, Census 2000 Brief, March 2001, pp. 3–5.

2. Bureau of the Census, "2006 American Community Survey," http://www.census.gov/acs/www/ (accessed October 1, 2007).

3. Office of Management and Budget, "Revisions to the Standards for the Classification of Federal Data on Race and Ethnicity," October 30, 1997, http://www.whitehouse.gov/omb/fedreg/1997standards.html (accessed June 6, 2007).

4. Bureau of the Census, "2006 American Community Survey."

5. Bureau of the Census, National Population Estimates, http://www.census.gov/popest/national/asrh/NC-EST2007-sa.html (accessed June 11, 2008).

6. Author's calculations based on Bureau of the Census, 2006 American Community Survey.

7. Bureau of the Census, "Families and Living Arrangements, Historical Time Series," http://www.census.gov/population/www/socdemo/hh-fam.html (accessed June 4, 2007).

8. Bureau of the Census, "America's Families and Living Arrangements: 2006," detailed tables, http://www.census.gov/population/www/socdemo/hh-fam/cps2006.html (accessed June 4, 2007).

9. Author's calculations based on ibid.

10. Office of Management and Budget, "Revisions to the Standards for the Classification of Federal Data on Race and Ethnicity."

11. Bureau of the Census, "National Population Estimates," http://www.census.gov/popest/national/asrh/ (accessed June 11, 2008).

12. Bureau of Labor Statistics, "Labor Force Statistics from the Current Population Survey," http://www.bls.gov/cps/home.htm (accessed June 11, 2008).

13. Bureau of the Census, "American Housing Survey for the United States: 2005, National Tables: 2005," http://www.census.gov/hhes/www/housing/ahs/ahs05/ahs05.html (accessed June 7, 2007).

14. Brian K. Bucks, Arthur B. Kennickell, and Kevin B. Moore, "Recent Changes in U.S. Family Finances: Evidence from the 2001 and 2004 Survey of Consumer Finances," *Federal Reserve Bulletin* 92 (February 2006): A8.

15. *Washington Post*/Kaiser Family Foundation/Harvard University, *Race and Ethnicity in 2001: Attitudes, Perceptions, and Experiences*, August 2001, p. 4.

16. HarrisInteractive.com, "Fewer Americans Than Europeans Have Trust in the Media—Press, Radio and TV," Harris Poll #4, January 13, 2005, http://www.harrisinteractive.com/harris_poll/index.asp?PID=534 (accessed July 20, 2007).

17. Martin Gilens, *Why Americans Hate Welfare: Race, Media, and the Politics of Antipoverty Policy* (Chicago: University of Chicago Press, 2000), p. 139.

18. Bureau of the Census, *Income, Poverty, and Health Insurance Coverage in the United States: 2006*, Current Population Reports P60–233, August 2007, p. 12.

19. Gilens, *Why Americans Hate Welfare*, p. 114.

20. Ibid., p. 140.

21. *Washington Post*/Kaiser Family Foundation/Harvard University, *Race and Ethnicity in 2001*, p. 25.

22. Lydia Saad, "A Downturn in Black Perceptions of Racial Harmony," Gallup Poll, July 6, 2007, http://www.gallup.com/poll/28072/Downturn-Black-Perceptions-Racial-Harmony.aspx (accessed July 22, 2007).

23. Survey Documentation and Analysis, Computer-Assisted Survey Methods Program, University of California, Berkeley, General Social Surveys, 1972–2006 Cumulative Data Files, GSS Variables FEELBLKS and FEELWHTS, http://sda.berkeley.edu/cgi-bin32/hsda?harcsda+gss06 (accessed October 2, 2007).

24. *Washington Post*/Kaiser Family Foundation/Harvard University, *Race and Ethnicity in 2001*, p. 26.

25. Ibid., p. 25.

26. Bureau of the Census, "Current Population Surveys, Historical Income Data," http://www.census.gov/hhes/www/income/histinc/histinctb.html (accessed October 2 2007).

27. Bureau of the Census, "Educational Attainment, Historical Tables," http://www.census.gov/population/www/socdemo/educ-attn.html (accessed July 27, 2007).

28. Bureau of Labor Force Statistics, "Labor Force Statistics from the Current Population Survey," http://www.bls.gov/cps/home.htm (accessed June 11, 2008).

29. Bureau of the Census, "Families and Living Arrangements, Historical Time Series," http://www.census.gov/population/www/socdemo/hh-fam.html (accessed July 27, 2007).

30. Eurobarometer, *Europeans and Languages*, Report 54, Executive Summary, February 15, 2001, p. 1.

31. Pew Hispanic Center/Kaiser Family Foundation, *2002 National Survey of Latinos*, December 2002, pp. 17, 29.

32. National Geographic–Roper Public Affairs, *2006 Geographic Literacy Study*, Final Report, May 2006, p. 42.

33. National Center for Education Statistics, *Digest of Education Statistics: 2007*, http://nces.ed.gov/programs/digest/d07/tables_2.asp (accessed June 11, 2008).

34. Eduardo Porter, "Stretched to Limits, Women Stall March to Work," *New York Times*, March 2, 2006, http://www.nytimes.com (accessed August 17, 2007).

35. Author's calculations based on Bureau of Labor Statistics, "Labor Force Statistics from the Current Population Survey."

36. "A New Baby-Boom? Why Americans Are Having More Kids," cover of *Life*, May 12, 2006.

37. Author's calculations based on National Center for Health Statistics, *Births: Preliminary Data for 2006*, National Vital Statistics Report, Vol. 56, No. 7, December 5, 2007, p. 10; and *Births: Final Data for 2000*, National Vital Statistics Report, Vol. 50, No. 5, February 12, 2002, pp. 28, 34–35.

38. Bureau of the Census, "National Population Estimates," http://www.census.gov/popest/national/asrh/NC-EST2007-compchg.html (accessed May 1, 2008).

39. Susy Buchanan and David Holthouse, "'Shoot, Shovel, and Shut Up'—144 'Nativist Extremist' Groups Identified," Southern Poverty Law Center, *Intelligence Report*, Spring 2007, http://www.splcenter.org/intel/intelreport/article.jsp?aid=763 (accessed August 19, 2007).

40. National Conference of State Legislatures, "2007 Enacted State Legislation Related to Immigrants and Immigration," August 6, 2007, http://www.ncsl.org/programs/immig/2007ImmigrationUpdate.htm (accessed August 19, 2007).

CHAPTER 16. SPENDING

1. Author's calculations based on unpublished tables from the Bureau of Labor Statistics 2005 Consumer Expenditure Survey.

2. Bureau of Labor Statistics, *100 Years of U.S. Consumer Spending: Data for the Nation, New York City, and Boston*, BLS Report 991, May 2006, p. 6.

3. Author's calculations based on Bureau of Labor Statistics, "2006 Consumer Expenditure Survey," standard tables, http://www.bls.gov/cex/home.htm (accessed December 2, 2007).

4. Bureau of Labor Statistics, *100 Years of U.S. Consumer Spending*, p. 28.

5. Bureau of the Census, "2005 County Business Patterns," http://censtats.census.gov/cgi-bin/cbpnaic/cbpdetl.pl (accessed July 10, 2007).

6. Author's calculations based on unpublished tables from the 2000 and 2006 Bureau of Labor Statistics Consumer Expenditure Surveys.

7. Author's calculations based on 1984 and 2006 personal consumption expenditures from Bureau of Economic Analysis, "National Economic Accounts, All NIPA Tables," http://www.bea.gov/bea/dn/nipaweb/SelectTable.asp?Selected=N (accessed December 2, 2007).

8. Author's calculations based on Bureau of Labor Statistics, 1984 and 2006 Consumer Expenditure Surveys, http://www.bls.gov/cex/home.htm (accessed December 2, 2007).

9. Jagadeesh Gokhale, Laurence J. Kotlikoff, and John Sabelhaus, *Under-*

standing the Postwar Decline in U.S. Saving: A Cohort Analysis, National Bureau of Economic Research, NBER Working Paper 5571, May 1996, pp. 44–45.

10. Author's calculations based on Department of Transportation, "2001 National Household Travel Survey," http://nhts.ornl.gov/ (accessed August 25, 2007).

11. Bureau of Labor Statistics, unpublished tables from the Bureau of Labor Statistics 2006 American Time Use Survey.

12. Veronica V. Soriano, "Converting Browsers into Spenders," *Research Review* 13 (2006): 10.

13. John P. Robinson and Geoffrey Godbey, *Time for Life: The Surprising Ways Americans Use Their Time* (University Park: Pennsylvania State University Press, 1997), p. 340.

14. Author's calculations based on unpublished tables from the Bureau of Labor Statistics 2006 Consumer Expenditure Survey.

CHAPTER 17. HOUSES

1. US Department of Housing and Urban Development, Federal Housing Administration (FHA), http://www.hud.gov/offices/hsg/fhahistory.cfm (accessed May 14, 2007).

2. Bureau of the Census, *Historical Statistics of the United States, Colonial Times to 1970, Part 2* (Washington, DC: US Government Printing Office, 1975), p. 646.

3. Bureau of the Census, "American Housing Survey National Tables: 2005," http://www.census.gov/hhes/www/housing/ahs/ahs05/ahs05.html (accessed December 2, 2007).

4. Alan Greenspan, "Understanding Household Debt Obligations," Remarks by Federal Reserve Board Chairman Alan Greenspan at the Credit Union National Association 2004 Governmental Affairs Conference, Washington, DC, February 23, 2004, http://www.federalreserve.gov/boardDocs/speeches/2004/20040223/default.htm (accessed May 13, 2007).

5. Bureau of the Census, "Historical Income Tables—Households," http://www.census.gov/hhes/www/income/histinc/inchhtoc.html (accessed September 22, 2007).

6. Bureau of the Census, "Construction Price Indexes, Constant Quality (Laspeyres) Price Index of New One-Family Houses Sold," http://www.census.gov/const/www/constpriceindex.html (accessed December 2, 2007).

7. Bureau of the Census, *Characteristics of New Housing*, Construction Reports, C25-75-13, 1985, and 1995. tables 21 and 22, http://www.census.gov/const/www/charindex.html#sold (accessed May 10, 2007).

8. Bureau of the Census, *Computer and Internet Use in the United States: 2003*, Current Population Reports P23–208, October 2005, p. 1.

9. Pew Internet & American Life Project, "Latest Trends, Usage Over Time," http://www.pewinternet.org/trends.asp#usage (accessed September 22, 2007).

10. Bureau of the Census, "American Housing Survey National Tables: 2005," http://www.census.gov/hhes/www/housing/ahs/ahs05/ahs05.html (accessed May 10, 2007).

11. Bureau of the Census, "Characteristics of New Housing, Characteristics of New One-Family Houses Sold," http://www.census.gov/const/www/charindex .html#sold (accessed June 11, 2008).

12. Answers.com, "Air Conditioning," citation from the *Encyclopedia of American History*, http://www.answers.com/topic/air-conditioning (accessed May 11, 2007).

13. Author's calculations based on Bureau of the Census, "National and State Population Estimates," http://www.census.gov/popest/archives/ (accessed June 11, 2008).

14. Pew Research Center, *Luxury or Necessity? Things We Can't Live Without: The List Has Grown in the Past Decade*, December 14, 2006, p. 2.

15. Roper Center for Public Opinion Research, "Gotta Have It: What Is Necessary, and What's Just 'Nice'?" *Public Perspective* 10 (February/March 1999): 26.

16. Bureau of the Census, "American Housing Survey National Tables: 2005," http://www.census.gov/hhes/www/housing/ahs/ahs05/ahs05.html (accessed May 12, 2007).

17, Bureau of the Census, "Housing Vacancies and Homeownership, Annual Tables," table 9, http://www.census.gov/hhes/www/housing/hvs/annual07/ann07 ind.html (accessed June 11, 2008).

18. Bureau of Labor Statistics, unpublished tables from the 2006 Consumer Expenditure Survey.

19. Bureau of the Census, "Historical Census of Housing Tables—Vacation Homes," http://www.census.gov/hhes/www/housing/census/historic/vacation.html (accessed May 29, 2007).

20. Bureau of the Census, *Housing Characteristics: 2000*, Census 2000 Brief, October 2001, p. 5.

CHAPTER 18. CARS

1. Bureau of Transportation Statistics, table 1–4, http://www.bts.gov/ publications/national_transportation_statistics/html/table_01_11.html (accessed June 11, 2008).

2. Federal Highway Administration, "Highway Statistics 2005, Licensed Drivers by Sex and Ratio to Population—2005," http://www.fhwa.dot.gov/policy/ohim/hs05/htm/dl1c.htm (accessed September 11, 2007).

3. Federal Highway Administration, "Traffic Congestion and Reliability: Trends and Advanced Strategies for Congestion Mitigation," September 1, 2005, http://www.ops.fhwa.dot.gov/congestion_report/executive_summary.htm #congestion_worse (accessed November 27, 2006).

4. US Department of Transportation, "2001 National Household Travel Survey," Online Analysis Tool, http://nhts.ornl.gov/index.shtml (accessed November 20, 2005).

5. Bureau of the Census, "2006 American Community Survey," http://factfinder.census.gov/servlet/DatasetMainPageServlet?_program=ACS&_submenuId=&_lang=en&_ts= (accessed September 13, 2007).

6. Ann Tatko-Peterson, "It Takes Organization, Planning to Reclaim Garage," *Oakland Tribune*, September 23, 2006, http://www.insidebayarea.com/ (accessed April 9, 2007).

7. Bureau of Labor Statistics, "2006 Consumer Expenditure Survey, Standard Tables," http://www.bls.gov/cex/home.htm (accessed December 2, 2007).

8. Brian K. Bucks, Arthur B. Kennickell, and Kevin B. Moore, "Recent Changes in U.S. Family Finances: Evidence from the 2001 and 2004 Survey of Consumer Finances," *Federal Reserve Bulletin* 92 (February 2006): A22–A23.

9. Information Please Database, "Population Density Per Square Mile of Countries," http://www.infoplease.com/ipa/A0934666.html (accessed December 3, 2007).

10. Bureau of the Census, "2006 American Community Survey," http://factfinder.census.gov/servlet/DatasetMainPageServlet?_program=ACS&_submenuId=&_lang=en&_ts= (accessed September 13, 2007).

11. Bureau of Transportation Statistics, "National Household Travel Survey Long Distance Travel Quick Facts," http://www.bts.gov/programs/national_household_travel_survey/long_distance.html (accessed November 27, 2006).

12. National Sporting Goods Association, "Sports Participation," http://www.nsga.org/public/pages/index.cfm?pageid=328 (accessed September 11, 2007).

13. Lawrence D. Frank, Martin A. Andresen, and Thomas L. Schmid, "Obesity Relationships with Community Design, Physical Activity, and Time Spent in Cars," SMARTRAQ, http://www.act-trans.ubc.ca/smartraq/pages/reports.htm (accessed December 3, 2007).

CHAPTER 19. TECHNOLOGY

1. John B. Horrigan, *Home Broadband Adoption 2008*, Pew Internet & American Life Project, June 2008, p. 11.

2. Christopher Baker and Ann McLarty Jackson, "Older Persons and Wireless Telephone Use," AARP, May 2005, http://www.aarp.org/research/utilities/phone/fs116_wireless.html (accessed July 12, 2007).

3. John B. Horrigan, *A Typology of Information and Communication Technology Users*, Pew Internet & American Life Project, May 7, 2007, p. 6.

4. Calculations by the author based on unpublished tables from the Bureau of Labor Statistics 1991 and 2006 Consumer Expenditure Surveys.

5. Survey Documentation and Analysis, Computer-Assisted Survey Methods Program, University of California, Berkeley, General Social Surveys, 1972–2006 Cumulative Data Files, GSS Variable NEWS, http://sda.berkeley.edu/cgi-bin32/hsda?harcsda+gss06 (accessed October 8, 2007).

6. Project for Excellence in Journalism, "The State of the News Media 2008," http://www.stateofthenewsmedia.org/2008 (accessed June 11, 2008).

7. Harris Poll, "TV Network News Top Source of News and Information Today," Harris Interactive, June 11, 2007, http://www.harrisinteractive.com/harris_poll/index.asp?PID=768 (accessed July 14, 2007).

8. Nielsen Media Research, "Average U.S. Home Now Receives a Record 104.2 TV Channels, According to Nielsen," March 19, 2007, http://www.nielsenmedia.com (accessed August 30, 2007).

9. Survey Documentation and Analysis, Computer–Assisted Survey Methods Program, University of California, Berkeley, General Social Surveys, 1972–2006 Cumulative Data Files, GSS Variable LIFE, http://sda.berkeley.edu/cgi-bin32/hsda?harcsda+gss06 (accessed October 8, 2007).

10. Stephen Battaglio, "TV Goes Gray," TVGuide.com, June 28, 2007, http://www.tvguide.com/Biz/tv-goes-gray/070628–01 (accessed July 16, 2007).

11. New Strategist Publications, *Household Spending: Who Spends How Much on What*, 5th ed. (Ithaca, NY: New Strategist Publications, 1999), p. 777.

12. Calculations by the author based on unpublished tables from the Bureau of Labor Statistics 2006 Consumer Expenditure Survey.

13. Lee Rainie and Scott Keeter, *How Americans Use Their Cell Phones*, Pew Internet & American Life Project, April 3, 2006, p. 1.

14. Stephen J. Blumberg and Julian V. Luke, *Wireless Substitution: Early Release of Estimates from the National Health Interview Survey, July—December 2007*, May 13, 2008, National Center for Health Statistics, p. 4.

15. Bureau of Labor Statistics, unpublished tables from the 2006 Consumer Expenditure Survey.

16. Scott Keeter et al, "Cost and Benefits of Full Dual-Frame Telephone Survey Designs," paper presented at the annual meeting of the American Association for Public Opinion Research, New Orleans, Louisiana, May 15–18, 2008, p. 8.

17. Bureau of Labor Statistics, Employment Characteristics of Families, http://www.bls.gov/news.release/famee.t04.htm (accessed June 25, 2007).

18. Ellen R. DeLisio, "Crafting a Workable Cell Phone Policy," *Education World*, February 22, 2005, http://www.education-world.com/a_admin/admin/admin393.shtml (accessed June 25, 2007).

19. United States Postal Service, Revenue, Pieces, and Weights Reports, http://www.usps.com/financials/rpw/ (accessed June 11, 2008)

20. Unpublished tables from the Bureau of Labor Statistics 2006 Consumer Expenditure Survey.

21. Blumberg and Luke, *Wireless Substitution*, p. 5.

22. Federal Communications Commission, *Trends in Telephone Service* (Washington, DC: FCC, February 2007), pp. 7–11.

23. See www.payphoneproject.com and www.payphone-directory.org.

CHAPTER 20. PLAY

1. Mark Aguiar and Erik Hurst, *Measuring Trends in Leisure: The Allocation of Time over Five Decades*, Federal Reserve Bank of Boston, Working Paper 06–2, January 2006, p. 44.

2. Valerie A. Ramey and Neville Francis, *A Century of Work and Leisure*, National Bureau of Economic Research, NBER Working Paper 12264, May 2006, p. 27.

3. Pew Research Center, *American Work Life Is Worsening, But Most Workers Still Content*, August 30, 2006, p. 1.

4. John P. Robinson and Geoffrey Godbey, *Time for Life: The Surprising Ways Americans Use Their Time* (University Park: Pennsylvania State University Press, 1997), p. 244.

5. Calculations by the author based on unpublished tables from the Bureau of Labor Statistics 1991 and 2006 Consumer Expenditure Surveys.

6. National Endowment for the Arts, *To Read or Not to Read: A Question of National Consequence*, Research Report 47, November 2007, p. 7.

7. New Strategist, *American Time Use: Who Spends How Long at What* (Ithaca, NY: New Strategist Publications, 2007), p. 30.

8. US Fish and Wildlife Service, *2006 National Survey of Fishing, Hunting, and Wildlife-Associated Recreation, National Overview*, May 2007, pp. 15, 17.

9. Suzanne M. Bianchi, John P. Robinson, and Melissa A. Milkie, *Changing*

Rhythms of American Family Life (New York: Russell Sage Foundation, 2006), pp. 64, 93.

10. Survey Documentation and Analysis, Computer-Assisted Survey Methods Program, University of California, Berkeley, General Social Surveys, 1972–2006 Cumulative Data Files, GSS Variable HUBBYWK1, http://sda.berkeley.edu/cgibin32/hsda?harcsda+gss06 (accessed September 4, 2007).

11. National Center for Health Statistics, *Fertility, Contraception, and Father-hood: Data on Men and Women from Cycle 6 of the 2002 National Survey of Family Growth*, Vital and Health Statistics, Series 23, No. 26, 2006, p. 118.

12. National Park Service, "Public Use Statistics Office," http://www.nature.nps.gov/stats/index.cfm (accessed April 27, 2008).

13. Orbitz, "Take 5 to Travel Survey," July 3, 2007, http://pressroom.orbitz.com/downloads/Take5_survey.pdf (accessed July 21, 2007).

14. Expedia.com, "2007 International Vacation Deprivation Survey," http://www.expedia.com/daily/promos/vacations/vacation_deprivation/default.asp (July 21, 2007).

15. National Sporting Goods Association, "Research and Statistics," http://www.nsga.org (accessed August 12, 2007).

16. Rhonda Clements, "An Investigation of the Status of Outdoor Play," *Contemporary Issues in Early Childhood* 5 (November 1, 2004): 72.

17. J. Duke, "Physical Activity Levels among Children Aged 9 to 13—United States, 2002," *Mortality and Morbidity Weekly Report* 52 (August 22, 2003): 785–88.

18. National Center for Health Statistics, *Summary Health Statistics for U.S. Adults: National Health Interview Survey, 2006*, Series 10, No. 235, Table 28.

19. National Sporting Goods Association, "Research and Statistics."

CHAPTER 21. HEALTH

1. Centers for Disease Control and Prevention, "Behavioral Risk Factor Surveillance System, Prevalence Data," http://apps.nccd.cdc.gov/brfss/index.asp (accessed June 12, 2008).

2. Beth J. Soldo et al., "Cross-Cohort Difference in Health on the Verge of Retirement," *PARC Working Paper Series*, WPS 06–13, Population Aging Research Center, University of Pennsylvania, September 2007, p. 17.

3. Ibid., p. 18.

4. Centers for Disease Control and Prevention, "Health Related Quality of Life, Prevalence Data," http://apps.nccd.cdc.gov/HRQOL/ (accessed December 4, 2007).

5. Bureau of Labor Statistics, "Employee Tenure," table 2, http://www.bls.gov/news.release/tenure.t02.htm (accessed April 24, 2007).

6. Bureau of the Census, "Current Population Survey Annual Social and Demographic Supplements," http://www.census.gov/hhes/www/income/histinc/incpertoc.html (accessed September 21, 2007).

7. Bureau of the Census, "Housing Vacancy Surveys," http://www.census.gov/hhes/www/housing/hvs/hvs.html (accessed April 24, 2007).

8. Bureau of the Census, "2007 Current Population Survey Annual Social and Economic Supplement, Health Insurance Coverage: 2006," http://pubdb3.census.gov/macro/032007/health/toc.htm (accessed September 21, 2007).

9. David G. Blanchflower, "Self-Employment: More May Not Be Better," paper presented at the Conference on self-employment organized by the Economic Council of Sweden, March 2004, p. 22.

10. *ABC News*/Kaiser Family Foundation/*USA Today, Health Care in America 2006 Survey*, Publication 7573, October 2006, p. 8.

11. Brigid McMenamin, "What Your Congressman Won't Tell You," SmartMoney.com, October 11, 2006, http://www.smartmoney.com/10things/index.cfm?story=november2006 (accessed April 26, 2007).

12. National Center for Health Statistics, *Health, United States, 2007* (Washington, DC: US Government Printing Office, 2007), p. 336.

13. Frank Lichtenberg, *Benefits and Costs of Newer Drugs: An Update*, National Bureau of Economic Research, NBER Working Paper 8996, June 2002, p. 1.

14. Ibid., p. 2.

15. Beth J. Soldo et al., "Cross-Cohort Difference in Health," p. 17.

16. Rand Corporation, "Obesity and Disability: The Shape of Things to Come," Rand Research Highlights, http://www.rand.org/pubs/research_briefs/RB9043–1/ (accessed April 29, 2007).

17. Robert F. Schoeni, Vicki A. Freedman, and Linda G. Martin, "Socioeconomic and Demographic Disparities in Trends in Old-Age Disability," February 2005, p. 16, paper presented at the conference Health in Older Ages: The Causes and Consequences of Declining Disability among the Elderly, October 8–11, 2004.

18. National Center for Health Statistics, *Trends in Hospital Utilization: United States, 1988–92*, Vital and Health Statistics, Series 13, No. 124, 1996, p. 33; and National Center for Health Statistics, *2005 National Hospital Discharge Survey*, Advance Data, No. 385, 2007, p. 12.

19. American Hospital Association Annual Survey of Hospitals, reprinted in National Center for Health Statistics, *Health, United States, 2007* (Washington, DC: US Government Printing Office, 2007), p. 352.

20. David Baker et al., "Trends in Post-discharge Mortality and Readmissions: Has Length of Stay Declined Too Far?" *Archives of Internal Medicine* 164 (March 8, 2004): 538–44.

21. Bureau of Labor Statistics, unpublished tables from the 2006 Consumer Expenditure Survey.

22. National Center for Health Statistics, *Summary Health Statistics for U.S. Adults: National Health Interview Survey, 2006*, Vital and Health Statistics Provisional Report, Series 10, No. 235, August 2007, table 38; and *Summary Health Statistics for U.S. Children: National Health Interview Survey, 2006*, Vital and Health Statistics, Series 10, No. 234, September 2007, p. 44.

23. National Center for Health Statistics, *Summary Health Statistics for U.S. Adults*, table 38.

24. National Center for Health Statistics, "Trends in Nursing Homes," http://www.cdc.gov/nchs/about/major/nnhsd/Trendsnurse.htm (accessed May 1, 2007).

25. Brenda C. Spillman and Kirsten J. Black, *The Size and Characteristics of the Residential Care Population: Evidence from Three National Surveys*, US Department of Health and Human Services, January 4, 2006, p. iv.

26. National Alliance for Caregiving and AARP, *Caregiving in the U.S.*, April 2004, p. 7.

27. Bureau of the Census, "Americans with Disabilities: 2002," detailed tables, http://www.census.gov/hhes/www/disability/sipp/disable02.html (accessed May 1, 2007).

CHAPTER 22. WEIGHT

1. National Center for Health Statistics, *Health, United States, 2007* (Washington, DC: US Government Printing Office, 2007), p. 290.

2. Pew Research Center, *Americans See Weight Problems Everywhere but in the Mirror*, April 11, 2006, p. 1.

3. Calculations by the author based on data in National Center for Health Statistics, *Mean Body Weight, Height, and Body Mass Index, United States 1960–2002*, Advance Data No. 347, October 27, 2004, p. 8.

4. Gallup Poll, "Personal Weight Situation," http://www.gallup.com/poll/7264/Personal-Weight-Situation.aspx (accessed June 12, 2008).

5. Pew Research Center, *Americans See Weight Problems*, p. 6.

6. Richard H. Steckel, "A History of the Standard of Living in the United States," EH.Net Encyclopedia, http://eh.net/encyclopedia/article/steckel.standard.living.us (accessed September 20, 2007).

7. John Komlos and Benjamin E. Lauderdale, "Underperformance in Affluence: The Remarkable Relative Decline in U.S. Heights in the Second Half of the 20th Century," *Social Science Quarterly* 88 (June 2007): 283–305.

8. National Center for Health Statistics, *National Ambulatory Medical Care Survey: 2005 Summary*, Advance Data No. 387, 2007, p. 30.

9. US Department of Health and Human Services, Agency for Healthcare Research and Quality, Medical Expenditure Panel Survey, Household Component, http://www.meps.ahrq.gov/mepsweb/survey_comp/household.jsp (accessed June 12, 2008).

10. Robert Wood Johnson Foundation, "Study Finds Most Doctors Don't Smoke; But They Don't Press Patients to Quit," June 2006, http://www.rwjf.org/portfolios/resources/grantsreport.jsp?filename=043562.htm&iaid=143 (accessed February 5, 2007).

11. Gary D. Foster et al., "Primary Care Physicians' Attitudes about Obesity and Its Treatment," *Obesity Research* 11 (October 2003): 1168–77.

12. Ibid., p. 1168.

13. Sara Bleich et al., *Why Is the Developed World Obese?* National Bureau of Economic Research, NBER Working Paper 12954, March 2007, p. 43.

14. National Center for Health Statistics, *Health, United States, 2007*, p. 285.

15. Inas Rashad, Michael Grossman, and Shin-Yi Chou, "The Super Size of America: An Economic Estimation of Body Mass Index and Obesity in Adults," National Bureau of Economic Research, NBER Working Paper 11584, August 2005, p. 12.

16. Bureau of Labor Statistics, unpublished tables from the 2006 Consumer Expenditure Survey.

17. Author's calculations based on Bureau of Labor Statistics, unpublished tables from the 2006 Consumer Expenditure Survey.

18. Theresa A. Hastert et al., "More California Teens Consume Soda and Fast Food Each Day Than Five Servings of Fruits and Vegetables," *UCLA Health Policy Research Brief*, September 2005, p. 5.

19. Shanthy A. Bowman et al., "Effects of Fast-Food Consumption on Energy Intake and Diet Quality among Children in a National Household Survey," *Pediatrics* 113 (January 2004): 115.

20. Pew Research Center, *Americans See Weight Problems*, p. 8.

21. Bleich et al., *Why Is the Developed World Obese?* p. 16.

CHAPTER 23. DEATH

1. Felicitie C. Bell and Michael L. Miller, "Actuarial Study No. 116, Life Tables for the United States Social Security Area 1900–2100," http://www.ssa.gov/OACT/NOTES/as116/as116_Tbl_6_1900.html#wp1072627 (accessed July 3, 2007).

2. Eileen M. Crimmins, Yasuhiko Saito, and Dominique Ingegneri. "Trends in Disability-Free Life Expectancy in the United States: 1970–90," *Population and Development Review* 23 (September 1997): 555–72.

3. National Center for Health Statistics, "Leading Causes of Death, 1900–1998," http://www.cdc.gov/nchs/data/dvs/lead1900_98.pdf (accessed July 4, 2007).

4. James F. Fries, "The Compression of Morbidity," *Milbank Quarterly* 83 (2005): 802.

5. Author's calculations based on National Center for Health Statistics, *Maternal Mortality and Related Concepts*, Vital and Health Statistics, Series 3, February 2007, p. 9.

6. National Center for Health Statistics, *Deaths: Preliminary Data for 2006*, National Vital Statistics Reports, Vol. 56, No. 16, June 11, 2008, p. 27.

7. National Center for Health Statistics, *Health United States, 2007* (Washington, DC: US Government Printing Office, 2007), p. 175.

8. Daniel J. Kruger and Randolph M. Nesse, "Sexual Selection and the Male:Female Mortality Ratio," *Evolutionary Psychology* 2 (2004): 80.

9. National Center for Health Statistics, *Health, United States, 2007*, p. 195.

10. David M. Cutler and Adriana Lleras-Muney, *Education and Health: Evaluating Theories and Evidence*, National Bureau of Economic Research, NBER Working Paper 12352, June 2006, p. 16.

11. Humphrey Taylor, "What We Are Afraid Of," Harris Poll #49, August 18, 1999, http://www.harrisinteractive.com/harris_poll/index.asp?PID=281 (accessed December 4, 2007).

12. National Safety Council, "The Odds of Dying From . . . ," http://www.nsc.org/research/odds.aspx (accessed June 12, 2008).

13. National Center for Health Statistics, "Mortality Tables," http://www.cdc.gov/nchs/datawh/statab/unpubd/mortabs/gmwki10.htm (accessed September 13, 2007).

INDEX